SERVICE FRANCHISING
A GLOBAL PERSPECTIVE

SERVICE FRANCHISING
A GLOBAL PERSPECTIVE

by

Ilan Alon
Crummer Graduate School of Management,
Rollins College, Winter Park, Florida

 Springer

Library of Congress Cataloging-in-Publication Data

A C.I.P. Catalogue record for this book is available
from the Library of Congress.

ISBN-10: 0-387-28182-7   e-ISBN-10: 0-387-28256-4   Printed on acid-free paper.
ISBN-13: 978-0387-28182-7   e-ISBN-13: 978-0387-28256-5

Printed in the United States of America.

9 8 7 6 5 4 3 2 1   SPIN 11500254

springeronline.com

Dedication

To Sophia, Joseph and Polya

Contents

List of Figures

List of Tables

Foreword
Service Franchising: A Global Perspective

Twenty years ago I was offered the position of assistant director of development for the International Franchise Association (IFA). At the time, I knew little about trade associations and even less about franchising, but the job seemed intriguing and the IFA was willing to take a chance on me. Little did I know this would propel me down a path dedicated to one of the most successful models for retail development ever created--franchising.

My first job at the IFA was to meet with franchised companies to learn about the challenges they faced in building their businesses and to sell them IFA memberships. Later, I created the international division for the IFA with the goal of helping members franchise outside the United States. At that time there had been little serious research, or useful writing on international franchising. I learned by observing, listening and working with franchisors as they pursued international franchising. When I was offered a position to help build the international division of a franchised company, I jumped at the chance. For the next fifteen years I learned firsthand the extraordinary power of the business format franchise model.

What I learned was that it is not easy to build a business. It is even more difficult to build a business in the retail sector. The expenses of marketing, real estate, labor costs and rapidly changing consumer habits are just a few of the factors that add to the risk and complexity of this business sector. Trying to replicate the success of a retail concept in a new country creates an even greater challenge. Now the business needs to learn how to operate in the new country with different legal and tax codes, consumer habits, labor laws, retail environment—no easy task as demonstrated by the numerous failed attempts.

It was exciting to experience how the use of a business format franchise system helped reduce the risk for all parties and increase the chances that the venture would be successful. The risks are reduced because the franchisor is transferring specific knowledge about management of the business to the franchisee (or master franchisee). But it is not just a one way relationship where the franchisor has all the answers. Because the franchisee is providing virtually all the capital to build the business, a unique relationship is created where the franchisor must listen and respond to the concerns and issues of the franchisee differently than if that franchisee were simply an employee of the organization. The right franchisee brings critically important local knowledge and experience to the relationship that accelerates the learning curve for the US franchisor. It is the franchisee that is in direct, daily contact with the customer and listening to what is happening on the line level.

This vital information sharpens the franchisor's awareness of changes in consumer needs, and enables a timely response to keep the product or service relevant.

It is important to remember that franchising is not an industry. Franchising is a business strategy for delivering a product or service to a customer. The IFA has identified over 75 different industries that use the methodology of franchising. According to the 2004 study sponsored by the International Franchise Association Educational Foundation and conducted by the National Economic Consulting Practice of PricewaterhouseCoopers, in the United States alone, more than 760,000 franchised outlets employ more than 18 million people providing nearly 14% of US private-sector employment. This generates $1.53 trillion in economic activity or nearly 10% of the private-sector economic output. Outside the United States franchising appears to be growing at an even faster pace.

At a time when use of this powerful business model for growth is expanding around the world, it is curious that there has been relatively little academic interest in the subject. Without empirical research it is difficult to evaluate the impact that franchising is having in a country. Again, franchising is not an industry, so the overall effect of the franchising model on an economy is hard to measure. Because franchising has been dominated by the fast food industry, many policymakers focus on the product rather than the model that franchising is and how it facilitates the transfer of best of business development strategies and processes. A successful franchise system teaches standardization, training, marketing, operational support—key areas that improve the competitiveness and development of a robust retail sector. It is not often understood that franchising creates important opportunities for local investment and employment. If policymakers better understood the positive impact of franchising on local and national economies and societies, particularly in emerging markets, then we might see a more supportive regulatory environment, one that works to nurture and protect the development of franchising as a business model. Ilan Alon's work examines the total impact of international franchising, and specifically the implications for emerging markets. He provides is an important addition to this sparsely covered topic.

From the US franchisor's perspective, many attractive opportunities encourage the franchisor to venture into markets beyond the United States. However, I have learned from direct experience the hardships and challenges that must be overcome in order to make a franchised business successful outside of the US. Most franchisors start with the strategy of finding the right local partner, or perhaps more accurately, the local partner finding them. They then embark upon the process of replicating the key elements of their franchise system and transferring them to the new franchisee. They must adapt the business model to local consumer habits and business customs. While at the same time they must make sure that there is enough capital in the enterprise to keep the cash flow of the business positive until franchise sales and the ongoing royalty becomes self-sustaining. These are complex and critical tasks that the franchisor must manage no matter which country he begins operations.

But there are key factors that can profoundly influence whether it even makes sense to begin in a certain country. The more knowledge that the franchisor has of the key factors, the more likely will be that company's success. With this book, Dr. Alon helps the franchisor to ask the right questions to determine whether a company is prepared to tackle risks and realize the rewards associated with doing business internationally.

Franchising is a business model that is becoming even more important in the 21st century. More and more countries' economies are dominated by the service and information sector. This is a sector ideally suited for the use of franchising. Today the influence of global brands reaches to furthest corners of our globe. Around the world technology continues to transform the way in which we live our lives and conduct our businesses. I have been amazed at the positive impact that use of technology has had in facilitating and dramatically reducing the cost of managing the complete transfer of a business system and the ongoing support required by the structure of franchising. Because of the scarcity of empirical research on international franchising, the knowledge gap is filled with anecdotal information that may or may not be accurate. Dr. Alon's work makes a significant contribution to the understanding of franchising as a powerful business model in international markets, and it is my hope that more academicians will recognize franchising as a topic worthy of serious research both as a strategy for expansion and as a method of development for emerging markets.

Peter D. Holt
San Diego, CA, USA
2005

Preface
Service Franchising: A Global Perspective

The roots of franchising are lost in antiquity. Some argue that English pubs were the first franchises when they were required to be licensed by the king in order to ensure that they met standards for the safety of travelers. Others contend that the original franchisor was the Roman Catholic Church, authorizing parish priests to collect tithes and remit a portion to the Pope. Regardless of whatever the starting date might have been, the global explosion of franchising is barely a generation old.

The growth of franchising has been truly remarkable. Few places in the world have not been touched by this organizational form. While critics attribute homogenization of cultures and economies to aggressive international franchising, the efficient distribution systems, business ownership opportunities, and contributions to society through employment and taxes are undeniable. Additionally, franchisors have proved themselves capable of thinking globally but acting locally by adjusting their product and service offerings to local markets.

But what do we know about franchising? Authors of books and articles about franchising come more frequently from practitioners than from objective researchers. Pioneers such as William Rosenberg of Dunkin' Donuts and Dave Thomas of Wendy's published their autobiographies, giving their views from personal experience. The point of academic research is to avoid personal biases by using an impersonal lens in examining how franchising works. It is here that Ilan Alon is making a critical contribution.

Alon has made major contributions to our understanding of franchising, both through his own research and through his compilations of studies by other scholars. Early studies of franchising were predominantly domestic investigations in English-speaking regions, North America, the United Kingdom, and, more recently, Australia. Alon pioneered research into the internationalization of franchising with his dissertation at Kent State University, then, in collaboration with Dianne Welsh, published studies from Asia, Europe, Latin America and other parts of the world.

This book represents a natural extension of his work to date. Here he has organized the best of what studies have documented about successful franchise operations. Alon succinctly extracts from observations about international franchising from both the scholarly and trade literature. Along with these citations, he adds insights that he has gained through research and experience. As a result, we have a book that advances the body of knowledge on international franchising for the academic community. This enables educators to provide high quality information to students and other audiences.

The book also contains guidance for franchisors and franchisees in their efforts to achieve success in the global marketplace, particularly through the case studies of Kodak and Marks & Spencer. Finally, Alon acknowledges that public policymakers are giving ever greater attention to franchising. This book provides factual information for those concerned with legislation and regulation of franchising. Whichever group you are in, to know franchising, you must have a global perspective.

Frank Hoy, Ph.D.
El Paso, Texas, USA
2005

Acknowledgements

This book is a product of over nine years of research on the subject of franchising, leading to numerous articles, books, and presentations on the subject. Collectively, the chapters of this book integrate much of my research on franchising as a global phenomenon.

It is needless to say that many people and organizations have been instrumental in my professional development and franchising research leading to this point. But, an acknowledgement of select contributors is worth mentioning. Key among them, of course, are my parents, wife, family, mentors, friends and colleagues. This book is dedicated to my family.

Franchising was introduced to me through Dr. John Ryans, a longtime Kent State University faculty member in international business and marketing and James R. Good Chair of Global Strategy at Bowling Green State University. It was Dr. David L. McKee Professor of Economics at the Graduate School of Management of Kent State University who supported, encouraged, and endured through my years of dissertation research, which led me on this path.

The path of franchising research is truly and fruitful one. Franchising has been largely developed by niche researchers who cut across the traditional disciplinary divides (e.g., marketing, management, law, economics, finance, international business, and entrepreneurship). Organizations such as the International Society of Franchising (ISOF), in particular, and USASBE, more generally, have united these researchers leading to new research interactions. I am particularly thankful to the various organizers of ISOF for showing the relevance and advancing knowledge on franchising globally.

Also, the following organizations have to be acknowledged: Blackwell Publishing, Sage Publication, St. Luis University, Journal of Business & Entrepreneurship, Academy of Marketing Science Review, and Thunderbird International Business Review for earlier versions of some chapters.

I would also like to thank my colleagues and co-authors namely Ralph Drtina, James Gilbert, David McKee, James Johnson, Noora Anttonen, Mika Tuunanen, Mark Munoz, and Igor Pavlin for having patience, working under pressure, and for their singular contributing to the emergent field of franchising. Included in this group of respected contributors are foreword writer Peter Holt, an executive and veteran of the industry, and the preface writer Frank Hoy, an influential franchising author. Their full biographical sketches are included in the back of this book.

Finally, we would like to thank Springer, the publisher, and, in particular, Sean Lorre, the editor, for showing flexibility and propelling the process of publishing this book.

I. Franchising Development

Chapter 1
Introduction

Ilan Alon

Crummer Graduate School of Business, Rollins College

In recent years, a plethora of articles have emerged discussing franchising in a global context. A basic search (conducted on June 9, 2005 by the author) on "international franchising" using the popular database of *ProQuest Direct* revealed 123 publications. However, only 25 of the 123 (about 20%) were in scholarly journals. *Franchising World, World Trade, International Marketing Review, Hotel and Motel Management, Nation's Restaurant News, Nation's Business, and Success* were the most relevant publications associated with the search. Of these, only *International Marketing Review* is a refereed journal. In the same fashion, recent years have also seen an increase in the number of scholarly books focusing on global franchising including:

1. *The Economics of Franchising,* Roger D. Blair, Francine Lafontaine (2005)
2. *Incentive Based Franchise- a New Model for World Governance,* Sondlo L. Mhlaba (2005)
3. *Economics and Management of Franchising Networks,* Josef Windsperger, Gerard Cliquet, George Hendrikse, Mika Tuunanen (2004)
4. *Franchising and Licensing: Two Powerful Ways to Grow Your Business in Any Economy,* Andrew J. Sherman (2003)
5. *Franchising,* Robert T. Justis, Richard J. Judd (2003)
6. *International Franchising in Industrialized Markets: Western and Northern Europe,* Ilan Alon, Dianne Welsh (2003)
7. *Franchising: An International Perspective,* Frank Hoy, John Stanworth (2002)
8. *International Franchising in Industrialized Markets: North America, Pacific Rim, and Other Countries,* Dianne Welsh, Ilan Alon (2002)
9. *International Franchising in Emerging Markets: Central and Eastern Europe and Latin America,* Dianne Welsh, Ilan Alon (2001)

10. *International Franchising in Emerging Markets: China, India, and Other Asian Countries,* Ilan Alon, Dianne Welsh (2001)

Increased interest in the global context of franchising is evident in the emergent literature on the subject. This book adds to the scant but growing academic literature on franchising globally by examining theoretical and practical aspects of franchising from the standpoints of franchisors and policy makers. The book is divided into four sections. Section I deals with franchising development explaining why franchisors use franchising, the social and economic benefits and costs of franchising to host markets, and measuring the economic impact of franchising on a locality. Section II focuses on financial impact of franchising to franchisors, how franchisors evaluate foreign markets, master international franchising, and how franchisors cluster. Section III evaluates franchising conditions in three emerging markets: Russia, the Philippines, and Slovenia. Finally, section IV examines two cases of companies using franchising internationally, one of Kodak in China and the other of Marks and Spensor internationally. A chapter by chapter review in each section follows.

SECTION I: FRANCHISING DEVELOPMENT

Chapter 2 examines when franchisors use franchising. The question of whether to franchise or to own has garnered research interest in recent years. Two popular approaches used to explain the proportion of franchising in the franchisor's system, resource-scarcity and agency theories, are explained and tested for the retailing sector. The chapter claims that a complete explanation of franchising needs both. The study combines both theories to explain the proportion of franchised outlets in the US retailing sector and tracks the statistics associated with this industry for seven years in the 1990s. The findings show mixed results with regard to previous studies and hypothesized relationships. It shows that the proportion of franchising used by retailers is positively related to size (number of outlets) and geographical scope, and negatively related to the rate of growth and the level of investment. Age and royalty rates are not found to be significant to the proportion of franchising. More sizable franchisors with greater scope of operation, and those with lower level of system growth and required level of investment, are more likely to use franchising in their future expansion.

Chapter 3 analyzes the economic and social impacts of international franchising on regional development from the perspective of the host market with emphasis on developing countries. The conventional wisdom that prevails in the West is that franchising provides a net benefit to the host market. In addition to the obvious economic benefits of employment, output and tax, franchising development contributes qualitatively by injecting expertise and training in various industries and increasing the entrepreneurial and managerial capabilities and skills of the labor force. On the other hand, the unique nature of international franchising creates some social pressures, such as a potential increase in a cultural clash and a perceived reduction in national culture. The chapter discusses the implications of franchising to the developing counties, assessing both the potential benefits and their associated costs. Using the framework of this chapter, researchers, policy makers, and franchising practitioners can better evaluate the total impact of franchising and its desirability in the less affluent world.

Chapter 4 seeks to understand the potential economic impact of franchising on a local economy. Using Economic Analysis in Planning (IMPLAN) model, the study measures the economic effects of spending in three service industries in which franchising prevails: (1) eating and drinking, (2) management consulting, and (3) hotel sectors. IMPLAN is an economic analysis system designed to measure the direct, indirect and induced effects of industry spending on economic output and employment, allowing planners to assess the industry-specific differences. This article examines the economic impacts of potential franchising investment in a small city in Upstate New York. The total economic output multipliers found were about 1.14 and varied little in the three sectors. In contrast, there were considerable variations in the employment multiplier. Eating and drinking places, with 38 jobs created for every million dollars spent in the local economy, had the highest employment multipliers among the three industries.

SECTION II: FRANCHISING STRATEGIES AND TYPES

Chapter 5 sheds light on the debate on franchising success/failure. This debate has developed among franchising practitioners, franchising researchers, and support groups relating to the promise of the franchising as an organizational form and a method of distribution. On the one hand, some espouse franchising as a strategy for growth that limits the risk of failure. This group is typified by franchisors, franchise associations, and selected industry observers. On the other hand, another group of researchers has departed from accepted notions of the franchising success, claiming that it is no less risky than other forms of business. Given the apparent disagreement between the two groups, the purpose of this chapter is to investigate the relationship between the use of franchising at the chain level and one measure of the chain's financial performance, return on equity (ROE), in the context of the DuPont model. The results show no appreciable difference in the financial performance of franchising vs. non-franchising firms in the restaurant sector among publicly-traded firms. Therefore, franchising form neither improves nor worsens the return on equity for brands in the restaurant sector.

Chapter 6 provides a prescriptive framework for analyzing the foreign environments of franchising for international expansion, mostly from an American perspective. The chapter develops a macro environmental model of international franchising that delineates the critical socio-economic country factors associated with the expansion of US international franchising. These factors divided into (1) economic, (2) demographic, (3) distance, and (4) political dimensions, and should be useful to both franchisors wishing to expand to foreign markets and academicians wanting to build empirical models explaining the internationalization of US franchising systems. In a related study, using correlation analysis to link environmental factors with international franchising activity, Alon, Toncar and McKee (2000) found that per capita GDP, level of population, urbanization, female labor-force participation, level of individualism, and sex role differentiation are positively related to international franchising, while political risk and, to a lesser extent, power distance and uncertainty avoidance, are negatively related to international franchising.

Chapter 7 investigates a common form of international franchising expansion, master international franchising. Master international franchising is the fastest growing and most prevalent mode of entry by U.S. based franchisors abroad. The purpose of the chapter is to develop propositions concerning the impact of select organizational variables on the use of master franchising agreements by business-format franchisors overseas. The article proposes that the organizational factors of master international franchising divide into resource-based, knowledge-based, and strategy-based explanations. Franchisors with modest resources, internationally unknown brand names, little experience in international markets, and know-how that is transferable are more likely to use master franchising as an international franchising mode of entry. These franchisors will also tend to charge more of the price upfront through the franchisee fee and less over time through royalties and to pursue a multi-domestic strategy.

Drawing upon Castrogiovanni & Justis' (1998) organizational configurations of franchising firms and the literature on master franchising, chapter 8 looks at how internationally-minded franchisor group together. The chapter empirically examines the typologies of internationally-minded franchisors at the system level and the mode of entry they are likely to use when expanding overseas. Applying cluster analysis to a sample of 261 US-based franchisors, we found evidence of three types of franchisors, corresponding to Castrogiovanni and Justis' *entrepreneurial, confederation,* and *carbon-copy* forms. We also found that master international franchising was the preferred expansion mode for the *confederation* form of franchisors, followed by *carbon-copy* and *entrepreneurial* franchisors. This research extends the study of franchise configurations to internationally-bound franchisors. The findings support the view that franchise groupings exist and that the characteristics of each may help explain variance in franchising strategies.

SECTION III: FRANCHISING IN EMERGING MARKETS

Section III presents contemporary reviews of franchising conditions of three emerging markets: Russia, Philippines, and Slovenia. Emerging markets embody the most dynamic opportunities for global franchisors (Welsh and Alon, 2001; Alon and Welsh 2001). Chapter 9 makes a contribution to the state of knowledge on franchising in Russia by analyzing Russia as a target market for international franchising entrepreneurship. First, past research and literature on franchising in Russia and other emerging markets is reviewed. The country's franchising environment is examined in relation to five environmental factors: (1) demographics, (2) economy, (3) social and political environment, (4) culture, and (5) legislation. Some preliminary information on a major franchising system in Russia is presented. A complete SWOT (strengths, weaknesses, opportunities, and threats) analysis for international franchising in Russia is provided in the conclusion section.

Chapter 10 analyzes the franchising environment in the Philippines, an emerging market in Southeast Asia with close and long historical ties to the US market. As part of the exploration of the potential challenges and opportunities in the Philippine market, the authors peruse the environmental factors franchising from political, legal, economic, financial and social standpoints, the competitiveness in the franchising sector, the four marketing P's, strategic control measures, and the modes of entry available to prospective market entrants. The research information and strategies provided is beneficial to academics and business people seeking to understand the franchising dynamics in a key emerging market in Southeast Asia. It provides the background needed for the creation of a country-specific international market entry plan for potential franchisors and franchisees wishing to operate in the Philippines.

Chapter 11 proposes that research of franchising in the EU requires a heuristic examination of operative networks in order to establish the existence of key parameters of franchising as contained in the European Franchise Federation's definition of franchising. The chapter discusses the conditions for franchising development in the Central European context of Slovenia. If many studies of franchising consider top-down approaches in replication of successful business formulae, this is a case of gradual development of a franchise network as it develops out of a voluntary chain. Transitional conditions may negatively influence the growth and the long-term well being of a franchise system, coupled with the change in the span of autonomy required for conversion of a voluntary chain into a franchise system.

SECTION IV: CASES IN INTERNATIONAL FRANCHISING

Section IV present two cases of companies utilizing franchising in their international operations: Kodak, an American imaging firm, and Marks & Spenser, a British retailer. What is interesting about these firms is that both do not utilize franchising in their domestic market, but *do* franchise abroad. The conditions under which these companies chose to use franchising are discussed in the context of these firms' internationalization strategies.

The first case in this section, presented in Chapter 12, is focused Kodak's franchising in China, the largest emerging market in the world. According to Kodak, China poses unparalleled opportunities for low-cost production in addition to opportunities to market products and services to the world's largest nation. According to the company's estimate, China will become the largest market in the world for photographic products and services within the next 10 years. The chapter reviews Kodak's operations in China and presents an interview with a local franchising manager in Shanghai - the largest and most dynamic city in China. It provides a unique glimpse into the inner working of the organization's franchising activities in China.

In contrast to chapter 12 which examines franchising arrangement in China for an American multinational company, chapter 13's case study describes the internationalization of Marks & Spencer (M&S), a giant British retailer, which in part involved the usage of franchising. In the late 1990s, the company suffered a series of misfortunes, both at home (Britain) and abroad. The case reviews the different modes of entry the company used in selected regions and markets. The company made large investments in Europe and North America. Franchising was primarily used in emerging markets.

REFERENCES

Alon, Ilan, Mark Toncar, and David McKee (2000), "Evaluating Foreign-Market Environments for International Franchising Expansion," *Foreign Trade Review*, 35 (1), 1-11.

Castrogiovanni, G. J. and Justis, R.T. (1998) "Franchising configurations and transitions." *The Journal of Consumer Marketing*, 15 (2), 170-187.

Alon, Ilan and Dianne Welsh, eds. (2001), *International Franchising in Emerging Markets: China, India and Other Asian Countries*, Chicago IL: CCH Inc. Publishing.

Welsh, Dianne and Ilan Alon, eds. (2001), *International Franchising in Emerging Markets: Central and Eastern Europe and Latin America*, Chicago IL: CCH Inc. Publishing.

Chapter 2
Why Do Companies Use Franchising?

Ilan Alon
Crummer Graduate School of Business, Rollins College

INTRODUCTION

Franchising has experienced unprecedented growth during the last two decades both in the United States and abroad (Alon and McKee 1999). In the United State of America, for example, according to the US Department of Commerce, the number of business format franchises increased almost tenfold between 1972 to 1988 (Kostecka 1988). While in 1992 franchise sales accounted for $803 billion in sales, the International Franchising Association (1995) predicted that franchise sales will reach $1 trillion by the year 2000. In 2004, the International Franchising Association reported that franchising accounts for 760,000 businesses generating $1.53 trillion, about 10% of the private sector economy.

The study on the use of franchising is relevant to small business across multiple industries. According to the Uniform Franchise Offering Circular (UFOC), there were 1,178 franchisors with over 320,000 outlets, representing over 18 different sectors, operating in the United States in 1997. Twelve percent had no franchisee-owned units, 16 percent had less than 10 outlets, and 27 percent had between 11-50 units. Those with the largest number of units (500 and above) made up only nine percent, the smallest concentration of franchised systems (International Franchise Association 1999). In this chapter's sample of retail franchises, about a third of the franchisors had less than 10 franchisees, while 10 percent had no franchisees at all in their system. The median age and size were 11 years and 30 outlets, respectively. Therefore, this chapter is especially relevant to small business management, particularly from the franchisor's standpoint.

This chapter uses two popular approaches, resource-scarcity and agency theories, to examine the proportion of franchising in the US retailing sector. Although there is some disagreement between resource-scarcity and agency theorists regarding the causal factors of domestic franchising, by integrating variables from both the agency and resource-scarcity theories researchers have developed models with greater explanatory power (Carney and Gedajlovic 1991; Combs and Castrogiovanni 1994).

Using previously established theories and variables, this research innovates by examining franchising over time (longitudinally), rather than at a point in time (cross-sectionally), and by focusing on one industry, namely retailing. Examining one industry over time allows the researcher to (1) obtain an in-depth understanding of the industry, (2) control for competitive and industry variations, and (3) increase the sample size associated with the studied industry. Dant and his co-authors (1996) proposed that industry aggregation may hide industry differentials and margins, masking the true nature of the causal factors between organizational variables and the proportion of franchising. Resource and agency variables may also impact the relative proportion of franchising depending on the industry studied. Indeed, the meta-analysis conducted by Dant and others in 1996 found that industry-specific differences were such that analyses that did not take them into account could have flaws in their conclusions. Furthermore, comparing franchising across industries elides the obvious facts that different industries have different motivations for franchise-based expansion and that there will be variations in the degree to which individual industries will tend to franchise.

In the conclusion of their meta-analysis, Dant and his colleagues (1996, p. 440) wrote that "as for future research, foremost, there is an urgent need to study ownership redirection in sectors other than restaurants." Our focus is on the retailing industry because (1) franchising has been associated with the retailing sector (Cross and Walker 1987); (2) much of retailing is franchised, accounting for $900 million in sales and 40 percent of aggregate retail sales in the US (Rubel 1995); and (3) franchising is expected to grow in importance for the retailing industry. Therefore, this chapter seeks here to expand Dant's suggestion that a focus upon one industry is appropriate, and moves from the perhaps stale ground of restaurant franchising into a focused analysis of the retail industry from a business-format franchising perspective (defined below), with appropriate sidelong glances at out-of-industry examples that illustrate our points.

DEFINITIONS OF FRANCHISING

Franchising divides into product/trade-name franchising and business-format franchising. "Product/trade-name franchising is a distribution system in which suppliers make contracts with dealers to buy or sell products or product lines" (Falbe and Dandridge 1992, p. 43). The International Franchise Association (IFA), the major business-format franchising trade association, defines franchising as "a continuing relationship in which the franchisor provides a licensed privilege to do business, plus assistance in organizing, training, merchandising and management, in return for a consideration from the franchisee" (Franchise Opportunities Handbook

1994, p. ix). Similarly, the US Department of Commerce defines franchising as "an ongoing business relationship between franchisor and franchisee that includes not only product, service and trade-mark, but the entire business concept itself--a marketing strategy and plan, operating manuals and standards, quality control, and continuing process of assistance and guidance" (Kostecka 1988, p. 3).

The difference between product/trade-name franchising and business-format franchising is that the latter offers a method of operation or business system that includes a strategic plan for growth and ongoing guidance (Falbe and Dandridge 1992). Because business-format (from hereon franchising) franchising is the basis for most franchising ventures, it is the focus of this chapter.

THEORETICAL ANTECEDENTS

The focus of resource-scarcity and agency theories is different, requiring different causal connections for their respective explanations of franchising. Resource-scarcity theories attempt to explain franchising as the desire to expand with scant resources, while agency theories postulate that firms franchise to minimize monitoring and shirking costs. Traditional measures of resources include size, age and rate of growth (Combs and Castrogiovanni 1994). According to resource-scarcity theorists, the more resources a firm has, the less it needs franchising to expand and, therefore, a negative relation is hypothesized between size, age, rate of growth and the proportion of franchising. Geographical scope of operation, investment and royalty hypotheses have all developed out of agency theory. To minimize the amount of monitoring needed, geographically dispersed units have a greater tendency to be franchised. As a further guarantor of investment and to maximize profits, companies will often demand higher initial investments from franchisees and will require large royalties to capture the value of intangibles such as brand-name, trade-mark and know-how (Combs and Castrogiovanni 1994). Table 2.1 shows the hypotheses derived from these competing theories. The section that follows provides a review.

Table 2.1: The Hypotheses, Variables, and Measurements

Hypothesis	Variable	Measurement	Relationship
H1	LSize	Log (total # of units)	Negative
H2	LAge	Log (years in operation)	Negative
H3	Growth	Yearly growth rate	Positive
H4	Scope	0=Local 1=National	Positive
H5	Investment	Mean start-up costs	Positive
H6	Royalties	Mean royalties	Positive

Resource-Scarcity Theories

Resource-scarcity theories state that companies franchise in order to extend scarce resources. Early research explained the existence of franchising through the need of franchisors for financial capital (Oxenfeldt and Kelly 1969; Hunt 1973). The trade-off is a familiar one: the franchisee provides an infusion of capital through fees and royalties and offers the franchisor (relatively) inexpensive growth. Subsequent research, however, tended to focus on the fact that firms used franchising because they also needed human capital (Norton 1988), managerial talent (Oxenfeldt and Kelly 1969; Combs and Castrogiovanni 1994), and local knowledge (Combs and Castrogiovanni 1994). Resource-scarcity theories were embraced because of their intuitive appeal and logic (Fladmoe-Lindquist 1996).

A central tenet of these theories is the belief that as franchise systems matured and accumulated resources, the need for franchising would inevitably decrease. Thus, franchising firms would tend to shift from franchisee-owned to company-owned outlets for expansion. Hunt (1973) showed that the trend in US fast-food franchising was toward company-owned franchises and that this trend was because franchisors no longer needed to extend their resources. Hunt used three pieces of support to back his hypothesis that a lack of capital was the major motivation behind decisions to franchise. First, the percentage of company-operated, fast-food franchises increased from about one to about ten between 1960 and 1970. However, most of the expansion (about 70 percent of the franchises) came from new development (Combs and Castrogiovanni 1994). Second, larger fast-food franchises had more company-operated units. Finally, older franchising systems had disproportionately higher percentages of company-owned units.

Combs and Castrogiovanni (1994) proposed that as franchisors matured and accumulated resources, they bought back the most profitable franchises to capture additional rents because clauses in the franchising agreement allowed them to do so. A telling observation by LaFontaine and Kaufmann (1994) recognized that resource-scarcity theories imply that firms have a life-cycle that starts with franchising to raise capital and ends with 'buy-outs' as the system matures. As a result, theories founded upon this premise are committed to the hypothesis that an increase in the resources of a given firm will tend to decrease both the motivation to continue franchising and the actual proportion of franchised outlets to company-owned units within the system as a whole. A recent study of 91 publicly-traded restaurant chains revealed that capital-restrained companies were more likely to use franchising for expansion (Combs and Ketchen 1999).

A Critique of Resource-Scarcity Theories

But resource-scarcity theories have come under sharp conceptual and empirical attack, not least because some critics (notably Rubin 1978 and Norton 1988) have proposed that the capital-scarcity explanation of franchising is at odds with finance theory. One obvious critique is the suggestion that selling the shares of the chain to finance expansion would be more efficient than buying back units. Brickley and Weisbach (1991, p. 28) stated that "the company's value would be higher if it sold residual claims on the overall organization rather than franchising individual units because of the lower risk premium." Norton (1988) pointed out that even if capital imperfections existed, the only time franchising would be preferable to outright ownership of a chain's stores is when the franchisor is more risk-averse than the franchisee. However, Martin (1988) claimed that, in fact, this assumption about the franchisor is generally unfounded. The franchisee is more risk-averse than the franchisor and this is why he/she prefers to own a proven business system, instead of developing one from scratch. Norton (1988) suggested that if a franchisor were more risk-averse than the franchisee, the latter would request a premium, limiting the profits of the franchisor from the unit.

Further research continued to undermine resource-scarcity theories as weak, and even conflicting, evidence was uncovered; the intuitive logic of the premises was eroding. Combs and Castrogiovanni (1994) observed that, in contrast to the predictions of resource-scarcity theory, larger firms actually used more franchising in their development. They also found a weak negative relationship between the age of the franchisor and the use of franchising and no relationship at all between the growth of the franchisor and the use of franchising. After locating their hypothetical foundations, LaFontaine and Kaufmann (1994) challenged the basic assumption of resource-scarcity theories--that companies prefer chain-ownership to franchising. Franchising was shown to be the preferred mode of operation even in larger, more established systems. Furthermore, Brickley and Weisbach (1991) noted that franchising was not limited to small and young firms by merely pointing to such corporate giants as McDonald's and Budget Rent-A-Car.

A Defense of Resource-Scarcity Theories

Even critics of such theories were quick to seize upon several valuable elements; naturally, one need not wholly reject a theory merely because pieces of it require adjustment. And it was in the salvaged parts of the resource-scarcity perspective that a synthesis between heretofore mutually exclusive paradigms began to take shape. In defense of resource-scarcity theories, LaFontaine and Kaufmann (1994) argued that the managerial lack of incentive to expand might necessitate higher returns in financial markets. Furthermore, obtaining financing through capital markets (going public) is an expensive and a time consuming process that may be as hard to implement as franchising. Thus, capital gained from franchisees can be more efficient than capital obtained from selling shares. Two findings supported LaFontaine and Kaufmann's argument: franchisors that operated over 16 years had higher percentages of company-owned stores and, second, franchisors that were subsidiaries of larger corporations tended to have higher proportions of company-owned stores.

Inevitably, many agency theorists rejected resource-scarcity theories solely due to the flawed initial assumption identified by Oxenfeldt and Kelley in 1969, namely that franchisors would seek full ownership of all stores once they matured and no longer needed the inputs--capital and otherwise--of the franchisee. Other salient factors salvageable from resource-scarcity models include the fact that it can be advantageous for a big firm to franchise in an isolated location, that demand variability can influence the decision to franchise, and that a lack of local knowledge and a desire to test a given market might be unquantifiable--though powerful--incentives to explore franchise options. Furthermore, skill and capabilities (resources) associated with managing franchisees are not necessarily transferable to managing company-owned outlets, but can be used to obtain competitive advantage (Combs and Ketchen 1999).

Agency Theories

"An agency relationship is present whenever one party (the principal) depends on another party (the agent) to undertake some action on the principal's behalf (Bergen, Dutta, and Walker 1992, p. 1). In the case of franchising, the franchisor is the principal and the franchisee is the agent. Agency theories assume that organizations want to minimize their organizational costs, "the costs of aligning the incentives of principals and agents, including bonding and monitoring and the related forgone output attributable to those activities" (Norton 1988, p. 202).

Because franchising is an organizational method that minimizes organizational costs--monitoring costs in particular--by rewarding a franchisee's efficiency with profits, it is clear that the role of the franchisee is both that of a sole-proprietor and that of a single-unit manager for a chain. Franchisees are "owner-managers who typically bear the residual risks of a local operation because their wealth is largely determined by the difference between the stochastic revenue inflows to the local operation and promised payments to other factors of production" (Norton 1988, p. 201). Since the franchisee has a residual claim and ownership in the franchised unit, shirking should be minimized.   Shane (1996a) proposed that franchising is a mechanism of minimizing agency problems of growth.   He found support for the twin hypotheses that franchising spurs growth and that it increases a firm's likelihood for survival.   Because of monitoring costs, the increase in potential income generally associated with direct ownership may be insufficient to offset the greater efficiency of the franchisee (Bergen et al. 1992).

Empirical Support for Agency Theories

Norton (1988) hypothesized a direct relationship between increases in monitoring costs and increases in the number of franchising contracts a firm would be willing to undertake.   The two variables Norton (1988) used as proxies for monitoring costs, population dispersion and labor intensity, were found to be positively associated with the percentage of establishments categorized as franchise-holders.

Brickley and Dark (1987) found support for the hypotheses that the proportion of franchising units increases with employee-monitoring costs and that industries characterized by non-repeat customers are less likely to franchise.   This second hypothesis highlights several downsides of franchising: the inequitable distribution of risk and the tendency of some franchisees to shirk their responsibilities and ride the coattails of the parent organization. Using US Department of Commerce data, which summarized the proportion of franchising in 15 industries in 1985, Brickley and Weisbach (1991) found statistical support for agency-theory assumptions.   It seems, therefore, that empirical evidence favors agency theory's explanations of franchising; however, even these explanations have not escaped criticism.

A Critique of Agency Theories

A major critique of agency theory is its ahistoric orientation (Carney and Gedajlovic 1991).   The assumption of agency theory that franchising companies have a known brand name was criticized on the grounds that many small and young firms that have neither an identifiable brand name nor uniform product quality are engaged in franchising (Carney and Gedajlovic 1991).   These same two researchers also observed that agency theory's concentration on minimizing shirking and monitoring through franchising often ignores the fact that franchisees also engage in creative problem-solving and tactical decision-making.

Another problem in agency theory is the assumption that the principal (franchisor) has unilateral control over the agent, or franchisee (Bergen and others 1992). In recent years, the power of the franchisor has decreased as the use of franchisee associations and councils has started to proliferate (Stanworth and Dandridge 1994).

Reconciliation

A number of researchers have tried to reconcile the differences in both theories by building a comprehensive model providing causal connections from both paradigms. Carney and Gedajlovic (1991) found support for both resource-scarcity and agency theories, and Combs and Castrogiovanni (1994) discovered similar results not long thereafter, suggesting that a full explanation of franchising may require variables from both resource-scarcity and agency perspectives. Combs and Ketchen (1999) found that capital scarcity can help agency theory explain franchising. They showed empirically that public restaurant chains which had less capital were more likely to use franchising, and provided anecdotal evidence that public firms, which have greater access to capital markets, are more likely to use company-owned outlets.

METHODOLOGY

This chapter utilizes ordinary least-square regressions to test six independent variables on the proportion of franchised units. Using data collected by *Entrepreneur* from 1990 to 1997, a sample of 361 observations representing all non-food retailing firms listed during the time period was compiled. *Entrepreneur*'s sample covers about half of all US franchisors; thus, this chapter examines a rather large portion of US franchised retailers and its findings are, therefore, applicable to many of the industry's participants. Retailers of all sizes are included in the sample which ranges from stores with less than 10 franchised outlets, such as Talking Book World and Street Corner News, to ones with thousands of outlets such as Blockbuster Video and Radio Shack.

Data

Entrepreneur's data set has been used in both domestic (Combs and Castrogiovanni 1994; Martin and Justis 1993) and international (Alon 1999; Shane 1996b) franchising studies. Although the inclusion of franchisors in the survey is voluntary, several researchers proposed that no serious biases exist (Shane 1996b; Combs and Castrogiovanni 1994). Furthermore, the magazine itself validates over 80 percent of the data through the Uniform Franchise Offering Circular (UFOC), a prospectus containing key information required by US regulations.

Measurements

The independent and dependent variables use the operational definitions of Combs and Castrogiovanni (1994) to measure the amount of resources. The dependent variable is the proportion of franchised units (PF). The independent variables are (1) logarithm of size, total number of units (LSIZE); (2) logarithm of age, years since firm began (LAGE); (3) growth, yearly growth-rate (GWTH); (4) scope, geographical scope of operation (SCOPE); (5) investment, average start-up costs (INVEST); and (6) royalties, average royalty-rates (ROY). Table 2.1 summarizes the variables, measurements, and hypotheses.

Results

The descriptive statistics and the correlation matrix are shown in Table 2.2. Table 2.3 shows the model of franchise ownership. The model is significant at 0.00000 level, which means that, collectively, the variables help explain the proportion of franchised units in the system. The R-squared is 0.22, suggesting that organizational variables explain 22 percent of the variation in the proportion of franchising in the studied sample.

Table 2.2: Descriptive Statistics and Correlation Table

Variable	Mean	SD	Minimum	Maximum
LSize	1.53	0.77	0.00	3.83
LAge	1.08	0.39	0.00	2.08
Growth	0.39	0.87	-0.88	7.35
Scope	0.62	0.49	0.00	1.00
Investment	159.12	150.18	2.00	1023.00
Royalty	4.89	3.09	0.00	50.00
PF	0.72	0.34	0.00	1.00

	LSIZE	LAGE	GWTH	SCP	INVES	ROY	PF
LSIZE	1.00						
LAGE	0.52	1.00					
GWTH	-0.15	-0.34	1.00				
SCOPE	0.31	0.05	-0.03	1.00			
INVES	0.32	0.34	-0.06	0.18	1.00		
ROY	-0.11	-0.03	-0.03	-0.05	-0.09	1.00	

	LSIZE	LAGE	GWTH	SCP	INVES	ROY	PF
PF	0.45	0.19	-0.15	0.22	0.05	-0.09	1.00

Table 2.3: Franchise Ownership Model

Dependent Variable	PF	Number of Observations	361
Mean of Dep. Variable	0.7250	Std. Dev. of Dep. Var.	0.3388
Std. Error of Regression	0.2989	Sum of Squared Residuals	31.6315
R - squared	0.2347	Adjusted R - squared	0.2218
F(6, 354)	18.0971	Prob. Value for F	0.0000

Variable	Coefficient	T-Ratio	P-Value
Constant	0.494		
H1: Size	0.211	7.913	0.0000
H2: Age	-0.043	-0.781	0.4352
H3: Growth	-0.041	-2.082	0.0381
H4: Scope	0.063	1.817	0.0700
H5: Invest	-0.003	-2.258	0.0245
H6: Royal	-0.006	-1.108	0.2688

The size variable was highly significant and positively related to the proportion of franchising. The bigger the retail operation, the more likely it is to use franchising in its expansion. This result is the opposite of what is expected from a resource-scarcity standpoint, but is consistent with the findings of at least one major study. Combs and Castrogiovanni (1994) observed that larger firms may have more franchised units because these firms utilized franchising when they were smaller, and this led to greater growth. Alternatively, agency theory suggests that the more units there are in the franchising system, the harder it is to monitor and control these units, and the more likely franchising then becomes.

Combs and Castrogiovanni (1994) suggested that industry variations may have masked the results of the size coefficient. Since this chapter uses a single industry research design, it has been able to confirm the results obtained by Combs and Castrogiovanni (1994), precluding the argument that industry variation accounts for the positive coefficient of size.

The results may reflect a current trend in the franchising sector, which is contrary to the resource-scarcity explanation. In the 1980s and early 1990s, for example, PepsiCo started buying many franchises in the belief that it would make higher profits by operating on margins as compared to franchisee fees and royalties. Recently, however, this trend has reversed itself. Pizza Hut, Taco Bell, and KFC (operating under Tricon corporate headquarters, a spun-off division of PepsiCo) announced they will increase the proportion of franchised units to 80 percent, following the example of industry leader McDonald's (Business Week 1998). This example illustrates that large firms are also inclined toward franchising, perhaps intentionally manipulating the proportion of franchising.

LaFontaine and Shaw (1999) explained the decline in the proportion of company ownership as a simple function of franchising expansion. All franchised firms start out as 100 percent company owned. As they become involved in franchising, the proportion of franchisee-owned units increases and later stabilizes between 80 to 90 percent. An illustrative example: Mister Money-USA Inc., a pawn shop operating out of Ft. Collins, Colorado, has grown from 15 company-owned stores and one franchise in 1996 (PF = 6 percent) to 12 company-owned and 17 franchises in 1998 (PF = 41 percent). Size, represented by the total number of outlets, has increased along with the proportion of franchising.

The age variable was negative as expected, although weakly so. Combs and Castrogiovanni (1994) also found a weak negative association between age and the proportion of franchising and predicted that, as these firms mature over time, this relationship will become stronger. Interestingly, the present study finds that the opposite has occurred: the relationship between age and the proportion of franchising has weakened. Age has no significant impact on the proportion of franchising in the retailing industry. As stated earlier, mature franchising firms have found that franchising is a long-term method of doing business that can lead to a more productive competitive stance. Franchising allows firms to grow faster, keep their entrepreneurial talent, and attract investment.

The growth rate variable was consistent with the theory of resource-scarcity, but inconsistent with the findings of Combs and Castrogiovanni (1994). While their study reveals a mildly significant (t=1.56) and positive relationship between the growth rate and the proportion of franchising, this chapter shows a strong negative relationship. The negative coefficient of the growth-rate suggests that firms with fewer resources rely more on franchising. Alternatively, the results suggest that the high growth-rate in the retailing sector is positively related to company expansion.

Similar to Combs and Castrogiovanni's findings (1994), the scope of operation is positive and significant. This finding is consistent with agency theory which explains that the greater the scope of operation, the more likely the franchisor is to use franchising to align the incentives of the franchisor and franchisee, lower monitoring costs, and reduce shirking. Companies that operate over a greater geographical area have a harder time monitoring their outlets and controlling their operations and, thus, will prefer to franchise rather than to own units in their system.

Unlike the prediction of agency theory and the findings of Combs and Castrogiovanni (1994), this chapter finds that investment, measured as the franchise fee, is negatively and significantly related to the proportion of franchising. Combs and Castrogiovanni (1994) proposed that higher investment would deter franchisees from violating the franchise agreement, due to fear of termination. The franchise fee is a component of what Shane (1996b) referred to as *ex ante* bonding. On the other hand, lower levels of investment will attract more prospective franchisees, increasing the potential proportion of franchising. A lower franchise fee, therefore, has the potential to increase the quantity of franchises demanded and, all other things being equal, the number of franchisee-owned units in the system.

According to the present study, the coefficient for royalties is negative but not significant to the proportion of franchising. From the franchisor's perspective, a moderately small increase in the royalty rates can significantly increase the present value of the franchise. Therefore, high royalties are conducive to franchising, increasing the desire of franchisors to supply their business format. As in the case of the franchise fee, franchisees, as buyers of the franchise, may require a lower price to stimulate the quantity of franchises demanded. Franchisees, however, can also benefit from greater royalties. Agrawal and Lal (1995) found that royalty rates positively affect (1) the incentive of the franchisor to invest in the brand name, (2) the incentive of the franchisee to invest in retail service, (3) the monitoring frequency of the franchisor, and (4) the ongoing support by the franchisor. The net effect equates to a greater probability of success for the average franchisee.

CONCLUSION

While the model as a whole presented herein is highly significant, the results at the variable level are mixed. Having a positive coefficient, the size variable contradicts the resource-scarcity thesis. The result for the size coefficient can be explained by agency theory. The more units a retailer has, the more difficult it is to keep track and monitor each unit, making franchising more likely. Also, as firms use more franchising, the proportion of franchises in their system must increase, resulting in a positive coefficient for size. Therefore, this research concludes that the number of outlets is positively related to the proportion of franchising in the retailing sector.

On the other hand, the negative coefficient of the rate of growth supports the idea that high-growth companies, with a greater resource base, will use less franchising, in line with the prediction of resource-scarcity theory. In summary, larger, slower-growing companies will tend to use more franchising, while smaller, faster-growing firms will use more company ownership. The increased competition in attracting potential franchisees has led smaller firms, with less recognizable brand names, to expand though company ownership. The data does not suggest that franchising is limited to young, small and high growth firms.

The results do not provide full support for the agency theory as well. While the coefficient of the scope variable provides support for the agency explanation, the investment and royalty variables do not lend the same backing. The positive coefficient for the geographical scope of operation is explainable through agency theory. A greater scope of operation reduces the monitoring capabilities of the firm, leading the firm to use more franchising to align the incentives of the franchisee (the agent) with the franchisor (the principal).

The significant negative coefficient of investment is peculiar. It suggests that the lower the level of investment, the greater the proportion of franchising. This result can be interpreted quite logically from the standpoint of the franchisee. That is, potential franchisees will tend to seek franchise systems that have a lower cost of operation and, in particular, lower up-front fees. The same logic applies to the royalty rates. However, risk-averse franchisees may be more willing to transfer a percentage of their future income receipts because these receipts represent the unpredictable portion of their future income associated with the intangible assets of the franchisor. Royalties also may increase the franchisee's chances for continuity as they motivate the franchisor to invest in several of the key success factors of unit sales, such as quality controls, new product innovation, and brand name equity.

Implications to Small Businesses

This study has several potential implications to small businesses in the retailing sector. First, small retailers may need to expand through company-owned outlets before being able to franchise successfully. This is because small firms are less likely to be successful in attracting potential franchisees compared to more established franchisors with well-known brands, such as Mail Boxes Etc., Blockbuster Video and Radio-Shack. In order for smaller retailers to attract franchisees, therefore, they must provide a better value by providing financial incentives such as discounted franchise fees and royalties. Franchisors with a national scope of operation are more likely to find franchisees because their potential market is larger. Some franchisors do not operate businesses in the 12 states that require the UFOC, probably because of the added regulatory burden, but these franchisors only own a minority (about 30 percent) of the total franchisees. Small franchisors who wish to increase the proportion of franchising in their systems should consider meeting the UFOC requirements and seeking franchisees throughout the United States.

Limitations

This study is not without limitations. The analytical method used cannot capture outside influences on the decision to franchise. In recent years, legal influences have severely limited franchisors' ability to transfer ownership from franchisees to the company or locate within a specified geographical region (Fortune 1995). Including external variables in the analyses can expand the explanation of the propensity to franchise. Second, the proxies used in this chapter to measure the resource-based and agency constructs are rather crude and are based on available secondary data and past literature. More refined measures of the constructs would greatly enhance our understanding of the relationships between firm-level variables and the proportion of franchising.

Future Research

This research suggests that researchers need to examine not only supply-side (franchisor-related), but also demand-side (franchisee-related) factors of franchising. The domestic market saturation of franchised retailers has led to greater competition for potential franchisees, increasing the latter's bargaining power. The increased power of franchisees has led to structural changes in the market, necessitating the need to examine the forces that govern the franchisee's selection of franchisors. The determinants of franchise ownership, therefore, may be related to factors within and outside the franchising system. Future research should examine this point in more detail.

The present study also suggests the use of disaggregate data because of variations between industries and data problems resulting from aggregation. Researchers should seek to explain franchising in other industries, allowing for a greater base of comparison.

REFERENCES

Agrawal, Deepak, and Rajiv Lal (1999), "Contractual Arrangements in Franchising: An Empirical Investigation," *Journal of Marketing Research*, 32 (2), 213-219.

Alon, Ilan (1999), *The Internationalization of U.S. Franchising Systems*, New York: Garland Publishing.

Alon, Ilan and David McKee (1999), "Toward a Macro Environmental Model of International Franchising," *Multinational Business Review*, 7 (1), 76-82.

Bergen, M., S. Dutta, and O. C. Walker (1992), "Agency Relationships in Marketing: A Review of the Implication and Application of Agency and Related Theories," *Journal of Marketing*, (July), 1-24.

Brickley, J. A., and F. H. Dark (1987), "The Choice of Organizational Form: The Case of Franchising," *Journal of Financial Economics*, 18 (2), 401-420.

Brickley, J. A., and M. S. Weisbach (1991), "An Agency Perspective on Franchising," *Financial Management*, 20 (1), 27-35.

Business Week (1998), "With All This Fizz, Who Needs Pepsi?" (October), 72-73.

Carney, M., and E. Gedajlovic (1991), "Vertical Integration in Franchising Systems: Agency Theory and Resource Explanations, *Strategic Management Journal*, 12 (8), 607-629.

Combs, James G., and Gary J. Castrogiovanni (1994), "Franchisor Strategy: A Proposed Model and Empirical Rest of Franchise versus Company Ownership," *Journal of Small Business Management*, 32 (2), 37-48.

Combs, James G. and David J. Ketchen Jr. (1999), "Can Capital Scarcity Help Agency Theory Explain Franchising? Revisiting the Capital Scarcity Hypothesis," *Academy of Management Journal*, 42 (2), 196-207.

Cross, James C., and Bruce J. Walker (1987), "Service Marketing and Franchising: A Practical Business Marriage," *Business Horizons*, 30 (6), 50-58.

Dant, Rajiv P., Audhesh K. Paswan, and Patrick J. Kaufmann (1996), "What We Know About Ownership Redirection in Franchising: A Meta-Analysis," *Journal of Retailing*, 72 (4), 429-444.

Entrepreneur (1990-1997), "Franchise 500," (March Editions).

Falbe, Cecilia M., and Thomas C. Dandridge (1992), "Franchising as a Strategic Partnership: Issues of Cooperation and Conflict in a Global Market," *International Small Business Journal*, 10 (3), 40-52.

Fladmoe-Lindquist, Karin (1996), "International Franchising: Capabilities and Development," *Journal of Business Venturing*, 11 (5), 419-438.

Franchise Opportunities Handbook (1994), US Department of Commerce Minority Business Development Agency, (October), Washington, D.C.

Fortune (1995), "Trouble in Franchise Nation," (March 6), 115-117.

Hunt, Shelbe D. (1973), "The Trend toward Company-Operated Units in Franchise Chains," *Journal of Retailing*, 49 (2), 3-11.

International Franchise Association (1999), "Second Franchise Study Offers Detailed Look at Concept," Washington, D.C.

International Franchise Association (1995), "Franchise Fact Sheet," (June), Washington D.C.

Kostecka, Andrew (1969-1988), *Franchising in the Economy*, Washington DC: U.S. Department of Commerce.

LaFontaine, Francine, and Kathryn L. Shaw (1999), "Company-Ownership Over the Life Cycle: What Can We Learn From Panel Data," in *Franchising Beyond The Millennium: Learning Lessons From The Past*, John Stanworth and David Purdy, eds., in 13th Annual Meeting of the Society of Franchising, Miami, Florida.

LaFontaine, Francine and Patrick J. Kaufmann (1994), "The Evolution of Ownership Patterns in Franchise Systems," *Journal of Retailing*, 70 (2), 97-114.

Martin, R. (1988), "Franchising and Risk Management," *American Economic Review*, 78 (5), 954-968.

Martin, R., and Justis R. (1993), "Franchising, Liquidity Constraints and Entry," *Applied Economics*, 25 (9), 1269-1277.

Norton, S. (1988), "An Empirical Look at Franchising as an Organizational Form," *Journal of Business*, 61, 197-217.

Oxenfeldt, Alferd R., and Anthony O. Kelly (1969), "Will Successful Franchise Systems Ultimately Become Wholly-Owned Chains?" *Journal of Retailing*, 44, 69-87.

Rubin, P. (1978), "The Theory of the Firm and the Structure of the Franchise Contract," *Journal of Law and Economics*, 21, 223-234.

Shane, S. (1996a), "Hybrid Organizational Arrangements and Their Implications For Firm Growth And Survival: A Study of New Franchisors," *Academy of Management Journal*, 39 (1), 216-234.

Shane, S. (1996b), "Why Franchise Companies Expand Overseas," *Journal of Business Venturing*, 11 (2), 73-88.

Stanworth, John, and Thomas Dandridge (1994), "Business Franchising and Economic Change: An Overview," *International Small Business Journal*, 12 (2), 12-14.

Chapter 3
What are the Social and Economic Benefits and Costs of Global Franchising?

Ilan Alon
Crummer Graduate School of Business, Rollins College

INTRODUCTION

According to a 2004 survey by the International Franchise Association, the positive economic impact of franchising on the U.S. economy is undeniable:

- Franchise businesses account for about half of retail sales, and 10% of the US private sector economy
- Franchise businesses directly employ over 9.8 million Americans, and generate a total of 18 million jobs (about 10% of the private sector workforce)
- Sales of franchised businesses have surpassed $1.5 trillion
- One out of 12 businesses is franchised

In a recent study of the US franchise sector conducted for the International Franchise Association, Franchise Recruiters Ltd (2003, p.2) concluded that "franchising is a foremost force in the creation of the US entrepreneurial revolution that continues to fuel the lethargic economy, producing new business owners and jobs."

Despite the impressive performance of franchising as an organization form in the U.S., internationally franchising has lagged behind and only over the last decade has picked momentum (Welsh and Alon, 2001). Emerging markets have offered a number of advantages to franchisors that include, but are not limited to, an expanding middle class, relatively unsaturated markets, urbanized and highly populated cities, a growing youth market, free trade zones, relatively friendly business laws, liberalized markets and transitioning economies, and a huge pent-up demand for western-style goods and services.

Policy makers in merging markets have observed the economic contributions of franchising in the developed markets and are increasingly seeking for ways to both develop and regulate this form of business. While in 1993 at least 24 nations developed trade association specializing in franchising (Preble and Hoffman, 1995), a decade later there are at least 55 national and regional franchise associations globally according to sources in the International Franchise Association. The attractiveness of emerging markets to the franchising sector coupled with the efforts by the host markets to stimulate economic development through franchising has led to the rapid diffusion of franchising globally (Hoffman and Preble, 2001).

Franchising is an organizational form primarily used in service industries and a method of transferring a business format via arm's length with minimum financial investment. Table 3.1 depicts the internationalization of U.S.-based franchising. What can be gleaned from the data is that franchisors exist in multiple industries and that these industries vary in terms of the internationalization of their franchising systems and their mode of entry. The data also suggest that most franchisors (63%) in the U.S. are seeking international franchisees. This data were calculated by compiling all the franchisors which appeared in *Entrepreneur Magazine* (a total of 640) by industry and counting those who indicated that they are interested in expanding overseas via franchising.

In recent years, expansion into emerging markets in Latin America, Eastern and Central Europe, and East Asia has accounted for much of the international expansion of franchising from industrialized world (Welsh and Alon, 2001; Alon and Welsh, 2001). Franchising has been used by emerging markets as a tool for economic development and for global integration. But since franchising in emerging markets is a new emerging phenomena (Alon and Welsh, 2001; Welsh and Alon, 2001), few papers have investigated a wide spectrum of social and economic concerns facing this nascent interaction. Therefore, the purpose of this chapter is to better understand the influence of franchising on development and transitioning in developing economies, discussing both the economic and social implications of the franchising mode of entry to low income countries. The rest of the paper is organized as follows: next, the link between globalization and franchising is established, setting the framework for the body of the paper which analyzes the economic and the social franchising environments. The chapter concludes with summary discussions and an agenda for future research.

Table 3.1: Industry Analysis of International Franchising in the U.S.

Industry	Number of Franchisors (By Category)	Seeking International (% Industry)	Canada Only (% Int'l)	Master Franchise Only (% Int'l)
1. Automotive	58	35 (40%)	8 (23%)	7 (20%)
2. Business Services	72	46 (64%)	10 (22%)	14 (30%)
3. Children Products	30	21 (70%)	5 (24%)	4 (19%)
4. Food (Quick Service)	94	40 (43%)	7 (18%)	35 (88%)
5. Food (Full Service)	30	18 (60%)	5 (28%)	5 (28%)
6. Food (Retail)	17	12 (71%)	0 (0%)	4 (33%)
7. Healthcare	6	4 (67%)	0 (0%)	1 (25%)
8. Home Improvement	59	36 (61 %)	9 (25%)	12 (33%)
9. Maintenance	68	47 (69%)	9 (19%)	14 (30%)
10. Personal Care	22	15 (68%)	8 (53%)	3 (20%)
11. Pet Business	7	5 (71%)	3 (60%)	1 (20%)
12. Recreation	25	18 (72%)	6 (33%)	3 (16%)
13. Retail	43	27 (63%)	12 (44%)	4 (15%)
14. Professional Service	74	49 (66%)	17 (34%)	15 (31%)
15. Technology Business	12	10 (83%)	0 (0%)	5 (50%)
16. Hotels and Motels	23	20 (87%)	1 (5%)	8 (40%)
17. Restaurant (4+5)	124	58 (47%)	12 (21%)	40 (69%)
18. Food Total (17+6)	141	70 (50%)	12 (17%)	44 (63%)
19. Total	640	403 (63%)	100 (25%)	135 (33%)

Calculated from Entrepreneur Magazine (2001), "22nd Annual Franchise 500," pp. 173-2

GLOBALIZATION AND FRANCHISING

Globalization – the trend toward a single, integrated, and interdependent global economy propelled by increases in international capital flows, international travel, cross-border exchange of information and ideas, and trade in goods and services – has prompted franchisors to think of the world as one market and to examine common needs within and across societies. The new global landscape has been shaped by organizational and strategic factors, industry structure, and environmental (economic, political, technological, etc.) and nationalistic differences. Cost differentials, greater connectivity (fueled to a large extent by the Internet), and emerging global consumer markets have made internationalization easier and more profitable. As a result, globalization has become a force that affects global consumption patterns in emerging nations by converging them with those of the West because of global mass media, tourism, immigration, pop culture and international marketing activities of transnational companies (Ger and Belk 1996). In particular, the youth market is increasingly integrated because its life is set in the context of greater globalization compared to the older generations. International franchisors often target this segment of the population when entering developing countries because they are more open to foreign franchising systems.

A seminal article by Levitt (1983) examined the globalization of markets and its impact on the organizations' internationalization strategy. Levitt suggested that global commonalities driven by advances in technology and communications have led to the standardization of products, manufacturing, and institutions of trade and commerce. These arguments have been echoed by Yip (1989, 1997) among others. The franchising sector has benefited from the trend toward the globalization of markets. As a result of this trend, the franchising firm can, for the most part, successfully duplicate its business format across multiple international locations. Therefore, franchising is often seen as an icon of (western-based economic) globalization.

The globalization debate transcends the discussions of international business, in general, and franchising, in specific. This paper focuses on elements of franchising that interact with the globalization debate. International franchising as an organizational form interacts with critical dimensions of globalization in terms of the cross-national particularly in terms of the associated global movements of goods and services, financial capital and ideas (e.g., knowledge, innovations, business formats, skills and capabilities), which will be discussed in more details in the economic and cultural impacts sections that follow. In order to set the context for cataloging the franchising impacts, the remainder of this section differentiates international franchising from other modes of international market entry, allowing the reader to understand how global franchising is different from licensing, exporting, and foreign direct investment. Such differences have an impact on the host market environments in which multinationals operate.

International franchising is a unique organizational form that is different from international licensing, exporting and foreign direct investment. Unlike licensing, franchising may provide tangible as well as intangible assets. The franchisor often gives the franchisee the products, machinery, and raw materials needed for the production process. Furthermore, a study by Arthur Andersen (1996) of US international franchisors found that the average investment in international franchising is $680,000. Often, investments in technology, management time, translations, supply chain, and professional advisors are significant before the company even opens its first outlet overseas. Furthermore, franchisors often prefer to own many of their international outlets as a means to test market their concepts and to control their intellectual property. Initial investment in company-owned outlets facilitate a later expansion by franchising in the host market. Unlike exporting, international franchising requires the development of a local supply chain and the acquisition of local trademarks and local knowledge. Finally, international franchising is also distinct from foreign direct investment in that it limits equity participation, exchange rate and country risks, and home country job loss, but retains a high degree of control that is difficult to emulate across cultures (Alon, 1999). From the host market perspective, Aydin and Kacker (1990) claimed that international franchising is less detrimental to the balance of payment than foreign direct investment because of minimal import content, little capital outflows, and relatively small repatriation of profits.

International franchising has a number of distinguishing features. The characteristics of the business stay the same regardless of ownership, and ownership can be transferred with relative ease without any change of operation and in relative secrecy (Burton and Cross 1995). Customers often do not know who the owner of the franchise is, although they often mistakenly assume it belongs to the multinational company, evident by occasional raids on high profile franchising outlets such as McDonald's, which symbolize the multinational company and portray the face of economic globalization. Given the mounting evidence of the uniqueness and importance of international franchising, Shane (1996, p. 86) concluded that "the use of franchise contracts appears to be an important long-term strategic choice in its own right for international service firms." The point is that economic and social impacts are specific to the mode of entry employed by the multinational company. The sections that follow examine the economic and social impacts in relation to international franchising in emerging markets.

ECONOMIC IMPACTS OF INTERNATIONAL FRANCHISING

The economic impacts of franchising are output and job creation, increase in the tax base, economic modernization, balance of payments adjustments, SME and entrepreneurship development, and the acquisition of dynamic capabilities and skills. In a statement made by the Chief Economist of the U.S. Department of Commerce, International Trade Administration, Dwivedy (2002) wrote that franchising brings about the transferring of technology and business methods, the development of SMEs, the creation of jobs, and the offering of quality goods at a reasonable price.

Output and Job Creation

Most scholars have pointed to the positive economic impacts that franchising exerted on the local economy including job creation and economic development (e.g., Preble and Hoffman, 1995; Alon and Welsh, 2001; Welsh and Alon, 2001). Domestic output is often increased through direct sales and its multiplier effects. The multipliers of franchising provide a sense of how much influence a given investment will have throughout the economy and depend on the industry and the company strategy. Cost and availability of supplies often drives the company decision to source locally. Companies that source most of their supplies locally are likely to have a greater positive economic impact on the host market. The franchising systems' labor force contributes to economic development through induced purchases. That is, by providing employment and income to their employees, franchisors stimulate local demand for a variety of goods and services.

Direct Employment

The direct employment impact of franchising can be calculated by multiplying the number of franchise outlets by the number of people working in each outlet and adding it to the number of jobs created by the parent company itself. For example, Kodak employed 5,556 employees in its Chinese factories in addition to the jobs created in the 5,000 Kodak Express franchising outlets (Alon, 2001). Since each franchised outlet employs multiple people, the direct employment impact is substantial. A study of African franchisors revealed that on average each franchisor has created about 32 direct jobs per year (Siggel et al., 2003).

Indirect Employment

The indirect economic impact of franchising is even more substantial, although less pronounced. Indirect job creation occurs through industrial linkages, e.g., suppliers and customers, and is often measured by the employment multipliers. By one estimate, every franchise unit creates and maintains an average of 33 jobs – 13 direct jobs and up to twenty or more indirect jobs related through other economic exchanges (Saunders, 2002). Another study of franchising in Africa calculated that for every $5,000 of spending by a franchisor, one job is created (Siggel et al., 2003).

Many emerging markets are contending with massive unemployment, underemployment and labor mobilization problems. Franchising helps to alleviate some of the employment problems. Table 3.2 summarizes the International Franchising Association statistics on franchising and its employment in selected developing countries in Asia, Europe, Africa, and the Americas. Underlying both output and employment growth is economic development. Sanghavi (2001) argued that franchising has been used as tool for economic development and showed evidence for a number of central European countries.

Table 3.2: Franchising Employment Statistics in Selected Emerging Markets

Country	Franchisors	Franchisees	Franchise Annual Sales (Mil $)	Employment
Asia				
China	368	3,000	n/a	n/a
Indonesia	261	2,000	n/a	n/a
South Korea	1,300	120,000	27,000	530,000
Malaysia	225	6,000	5,000	80,000
Philippines	500	4,000	105	100,000
Thailand	150	3,000	1,300	15,000
Europe				
Bulgaria	18	n/a	n/a	n/a
Hungary	250	5,000	n/a	100,000
Russia	50	300	n/a	2,000
Americas				
Argentina	150	1,500	1,100	n/a
Brazil	894	46,534	12,000	226,334
Chile	50	300	250	n/a
Colombia	80	600	n/a	11,000
Dominican Republic	180	800	n/a	5,000
Mexico	500	25,000	8,000	n/a
Peru	59	440	375	3,250
Uruguay	148	340	360	3,600

Sources: Culled from the International Franchise Association website (www.franchise.org, 2003)

Tax Revenue

Raising taxes helps emerging markets develop their social overhead capital and institutional infrastructure. International franchisors raise the tax base directly through their involvement and indirectly through their franchisees and small business network. The tax multipliers are proportional to the output and employment multipliers. Multinational franchisors are more likely to pay their taxes as model corporate citizens compared to local companies that are either "connected," evasive, or unprofitable. Kodak, for example, paid more taxes in the first 6 months of operations in China than Fuda Co., one of its purchased companies, has paid in 14 years. In one of the cities in which the company located, Xiamen, it is the largest tax payer (Alon, 2001).

Economic Modernization

Economic modernization is closely linked with economic development and the globalization of the economy. When large companies, such as McDonald's, Allied Domecq and Kodak, have entered emerging markets, they have also invested heavily in the local markets in order to bring their products and services in line with the companies' standards. For example: in Russia, McDonald's invested in ancillary industries, food processing facilities, and meat and potato plants, while Allied Domecq (the franchisor of Baskin Robbins and Dunkin' Donuts in Russia) invested over $40 million in supporting infrastructure, production facilities, and various business along the supply chain (Alon and Banai, 2000).

Economic restructuring is, however, often painful and associated with a loss of certain jobs, especially ones deemed inefficient by worldwide standards, and the destruction of some existing businesses. In the case of Kodak, for example, the company consolidated and closed several state-owned plants to modernize the imaging sector in the country, but invested $1.2 billion in building new state-of-the-art manufacturing facilities that are capable to rival the most advanced facilities anywhere in the world in terms of the technology and output.

Another aspect of economic development and modernization is economic clustering. Economic clustering is often an outcome of external economies of scale which are produced by demand pull and supply push forces inherent in economic transformation (Siggel et al., 2003). In the franchising arena and the services sector, such clustering is evident in the formation of shopping malls, which tend to attract a wide variety of service franchises and help local economic development through taxes, shopping alternatives, and the availability of local jobs. Economic concentration is a function of economic modernization which is advanced by international franchisors.

Balance of Payments

The impact of franchising on the Balance of Payments (BOP) is more elusive. On the surface it seems that franchising is less beneficial than foreign direct investment as far as the BOP is concerned, and that there is an asymmetry between the benefits accrued by the home and host markets. To the home market, franchising helps the BOP because local production is not substituted, imports do not increase, and net capital inflows increase due to repatriated profits/royalties. The net benefit of international franchising to the home country can explain why the US government has been very supportive of the International Franchise Association, a group that primarily represents US-based franchisors and their internationalization efforts. The Overseas

Private Investment Corporation (OPIC) and the US Department of Commerce have dedicated personnel dealing with international franchising expansion.

To the host market, the story is slightly different. Teegan (2000) correctly pointed that imports to the host country often rise as a result of foreign franchising development because franchisors often export part of their product or service abroad. However, over time franchisors often try to find or develop local sources for host markets' franchisees in order to become more responsive and price competitive. Mail Boxes Etc., for example, uses this type of strategy in its international operations, first importing key materials and later finding local sources. Invariably, local economic development follows. While temporary BOP deficits may occur because of franchising, these capital flows are mitigated by a transfer of technology, specialized knowledge, and human capital by the foreign franchisor. Another argument advanced by international franchising practitioners is that franchising reduces capital flight by providing opportunities to invest in the developing country. This argument is plausible since international capital is highly mobile.

Local SME and Entrepreneurship Development and Innovation

One of the big promises of franchising is its ability to develop a host market's small and medium enterprises (SMEs) and bolster local entrepreneurship. Perhaps lesson from US franchising history can help in understanding the entrepreneurial dynamics of industrializing countries today. Hunt (1972) evaluated the impact of franchising on the US when franchising accounted for about 25% of total consumer goods' expenditures. Central to his evaluation was the ability of franchising to stimulate local independent businesses. His study revealed that franchisees believed that they are independent since they controlled key operating areas such as hours of operation, book keeping, local advertisement, pricing, standards of cleanliness and number of employees. Secondly, 52% reported that without franchising they would not be self employed. Thus, if the US experience is any indication franchising development in developing countries, franchising has the potential to increase the opportunities for SME development by providing an opportunity of business ownership to those who would otherwise not take the risk.

Related to SME development, Siggel et al. (2003) suggested that franchising entrepreneurs are sources of risk taking and innovation in emerging markets. Using a sample of 52 franchisors from four countries in Africa, these authors showed that franchisors generated an average of 7.5 franchises per year over a period varying between two years and 25 years. These statistics, however, were different by industry and country. For example, fast food, automotive, building and home services generated more than 14 franchising units per year in South Africa, while the same industries generated less than 2 units per franchisor in Morocco, suggesting the in Morocco franchising is less developed form of organizational development.

In many developing countries, entrepreneurs and their small and medium sized businesses only recently became recognized for providing employment and economic development, increasing the productivity of the economy, and bridging the gap between technology efforts and the commercialization of innovation. Most franchisees are SMEs and franchising is becoming dominant in certain service industries such as the fast food, retailing, and hotels.   Table 3.2 also shows the number of franchisors, franchisees, and turnover of franchising in selected developing countries to illustrate the impact of franchising on SME development.

Many franchisors in developing countries also sell multiple-unit franchising contracts (also called area franchising and master franchising). These types of contracts involve a higher level of risk due to the higher level of needed investment and skill level. Siggel et al. (2003) referred to this as advanced entrepreneurship and found that on average 19 percent of franchisees owned more than one outlet in the African nations they examined. Teegan (2000), on the other hand, viewed this advanced entrepreneurship as excluding private investors/entrepreneurs who can benefit the most from franchising affiliation and who form the bulk of franchisees in the United States.

Innovation as a byproduct of entrepreneurship is also created via franchising in developing countries. In the African context, Siggel et al. (2003) claimed that franchising allowed for new technologies to be disseminated, brought new business models to the local market, contributed to the productivity growth of the economy, and generated external economies. They distinguished between business-oriented and consumer-oriented innovations, claiming that the former raises the level of productivity and the latter raises the level of consumer satisfaction. As an example of innovation, the authors cite one of the interviewee, a domestic franchisor in the automotive and home building sub-sector, who purported that the franchisee of its system need to regularly come up with new and artistic proposals for improving the design of its products. Also noted in their study is that domestic franchisors, domestic suppliers and franchisees account for 25%, 20%, and 15% of all innovations, while foreign franchisors and suppliers account for 20% each.

Education, Dynamic Resources and the Acquisition of Skills

Related to entrepreneurship development are the qualitative improvements in the marketplace and labor force of developing countries through education, dynamic resources, and the acquisition of skills.

Franchising Education

Critical to entrepreneurship and small business development is education. Franchising education occurs directly through formal training and indirectly through imitation. Formal training is provided by developmental agencies and the franchisor. In some countries, specialized educational institutions are set up to educate the public about franchising. In China, for example, the Chinese Normal University in Beijing recently opened franchising educational centers to train future managers of franchising and stimulate the concept across various sectors.

Franchisee Education

The franchisee benefits directly through its affiliation with the franchisor. The benefits to (host market) franchisees are well documented in the franchising literature and include access to sophisticated systems and operating processes, experiential training in running a business, a global brand name, ongoing operational support, periodic system-wide improvements, new product innovation, and superior market research and financial capabilities. The basic assumption inherent in international franchising is that it enhances the chances of local entrepreneurial success due primarily to the transference of a business format that has proved itself and a well-known brand name. The franchisee, thus, will reap risk-reducing benefits by adopting the franchise format (Kaufmann and Leibenstein, 1988). Pavlin (2001, p. 24) wrote that in Slovenia private entrepreneurs discovered the power of association with international franchisors which include a safer future, good purchasing opportunities, bulk supplies, strategic partnership, international marketing involvement, and high visibility. The franchisor is also responsible for providing resources to train the franchisee's employees.

Entrepreneurship Education

Foreign franchisors entering into a host country teach local entrepreneurs to about franchising, giving rise to imitation based on demonstration. This 'demonstration effect' has a significant yet hard to measure impact on the local development of SMEs. Sanghavi (2001) wrote that local entrepreneurs in transitioning countries learn from franchising about the management of brand name, goodwill and reputation, and loyalty to the corporation, since many have not had the chance to experience doing business in a competitive environment where business ethics counts. Alon and Banai (2000) showed that franchising in Russia taught entrepreneurs to appreciate the concept and to emulate it in their own businesses.

Franchising Life Cycle

SME development through international franchising in emerging markets often occurs in steps. First, foreign franchisors enter the market though master franchising, joint ventures, or sole ventures. These entities, in turn, are used to launch local franchising through direct or area franchises. Small businesses in the form of franchisees are then ready to develop throughout the country. Local entrepreneurs learn from these new business systems, emulate and adapt them to local conditions and, over time, attempt to internationalize them to trading partners. In this way, franchising follows a global life cycle that begins with developed countries, passes to and matures in developing countries, and ends with the developing countries exporting their own concepts.

Local entrepreneurs observing the success of the foreign franchises imitate and adapt the foreign franchising systems to local tastes and quickly become powerful competitors by developing their own brands and business formats. They compete with the foreign franchises both for customers and for qualified franchisees. Ultimately, local franchise entrepreneurs can overcome the foreign franchise systems. For example, in South Africa, the majority of franchise systems (82% of franchisors) are locally developed and they, in turn, average about 49 units per franchisor (Toit, 2002). India and Brazil, two big emerging markets, have a vibrant franchising sector domestically and a rather limited participation by foreign franchisors. These markets can be classified as receptive to franchising, but difficult to do business with due to environmental differences.   Once established in their own markets, franchisors from these host markets may end up attacking the foreign franchisors in their home market or other markets, thereby increasing the global competition in franchising.

Franchising, however, is no panacea for success, neither domestically nor, most certainly, internationally. In the U.S., where franchising has experienced the explosive growth, one-third of franchisors stop franchising within 4 years of operation and three-quarter of franchisors stop within 12 years (Light, 1997). The statistics on international franchising failure should be much glimmer because a lack of brand-name recognition in the foreign market, mistrust of foreign interests, lack of qualified franchisees and financial capital, and misunderstanding of the cultural, economic and political host market environments.

Dynamic Resources, Capabilities, Routines and Skills

International franchising often transfers knowledge, technology and human capital and increases the skills and abilities of the labor force. The transfer of technology as it relates to franchising refers to the transfer of the 'learning organization' and labor skills in addition to the hardware and machinery that franchisors provide and can be viewed on three levels: (1) operating capabilities, (2) investment capabilities, (3) innovative capabilities (Stanworth, Price and Purdy, 2001). Operating capabilities to operate and maintain a business, investment capabilities to increase productivity and create new units, and innovative capabilities to modify and improve methods and products are a part of the dynamic resources, capabilities, routines and skills franchising offers to developing countries (Stanworth, Price and Purdy, 2001). As mentioned earlier, it is important to note again that these dynamic capabilities extend beyond the franchising concept. Entrepreneurs can copy the skills and routines they see in the franchise operation and employ them in other businesses.

Arguing against the benefits of skill enhancement through franchising, Teegan (2000) wrote that many of the jobs in franchising are menial in nature and produce little capabilities in local personnel. If one considers the skill development of a local cook in a McDonald's restaurant, for example, he/she may not be impressed with the transfer of know-how. To counter this argument, one has to consider that if someone has no skills, learning how to cook, serve customers, earn a living, run a retailing operation, work in a team or stay out of crime and the underground economy is an economic contribution. Also, the transfer of technology and know-how by the franchisor should be viewed more holistically from a country level perspective and not from the vantage point of a particular job. Siggel et al. (2003) suggested that franchising is responsible for the upgrading of skills in the labor force. Their study of Africa reveals that 48 percent of the jobs were high skilled (as defined by the respondents). The numbers varied by industry, however, from 33 percent in the fast-food restaurant sector to over 50 percent in the automotive, building, home services, and business education and training businesses.

THE SOCIAL IMPACTS OF FRANCHISING

It seems from the above economic analysis that the positive economic impacts outweigh the negative ones and that franchising can contribute to the wellbeing of the host market growth prospect and global integration efforts. The social impacts of franchising are more debatable. Four interrelated salient cultural issues relating to international franchising in developing countries include standards of living and the rationalization of consumer choice, the *McDonaldization* of Society, franchising and social conflict, and cultural homogenization/Americanization. Franchising as an element of globalization plays an important part in the cultural-globalization debates because franchising industries are often viewed as "non-essential" consumer-oriented discretionary-income-based industries that are market seeking and because of the franchisors' interaction with consumers is visible and likely to draw the attention of special interest groups and some government officials alike.

Standards of Living and Rationalization of Consumer Choice

Franchising supports a higher standards of living and a greater consumer choice, and is affected by changing demographic and psychographic trends in society. Demographic changes such as the aging population and psychographic changes such as the increase in the female labor force participation have changed the lives of individuals and the required services by consumers. For example, as female labor participation increased, family incomes increased accordingly, and new areas of demand have opened up for international franchisors.

Overall, franchising worldwide has had the effect of offering consumers lower prices through efficient distribution of goods and services, and consistent quality through standardization. As an example, English, Alon and Xau (2001) examined the prices of 18 menu items in a McDonald's in China in 1994 and in 2000. What they found is that on average prices in dollars decreased about 18% during this period, while the same items increased by an average of about 5% in the US during the same period. It is questionable whether without franchising efficiency of distribution and consistency of quality would have improved at the rate that they have throughout the world

On the other hand, some nationalists advocate that large franchising firms rationalize consumer choice by presenting barriers to entry through monopolistic powers, diffusing standardized products, and displacing local "mom and pop" operations. The cultural identification of franchises with a particular country of origin impacts the perception of local consumers and, thus, the acceptance of the franchise. For example, Italian apparel franchisors, such as *Benetton*, have enjoyed a positive image because Italian fashion is highly regarded around the globe. Global communications has allowed international consumers to identify franchising service leaders and modify their preferences in favor of the services that are offered by franchising oligopolistic corporate entities. Local consumers often seek international goods at the expense of local goods because they are lured by international media and aspire to a western lifestyle. In China, for example, KFC and McDonald's are frequently attended by young consumers who wish to embrace the "Western way" despite the fact that these franchises are often more expensive than the local alternatives. What American franchising sells in developing countries is not only a particular service or product, but also a cultural export: Americana. American franchisors have attracted customers who wish to identify themselves with American consumerism and western values and qualities.

The same factors that were responsible to the growth of franchising in the US in the 1960s and 1970s are now present in many of the industrializing countries: incomes are increasing, female labor participation is on the rise, time is becoming increasingly scarce, and consumer demand patterns are changing. These reasons explain in part why many American franchises entering emerging markets have experienced pent up demand for their products and services and were able to charge higher prices. In Russia, Alon and Banai (2001) noted that despite a higher price for foreign franchises in relation to local producers, there is a perception among local consumers that these franchises provide a better quality and, thus, a better value. For example, a pair of glass in an American eyeglasses franchise, Vision Express, cost about $60, half what it costs in the US, but 60 times more than what a pair of glasses cost in a government store. In sum, franchising has offered desired services to the changing demand of consumers in developing countries, at an acceptable price and quality, but these services have often been priced higher than local alternatives.

Cultural Modernization and the *McDonalization* of Society

Franchising brings about cultural transformation that is rejected by traditional elements of society. By bringing in new foods, new customs and new services to a traditional society, the franchisor is an agent of change, modernizing lifestyles and consumer demand. Teegan (2000) discussed this cultural modernization in the context of franchising in Mexico. In that market, the term *malinchismo* (selling out) is often used to express the preference of some for foreign-made rather than domestic-made products. The term comes from the Mexican woman, La Malinche, who betrayed the country by providing valuable services to the invading Spanish forces in Mexico. *Malinchismo* behavior in Mexico is associated with higher income and education levels, younger age, and larger households.

A number of sociologists have termed the trend toward westernization and homogenization of consumerism as the *McDonaldization* of Society, equating the processes used by the fast-food franchise giant with those of modernization and globalization. Beck (2000, p. 42) defined *McDonaldization* as "an ever greater uniformity of lifestyles, cultural symbols and transnational modes of behavior." Accordingly, the *McDonaldization* of society uproots and replaces local cultures and identities with the symbols of marketing departments of multinational corporations. Alfino, Caputo and Wynyard (1998, viii) defined *McDonalidzation* as "increased efficiency, calculability, predictability, and control through substitution of human labor power with technology and instrumental rationalization." The

McDonaldization thesis was popularized by the sociologist George Ritzer. Ritzer (1998) focused not only on fast-food restaurants, but also on the new means of consumption and socioeconomic life. In Ritzer's eyes, *McDonaldization* is the modern-day equivalent of Max Weber's and Karl Mannheim's processes of rationalization, bureaucratization, and dehumanization inherent in rational centralized planning of corporations.

According to Alfino and his colleagues (1998), the four fundamental tenets of Ritzer's *McDonaldization* theory are: (1) efficiency, (2) calculability, (3) predictability, and (4) control. These factors, they claim, create the undesirable outcome of the dehumanization of both workers and consumers and the phenomenon they coined the 'irrationality of rationality.' Efficiency involves organizing work to achieve the highest output per input and, thus, requires following procedures imposed by others. Calculability emphasizes the use of numerical measures for all aspects of production (portion sizes, material costs, waiting time, etc.), encouraging quantity over quality. Predictability entails routinization, standardization and uniformity of production and consumption, encouraging consistent mediocrity and scripted interactions. Control substitutes human with nonhuman technology including the use of mechanized processes and the reduction of employees and customers to automatons (Holbrook, 1999).

According to some sociologists, franchising systems through their adherence to standardized rules and business formats rob workers of their need to think intelligently, functioning mindlessly as automated robots, and push various elements of society toward increased rationalization, which is dehumanizing. Steijn and Witte (1996) found empirical support for the *McDonalization* of the laborforce thesis in the Dutch labor market after examining 1,022 employed respondents. They explained that the interaction between producers and consumers is devoid of "real" humanity and "authentic" products and is instead replaced by simulated interactions and products. Ritzer (1998) gave the example of an accounting practice: at franchising chains like H&R Block employees offer tax services often on the basis of only a brief training course, in contrast to the services that a trained and experienced accountant which are much less simulated and standardized.

The *McDonaldization* thesis advanced by selected sociologists paints franchising in a negative light almost demonizing its features of efficiency, calculability, predictability through standardization and control. It should be noted that these same features have been hailed by marketers, economists, and management scholars, and franchise practitioners who defend franchising on economic grounds. The very success of hundreds of international franchisors abroad is also an indication that large segments of consumers want the standardized (perhaps Americanized) and efficient products and services that franchising have to offer.

Franchising and Cultural Conflict

Inherent in globalization is a tension between the particular needs of nations, groups and individuals and the universal pressure to conform to a nascent global capitalistic environment. The nexus of globalization, therefore, is a juxtaposition of competing cultural paradigms: traditional vs. modern, idealism vs. materialism, relativism vs. universalism, old vs. young, disconnected vs. connected, localism vs. globalism, the olive tree vs. the Lexus, heroic life vs. everyday life, and Jihad vs. *McWorld*. While in the Western world globalization is often synonymous with modernization, progress, efficiency, growth, and economic opportunity, it is often viewed as a form of exploitation, forced Americanization, and cultural homogenization to disenfranchised groups in developing countries and special interest groups in developed countries. Those who oppose economic globalization usually also oppose global franchising, which is iconic of the global capitalistic system.

One book that uses McDonald's as the icon of the expansion of global capitalism is *Jihad vs. McWorld* (Barber, 1995). According to this book, the globalization of markets has created a multitude of complex socio-economic and policy problems that have led to debates and discussions on the impact of globalization on the welfare of society and on its desirability by the citizenry of the less affluent world (Robertson, 1992; Barber, 1995; Featherstone, 1995; Friedman, 2000). Ger and Belk (1996) suggested that the newly formed global material culture has led to social discontent, socio-economic inequality and polarization, consumer frustrations, stress, and threats to the environment, the working conditions, and living standards in developing countries. Global capital undermines the power of the state by seeking markets that minimize taxes, labor and distribution costs, and regulatory oversight (Beck, 2000). Stiglitz (2002) criticized the present global capital system and the institutional context under which it operates. The franchising company, as the holder of brand-name and financial capital, is often regarded as one of the culprits of globalization.

Social discontent with globalization and American foreign policy, in general, and franchising, in specific, is sometimes expressed violently and against leading international franchisors. For example, on December 15, 2001, a terrorist bomb went off in a McDonald's located in *Xi'an*, an ancient city in the People's Republic of China containing the famous terracotta warriors. According to Reuters (2001) the fact that the bomber targeted McDonald's, an icon of American influence, in a city with a substantial Uighur population (ethnic local Turkic people who claim descent from Genghis Khan, speak a Turkic language and follow the Muslim religion) could point to more than simple revenge by disgruntled workers or jilted lovers as the Chinese claimed as a motive for the attack.

Other example of cultural blunders by franchisors abound. Burger King through its location decision became entangled in the Arab-Israeli conflict after opening a franchised restaurant in 2002 in a new shopping mall in *Maaleh Adumim*, a Jewish settlement of 25,000 residents three miles east of Jerusalem that is located on the land Israel captured in the 1967 war. After becoming the target of the wrath of various Arab and Muslim interest groups, the company decided to revoke the license of the local Israeli franchisee. This move angered Israelis and Jewish interest groups who denounced the company caving to the Arab boycott as "a shame and an abomination" and called on Jews around the world to boycott Burger King in return (ABC News, 2002).

Protesters in France have targeted McDonald's as a symbol of unchecked globalization. The company was accused of

- Trampling local culture -- such as French cuisine
- Destroying local-cheese-farmers jobs -- due to a surcharge on Roquefort one of the many EU luxury products penalized by the United States after the World Trade Organization ruled the European Union improperly discriminated against U.S. hormone-treated beef and genetically modified crops
- Feeding bad foods to its children (Associated Press, 2001).

Ironically, France is a leading European market for McDonald's with per capita consumption exceeding most of its European neighbors including Germany, Italy, Spain and the Netherlands. The company opened an average of 30-40 outlets per year, operates over 900 restaurants, and is the leading restaurant chain in the country (The Economist, 2002).

Economic inequality both within and between countries is a feature of globalization. Those who do not have skills that are marketable in the global economy are increasingly marginalized by globalization and are likely to support nationalistic, ethnocentric, isolationistic policies and to resort to socio-political influences and even terrorism to prevent protect their markets and cultures (Friedman, 2000). The new global arena is marked by a plurality of cultures, nationalities, ethnicities, religions, and identities, which have led to particularistic and relativistic interpretations of reality (Robertson 1992). Franchising offers a "one for all formula" that downplays relativistic, nationalistic, and regional sentiments, homogenizing and, perhaps, Americanizing foreign tastes, values, and traits, hence the social tension.

Globalization – marked in part by global franchising – has the potential to create socioeconomic tensions that, according to some social scientists, will adversely affect the host markets' consumers, workers, and political organization. According to Beck (2000) economic globalization has fell just short of declaring war on the nation state forcing it to abandon its principle doctrines: (1) the equation of state and society and (2) exclusive territoriality of state and society. Beck (2000, p. 111) writes: "Admittedly there is no actual enemy, but the foundations are removed from a politics based upon the national state – and in a way that appears to be even worse, since globalization is often viewed almost as a virtual declaration of war (imperialism, Americanization) and responded to with protectionism." To end on a positive note, alternatively, Friedman (2000) advanced the Golden Arches theory suggesting that no two nations containing a McDonald's have fought a war. This highly contested proposition suggests the nations with McDonalds are free nations with a rising middle class and with similar aspirations and economic ties; and, thus, will prefer peaceful co-existence and socio-political cooperation over war.

Cultural Homogenization and the Americanization of Culture

As discussed earlier, franchising is an agent of economic globalization that seeks commonalities across nations and cultures. The literature on globalization debates whether such a commonality exists. Guillen (2001) has reviewed the question "is a global culture in the making?" and provided evidence from the sociological, economics, and business literature that while a segmented emerging global culture is in the making, mass consumption is diverse, particularly at the experiential level, and can provoke resistance, irony, selectivity, resurgence affirmation of identities, and cross border activism. Market researcher Levitt (1983) and sociologist Sklair (1991) suggested that the world is increasingly populated by cosmopolitan consumers whose tastes and desires are becoming standardized. These global commonalities are driven by advances in technology and communications, international trade and investment, and movement of people and ideas across nations. Comparing the cultural environments facing global franchising in 1988 and 2000, Kaufmann (2001) wrote that while cultural differences exist, there are fast disappearing due to advances in technology, international broadcasting, commercial messages and global brands. He added, however, that the social costs of losing one's local identity are sill relevant in the turn of the century and, if anything, magnified.

The Americanization thesis contends that American cultural value and icons dominate and often swamp local cultures and that American consumer culture is widespread. Accordingly, people around the world (particularly the youth) aspire to go to Disney world, wear Nikes and Levis, drink Coca-Cola, listen to Britney Spears and Eminem, and eat at McDonald's and KFC. Consider a few industries key to globalization and how strongly they influence the cultural framework of a country: TV, Media, and Cinema. Nearly three quarters of American TV drama is exported worldwide; American media companies AOL Time Warner, Disney, Viacom and News Corporation are among the largest in the world; American Hollywood controls the movie market dominating more than half the Japanese market, and two-thirds of the European market (Legrain, 2003). Another American cultural export, its language, is becoming global. English is spoken as a first language by 380 million and as a second language by 250 million, is studied by about one billion, and is estimated to be spoken by half of the world's population by 2050 (Legrain, 2003). The trend toward a global American culture globally has been referred to as American cultural imperialism. Franchising, in specific, is just one element of this American global acculturation.

Proponents of a standardized global approach envisioned an environment in which worldwide consumers with homogenized tastes and lifestyles can be satisfied with a single product and reached with a single message: a world in which the relentless pursuit of production efficiency, low cost, and reliable products overwhelms idiosyncratic differences among countries and cultures. International marketing researchers who believe the cultural homogenization thesis espouse integrated global marketing strategies which move away from country specific marketing mix adjustments to global cross functional integration (Sheth and Parvatiyar, 2001). Franchising is an efficient technological and cultural innovation that targets the cosmopolitan consumer and seeks common needs among consumers across national boundaries.

Not everybody agrees with the cultural homogenization and Americanization theses. As discussed before, some researchers have pointed out to the plurality of cultures, nationalities, ethnicities, religions, and identities, which have led to relativistic, often inconsistent, and sometimes conflicting interpretations of reality (Robertson 1992; Beck 2000). According to these thinkers, the world is culturally divided and will continue to be so. Others have looked at the positive side of diversity in the global economy. Legrain (2003) suggested that consumption patterns only reflect skin deep commercial artifacts that are not reflective of the more traditional elements of culture – shared beliefs, ideas, knowledge and art – citing observations of Taliban in Afghanistan sporting Nike bags. Globalization according to him brings about a lovely plethora of cultural mixing and exchange that gives life to the co-existence of a multitude of cultural symbols, offerings, and artifacts, freeing people around the world from the 'geographic tyranny' in which they live. Legrain challenged the American cultural imperialism thesis and suggested that in some ways, America is more of a peculiar outlier, rather than the norm of global behavior. Included in his examples are the American measurement system, American football, American debates of creationism, and other countries global roles in fashion (ex., Italy and France), Music (ex., Mexico's Carlos Santana), and publishing (Germany's Bertelsmann). Additionally, many of the so-called American ideas are actually not at all American. For example, "two of AOL Time Warner's biggest recent hit franchises, Harry Potter and The Lord of the Rings, are both based on British books, have largely British casts, and in the case of The Lord of the Rings, a Kiwi Director." Franchising itself is not an American idea. It was traced back to 1942 Spain when Queen Isabella granted Columbus a travel and trade franchise and to 19th century by British brewers who sought commercial distribution. It was first used in America in the 1850s by the Singer Sewing Machine, and popularized by Americans in the 1950s and the 1960s by the fast food chains. Thus, cultural borrowing, either in the form of commercial innovation or cultural icons, is a function of cultural dynamism that is reflected in the desires of free people in developing as well as developed countries.

Even if incomes around the world converge, there is no evidence the culture will also converge. One study found that converging incomes in a number of European countries have actually led to diverging consumer behavior, challenging the assumption that economic development would result in standardization of marketing practices (Mooij, 2000). The study claimed that economic prosperity leads to freedom of expression which, in turn, leads to particularistic consumer behavior across different nationalities. Using a sample of Belgians, Brits and Dutch, the author showed how demand for mineral water, cars, and the internet varied despite converging incomes in the European Union. He concluded (Mooij, 2000, p. 112) "disappearing income differences will not cause homogenization of needs. On the contrary, along with converging incomes, the manifestation of value differences becomes stronger."

Since the franchising concept embraces a uniform business model and a standardized marketing strategy, it is a force that continues to push for/look for cultural commonalities. This is not to say that franchisors do not need to make adjustments to their marketing mix or fine tune their strategies. Global marketing is not inconsistent with country-based marketing adjustments (Sheth and Parvatiyar, 2001). Pine et al. (2000), for example, has shown that hotels doing business in China often need to modify their marketing strategy. McDonald's sells beer in France, Chili in Mexico, and lamb in India (Legrain, 2003). According the company's own source it will take McDonald's about 9 years (since opening in 1996) before it will have a totally relevant Indian menu. The company already made significant modifications its food offering including the Paneer Salsa Wrap, McCurry Pan, McAloo Tikki (the mutton speciality for a country which does not eat beef), and the Chicken Maharaja Mac (BBC, 2003). Due to cultural sensitivities in France, McDonald's changed its promoter from Ronald McDonald, the firm's Disneyesque mascot, to its French Asterix, a French comic-strip character with a distinctive moustache who, ironically, symbolizes local resistance to imperial forces and resembles Mr José Bové, a militant sheep farmer and a fellow member of the radical union Farmers' Confederation who was convicted in a French court for leading an attack against a McDonald's in the southern town of Millau (The Economist, 2002).

Founder of Subway Fred DeLuca (2002) described some of the modifications the Subway system needed to make around the world. Due to religious prohibition to eat pork (Muslim) and eat beef (Hindu) in India, for example, no pork or beef products are used in any of the sandwich. Instead, these ingredients were substituted with lamb, chicken and turkey, and a variety of new vegetarian subs, such as hummus and falafel. The preparation format has changed a bit too. Subway India separated the counter area and preparation area since Vegetarians do not like to be served from the same place that non-vegetarian foods are prepared. Despite the cultural differences, according to DeLuca, India has the potential to be Subway largest market outside North America, and the company is planning to open 55 outlets in Mumbai and Delhi in the next seven years. McDonald's shares the same enthusiasm about the Indian market investing about 7bn rupees in India since it entered the market in 1996 and reporting an annualized growth of about 40 percent (BBC, 2003).

Not all attempts to enter the Indian market were met with cultural receptivity. KFC ran into several problems. In 1995 when it entered the country, it was attacked by protests from farmers in Bangalore who were against globalization and accused by a non-governmental organizations of serving chicken with high level of monosodium glutamate, forcing it to close its New Delhi outlet. More recently, animal rights activist in India protested outside the only KFC remaining outlet in India, (located in Bangalore) accusing it of cruelty and the unacceptable killing of more than 700 million (mistreated) chickens (Yahoo News, 2003). Despite these setbacks, according to the Director of Indian Marketing, the company serves 2,000-2,500 customers daily and is growing at an annualized rate of 18 percent yearly.

A series of four edited volumes on international franchising in developing and developed markets is fraught with cases of international franchising and examples from the cultural environment facing global franchising (Alon and Welsh, 2001, 2003; Welsh and Alon, 2001, 2002). Differences in culture make it difficult for franchisors to apply a uniform franchising format across varying nations. This is true particularly when the cultural distance is high between the home market of the franchisor and the host country. Developing countries, therefore, are especially challenging to franchisors from the Western world. Thompson and Merrilees (2001) touted a modular approach to franchising into emerging markets suggesting that some of the core franchising elements can be maintained and standardized across nations – operations, manuals, monitoring procedures, trademarks – while other peripheral elements can be adapted to the culture, including language, color schemes, product variations, prices, packaging, displays, and advertising.

CONCLUSION

The jury is still out on whether the rapid rate of globalization – through franchising as well as other forms of entry into developing countries – could have negative social consequences, as suggested by some, of such magnitude that the long-run benefit to the host country and to the world could be negative. This concern lies at the heart of the current populist debate on globalization. A detailed empirical study of franchising in transition economies, with an emphasis on both positive and negative externalities, will provide powerful knowledge for resolving some of the key debates over globalization.

This paper concludes that franchisors need to think about the economic and the social implications of their investment in order to maximize their chances for acceptance. Franchising seems to offer some economic benefits to the host nation, but at a cost of possible social discontent, that may make franchising investment prohibitively expensive. The economic transformation that follows franchising is, by western standards, necessary for growth and prosperity. Policy makers are thus advised to examine the cost-benefit of franchising and to put into place processes to promote franchising expansion, on the one hand, and to minimize its disruptive influences, on the other. Table 3.3 summarizes the positive and negative implications for franchising in developing countries from economic and social standpoints. The paper concludes with a suggested research agenda which includes six salient issues relating to the socio-economic environments of franchising.

Table 3.3: Impacts Of International Franchising

Economic Positives	Economic Negatives
• Output creation (direct, indirect and induced) • Job creation (direct, indirect, and induced) • Tax base is increased due to more output, higher efficiency of new businesses, more accurate reporting • Tariff on imports associated with international franchising may also increase • Economic modernization and infrastructure development • Economic clustering/concentration • Long term economic growth • Reduction in capital flight • Higher level of entrepreneurship and SME development • Advanced entrepreneurship via multiple-unit franchising provides higher growth • Franchising diffuses innovations across the system of outlets • Franchising education and skill transfer • Enhancement of the labor force • More expertise, managerial and labor training • Western business models	• Output destruction due to replacement of non-franchised businesses • Job destruction due to replacement of non-franchised businesses • Tax loss due to "mom-and-pop" businesses and other SMEs not being able to compete • Imports may substitute local producers who pay taxes • Pains of economic transitioning such as the displacement workers employed in inefficient/outdated industries • Uneven economic development • Short term BOP deficits due to imported goods and capital outflows • Possible increased inequality of income due to the new entrepreneurial class • Advanced entrepreneurship takes away opportunities from individuals investors/entrepreneurs who need franchising the most • Franchising does not guarantee success • Many jobs are menial in nature, requiring a low need for skill development • Loss of "humanity" in the consumption and production process due to standardized and mechanistic approach of franchising
Social Positives	Social Negatives
• Increase in consumer choice • Consistent prices and quality • Golden Arches Theory • Cultural alternatives increase consumer choice	• Prices of foreign franchisors are often higher than local alternatives • Increase potential for cultural conflict • Cultural homogenization/Americanization • *McDonaldization* of Society • Rationalization of choice

Output and Employment Impacts of Franchising

Both output and employment multipliers need to be developed to measure the economic impact of franchising on the host nation. These economic multipliers are likely to be affected by the economic structure of the host nation as well as the industry in which the franchisor operates. Makhija, Kim and Williamson (1997) showed that the extent of an industry's international linkages and integration of value-added activities within the industry is related to its level of globalization. The level of global integration, in turn, affects the impact that franchising will have on the host market environment. No known study has shown the differential impact of franchising industries on development. Such knowledge can answer vexing questions relating to industry-specific franchising development. For example, is the economic benefit of the hotel franchising sector likely to be larger in tourist destinations as compared to restaurant franchising? Are there facilitative sectors in which franchising can play a role that will further the needs of the local government? More studies are needed to measure the direct and indirect economic impacts of various industries utilizing franchising on the host market environment.

Franchising Competitiveness and the Service Sector

The competitiveness of the franchise sector will continue to have a ripple effect on the economy from a number of standpoints. A vibrant and competitive domestic franchising sector will be able to ward off foreign competition and at the same time stave off some of the negative economic consequences such as the balance of payments impact. Secondly, a competitive domestic franchising environment can revive the service sector and its supporting industries. Most of the developed countries' GDPs consist of services, and some, such as the United States, have an unusual balance of payments surplus in services. Does franchising have the potential to modernize the service sectors of developing countries and, if so, what sectors are likely to benefit the most? Increasingly, local franchising systems compete effectively with international ones in their local and regional markets. More research is needed on the type of franchising systems that would be most desirable to the host nation as well as how local franchisors can be developed to effectively compete with foreign franchises in global markets.

Franchising vs. Non-Franchising Businesses

The franchising literature is replete with papers examining the causes of the firm's decision to franchise. The impact of this decision on the host market was to our knowledge never advanced. Castrogiovanni and Vozikis (2000) suggested that franchisors are more likely to use a greater proportion of franchising in their foreign outlets due to the increased risk. To minimize their risk exposure, American franchisors are also more likely to use area-based and multi-unit franchising arrangements, instead of direct franchising or wholly owned operations in emerging markets. Is there a difference in the economic and social impacts between franchised and non-franchised firm on the regional economy? One way to addresss this issue is to compare, as Siggel et al. (2003) suggested, for example, the employment, or output, or labor intensity impacts in franchised-based businesses and independently owned businesses in the same sector. Such analyses would allow us to explore in more detail not only whether franchising has a particular impact, but also whether this impact is differentiated from non-franchising-based forms of developments.

Cultural Problems Facing Franchising

Despite their importance to franchising acceptance, the society impacts of franchising have been largely ignored in the marketing literature. The *International Franchise Association* recently (August, 2002) commissioned a study on the economic impact of franchising and routinely publishes articles for the promotion of franchising globally. Yet few articles discuss the cultural significance of a franchising concept. Many questions remain relating the impact of franchising on the social environment. For example, is cultural homogenization/westernization through franchising part of a trend toward globalization and, if so, is it a desirable/controllable? Is cultural conflict inherent in the interaction of global franchising with local interests? If so, what are the ways to cope with such divergence?

Franchising Country of Origin Effect

Franchising – even in the same system – is interpreted differently in different countries and the meaning of franchising brand is locally construed. For example, in the U.S. McDonald's can be perceived as a source of cheap fast-food on the road, while the same system in China can be perceived as a higher class, foreign, and trendy restaurant. The country from which the franchise concept emanates (or thought to emanate from) has an impact on global franchising. According to Teagan (2000), franchisors from developed markets benefit from positive country-of-origin perception in their international endeavors as compared to franchisors from emerging nations. On the other hand, the foreign consumer may also think that Pizza Hut is "Italian" and that Taco Bell is "Mexican" and ignore their corporate origin. What are the country-of-origin perceptions of foreign franchisors from different countries, and how do they affect success in emerging markets? Franchisors are advised to understand the local meaning of their concepts and brands. In this way, they can more easily adapt to the local environment.

Regulation of International Franchising

Some countries' governments at various points in time have shown concerns about the imbalance of power inherent in the franchise contract between the franchisor and the franchisee and the possible pyramid type scams that can be marketed under the guise of franchising. As a result, their governments attempted to draft regulation addressing the legal "inadequacies" of franchising, often at the detriment of stunting franchising growth. Little empirical evidence is available on the impacts of these regulations on franchising development. Host governments should attempt to devise regulations which will foster franchising while minimizing its negative impacts. More research on this topic is certainly likely to increase the effectiveness and efficiency of franchising regulations on the regional economy. What type of regulation/s, if any, should be employed by governments to promote and at the same time control the impact of franchising organizations within their borders? Teagan (2000) proclaimed that while franchisors prefer minimum regulation, this condition creates information asymmetry, promoting opportunistic behavior on the part of the foreign franchisor. On the other hand, over-regulation will tend to repel international franchisors from making investments in the host market. Thus, governments need to be sensitive in both protecting local interests of entrepreneurs and, at the same time, provide an auspicious environment in which franchising can thrive. Countries in both the Far East and Central Europe have achieved franchising growth through deregulation, adoption of international commercial law, and formation of local franchising associations. Attempting to develop a model for optimal franchising development that is relevant to the host nation culture can be a fruitful future research project.

In conclusion, this chapter has provided a framework for examining the impact of franchising on the economic and the social environments of marketing at the macro level. We hope that in this way we can stimulate additional research on the interface of development and the host country environments. Research that bridges the macro-micro gap and moves across levels of analysis, and focuses on specific industries, across nations, or over time, will help further our understanding of the debate on globalization. Detailed case studies of specific developing countries which will show the spectrum of economic, social and political implications of franchising will also be helpful. Franchising development research will have the potential to further not only marketing-based research, but, perhaps more broadly, improve our conceptual understanding of the benefits and drawbacks of globalization in general. Perhaps after additional investigation we will find whether the idea advanced by political philosopher John Stuart Mill in the 1800s applies to franchising development today. "The economical benefits of commerce are surpassed in importance by those of its effects which are intellectual and moral. It is hardly possible to overrate the value, for the improvement of human beings, of things which bring them into contact with persons dissimilar to themselves, and with modes of thought and action unlike those with which they are familiar...It is indispensable to be perpetually comparing (one's) notions and customs with the experience and example of persons in different circumstances...There is no nation which does not need to borrow from others" (as quoted in Legrain, 2003, p. B7).

NOTES

[1] Two current debates – one published by the World Bank (2002) between Stiglitz (the 2001 Nobel Prize economist and former World Bank chief who is anti-IMF) and Rogoff (economic counselor and director of the Research Department at the IMF who is pro-IMF) and one published by Foreign Policy (1999) between Friedman (foreign affairs columnist for the *New York Times* and author of The Lexus and the Olive Tree who is pro-globalization) and Ramonet (editor of *Le Monde diplomatique* who is anti-globalization) – exemplify some of the existing divergent thinking on the topic of globalization.

REFERENCES

ABC News (2002), "Of Burgers and Boycotts: Burger King Becomes Entangled in Arab-Israeli Debate," http://abcnews.go.com/sections/world/DailyNews/burger_king990827.html# (retrieved June 4, 2003)

Alfino, Mark, John S. Caputo, and Robin Wynyard (1998), *McDonalidization Revisited: Critical Essays on Consumer Culture*, Westport CT: Praeger.

Alon, Ilan (2001), "Interview: International Franchising in China with Kodak," *Thunderbird International Business Review*, 43 (6), 737-754.

Alon, Ilan (1999), *The Internationalization of U.S. Franchising Systems* (Transnational Business and Corporate Culture Problems and Opportunities), New York: Garland Publishing.

Alon, Ilan and Moshe Banai (2000), "Executive Insights: Franchising Opportunities and Threats in Russia," *Journal of International Marketing*, 8 (3), 104-119.

Alon, Ilan and Dianne H. B. Welsh (2001), *International Franchising in Emerging Markets: China, India, and Other Asian Countries*, Chicago: CCH Inc.

Alon, Ilan, and David L. McKee (1999), "Towards a Macroenvironmental Model of International Franchising," *Multinational Business Review*, 7 (1), 76-82.

Alon, Ilan and Dianne Welsh, eds. (2003), International Franchising in Industrialized Markets: Western and Northern Europe, Chicago IL: CCH Inc. Publishing. (ISBN# 0-8080-0963-X)

Associated Press (2001), "French Farmer José Bové Leads New McDonald's Protest," retrieved from http://www.commondreams.org/headlines01/0813-01.htm (July 9, 2003).

Barber, Benjamin (1995), *Jihad vs. McWorld*, Times Books, New York.

BBC (2003), "McDonald's plans Indian expansion," http://news.bbc.co.uk/1/hi/business/2924185.stm (retrieved July 3, 2003).

Beck, Ulrich (2000), *What is Globalization?* Cambridge UK: Polity Press.

Castrogiovanni, Gary J., and George S. Vozikis (2000), "Foreign Franchisor Entry into Developing Countries: Influences on Entry Choices and Economic Growth," *New England Journal of Entrepreneurship,* 3 (2), 9-19.

Dwivedy, Raj (2002), "Franchising Indeed Could Become the Business Ambassador of World Peace through Global Economic Prosperity," *Franchising World*, (April), 17.

(The) Economist (2002), "McDonald's in France Delicious irony: A nation of burger-munchers," http://www.economist.com/displayStory.cfm?Story_ID=S')H(%2CQQ%5B!!%20%23%5C%0A (retrieved July 9, 2003).

English, Wilke, Ilan Alon and Chin Xau (2001), "Price Comparisons Between China and the U.S.," in *International Franchising in Emerging Markets: China, India and Other Asian Countries*, Ilan Alon and Dianne Welsh, eds., Chicago, IL: CCH Inc.

Featherstone, Mike (1995), Undoing Culture: Globalization, Postmodernism and Identity, Sage Publications, London.

Foreign Policy (1999), "Dueling Globalizations: A Debate Between Thomas L. Friedman and Ignacio Ramonet," *Foreign Policy*, (Fall), 110-127.

Franchise Recruiters Ltd. (2003), "2003 Franchise Business Development Forecast and Industry Trends Analysis," A study presented to the IFA 2003 convention.

Friedman, Thomas L. (2000), *The Lexus and the Oliver Tree* (Newly Updated and Expanded Edition), Anchor Books, New York.

Ger, Guliz and Russell W. Belk (1996), "I'd Like to Buy the World a Coke: Consumptionscapes of the 'Less Affluent World,'" *Journal of Consumer Policy*, 19, 271-304.

Guillen, Mauro F. (2001), "Is Globalization Civilizing, Destructive or Feeble? A Critique of Five Key Debates in the Social Science Literature," *Annual Review in Sociology,* 27, 235-260.

Hoffman, Richard C. and John F. Preble (2001), "Global Diffusion of Franchising: A Country Level Examination." *Multinational Business Review,* (Spring) 66-76.

Holbrook, Morris B. (1999), "Higher Then the Bottom Line: Reflections on Some Recent Macromarketing Literature," *Journal of Macromarketing,* 19 (1), 48-74.

Hunt, Shelby D. (1972), "The Socioeconomic Consequences of the Franchise System of Distribution," *Journal of Marketing,* 36 (July), 32-38.

Kaufmann, Patrick J. and Harvey Leibenstein (1988), "International Business Format Franchising and Retail Entrepreneurship: A Possible Source of Retail Know-How for Developing Countries, *Journal of Development Planning,* 18, 165-179.

Kaufmann, Patrick J. (2001), "Post-Script 2000," in *International Franchising in Emerging Markets: Central and Eastern Europe and Latin America,* Welsh, D. and Alon, I., eds., CCH Inc.: Chicago, 80-86.

Legrain, Phillippe (2003), "Cultural Globalization Is not Americanization," *The Chronicle of Higher Education,* 49 (35), B7.

Levitt, T. (1983), "The Globalization of Markets," *Harvard Business Review,* 61 (3), 92-102.

Light, David (1997), "Franchising: Getting It Right form the Start," *Harvard Business Review,* (May-June), 14-15.

Makhija, Mona V., Kwangsoo Kim, and Sandra D. Williamson (1997), "Measuring Globalization of Industries Using a National Industry Approach: Empirical Evidence Across Five Countries Over Time," *Journal of International Business Studies,* (Fourth Quarter), 679-710.

Mooij, Marieke de (2000), "The Future is Predictable for International Marketers: Converging Incomes Lead to Diverging Consumer Behavior," *International Marketing Review,* 17.

Pavlin, Igor (2001), "Central Europe: Franchising in Slovania," in *International Franchising in Emerging Markets: Central and Eastern Europe and Latin America,* Welsh, D. and Alon, I., eds., CCH Inc.: Chicago, 189-202.

Preble, John F. and Richard C. Hoffman (1995), "International Note: Franchising Systems Around the Globe: A Status Report," *Journal of Small Business Management,* 80-8.

Reuters (2001), "One Killed in Bombing of McDonald's in China," http://www.ict.org.il/spotlight/det.cfm?id=719 (retrieved May 26, 2003).

Ritzer, George (1998), *The McDonaldization of Society: Explorations and Extensions,* London: Sage Publications.

Robertson, Roland (1992), *Globalization: Social Theory and Global Culture,* Sage Publications, London.

Sanghavi, Nitin (2001), "The Use of Franchising as a Tool for SME Development in Developing Economies – The Case of Central European Countries," ," in *International Franchising in Emerging Markets: Central and Eastern Europe and Latin America,* Welsh, D. and Alon, I., eds., CCH Inc.: Chicago, 171-188.

Saunders, David J. (2002), "Franchising Opportunities: Unlocking Africa's Potential," retrieved from www.africa-ata.org/franchising.htm (June 5, 2002).

Sheth, Jagdish N., and Atul Parvatiyar (2000), "The Antecedents and Consequences of Integrated Global Marketing," *International Marketing Review,* 18 (1), 16-29.

Siggel, Eckhard, Perry Maisonneuve, and Emmanuelle Fortin (2003), "The Role of Franchising in African Economic Development," Presented at the 17th Annual *International Society of Franchising Conference,* San Antonio, Texas, February 14-16.

Sklair L. (1991), *Sociology of the Global System,* New York: Harvester Wheatsheaf.

Stanworth, John, Stuart Price, and David Purdy (2001), "Franchising as a Source of Technology Transfer to Developing Economies," in *International Franchising in Emerging Markets: Central and Eastern Europe and Latin America,* Dianne Welsh and Ilan Alon, eds., Chicago: CCH Inc.

Steijn, B. & M. de Witte (1996), "The Dutch labor market: Threatened by McDonaldization?" *Sociale Wetenschappen,* vol 39, no 4, pp 45-58.

Stevenson, Lois, and Anders Lundström (2001), *Patterns and Trends in Entrepreneurship/SME Policy and Practice in Ten Economies* (Volume 3 of the Entrepreneurship Policy for the Future Series), Swedish Foundation for Small Business Research, Stockholm.

Stiglitz, Joseph E. (2002), *Globalization and Its Discontents,* New York: W.W. Norton Company.

Thompson, Megan and Bill Merrilees (2001), "A Modular Approach to Branding and Operations for International Retail Franchising Systems in Emerging Markets: An Australian Perspective," in *International Franchising in Emerging Markets: Central and Eastern Europe and Latin America,* Welsh, D. and Alon, I. (eds). CCH Inc.: Chicago, 105-118.

Teegan, Hildy (2000), "Strategic and Economic Development Implications of Globalizing Through Franchising: Evidence from the Case of Mexico," *International Business Review,* 9 (4), 497-521.

Transitions (2002), "Stiglitz-Rogoff Debate on "Globalization and Its Discontents," *Transitions* (May-June), 10-13.

Welsh, Dianne and Ilan Alon, eds. (2003), *International Franchising in Industrialized Markets: North America, Pacific Rim, and Other Developed Countries,* Chicago IL: CCH Inc. Publishing.

Welsh, Dianne H. B., and Ilan Alon (2001), *International Franchising in Emerging Markets: Central and Eastern Europe and Latin America,* Chicago: CCH Inc.

Yahoo News (2003), "Indian animal rights groups demand closure of KFC," http://story.news.yahoo.com/news?tmpl=story&u=/afp/20030627/wl_sthasia_afp/india_protest_kentucky_030627120100 (retrieved July 3, 2003).

Yip, George S. (1997), "Patterns and Determinants of Global Marketing," *Journal of Marketing Management,* (January), 153-165.

Yip, George S. (1989), "Global Strategy...In a World of Nations?" *Sloan Management Review,* (Fall), 29-42.

Chapter 4
What is the Economic Impact of Service Franchising Investment?

Ilan Alon
Crummer Graduate School of Business, Rollins College

INTRODUCTION

Economic development is a challenge to small communities across the world. A central question that arises is how to stimulate a remote and small economy. One method is to allow local entrepreneurs to open service businesses. The problem with this approach is that the skill base and training in opening and managing businesses is often missing from the community and from the people who most need it. Franchising may help in this respect. This article aims to empirically asses the economic impact of three franchising-related industries using a small city in Upstate New York as a case study.

Franchising has long been touted as a method of development for small economies. Franchising brings to a local economy a wealth of expertise and a system of doing business that may not be available otherwise. While these intangible effects have been discussed in the literature and by the International Franchising Association (Shay, 2002), no known study to date attempted to empirically assess these impacts across various industries. Alon (2004) conceptually analyzed the socio-economic benefits and costs of franchising from a global perspective. According to his analysis, among the economic impacts are job creation, output creation, tax revenue creation, economic clustering, economic modernization, entrepreneurship development, labor force improvements, as well as increases in innovation, competition, and efficiency.

Economic development in remote local economies is most daunting due to the lack of national economic integration. Often few industrial linkages exist between the remote local economy and key national industries and, thus, economic growth stems from transient travelers and tourists. Industries that facilitate the exchange between locals and tourists can boost local economic development by bringing in income from outside the region and integrating the local economy.

For the purpose of this chapter, we examine three industries in which franchising takes a role: eating and drinking places, hotels, and management consultants. The first two are directly related to tourists and travelers while the last is related to facilitative industries for businesses in general. We chose these industries because of their variance in terms of needed capital, infrastructure, and labor skills. Franchising examples in the eating and drinking sector include Denny's Inc., Friendly's Restaurants, and Arby's; in the hotel sector Super 8 motels, Day's Inns Worldwide Inc., and Howard Johnson Int. Inc.; in the management consulting sector Express Personnel Services, Labor Finders, and Management Recruiters. The industry specific influence on a local economy is important as it allows city planners to target the industries that have the maximum economic impact in terms of output and employment. We then discuss the methodology of IMPLAN in detail explaining to non-specialists about input-output analysis and multiplier effects. This is followed by a case study of three industries in one small city, discussions, conclusions, and future research.

LITERATURE REVIEW: ECONOMIC IMPACT STUDIES

Economic impact analyses vary greatly in terms of industry, region, and methodology. Many economic impact studies have concentrated on tourism (e.g., Upneja et al., 2001; Crompton et al., 2001; Tyrrell and Johnston, 2001; Chase and Alon, 2002), professional sports events (e.g., Crompton, 1999; Hudson, 2001), and non-profit and government organizations (e.g., Bradshaw, 2001; Alon et al., 2001; Hudson, 2001; Woller and Parsons, 2002).

Tourism and Hospitality Economic Impact Studies

Perhaps the largest body of economic impact studies revolves around the impact of tourism and sports. The reason is simple: tourism is the largest industry in the world, contributing from 10-12% to the world's GDP (World Tourism Organization 1998).

Tourism has a significant economic impact on the economies of some countries and regions. For instance, countries like Singapore attract millions of visitors per year and injections of tourist spending directly provide revenues to airlines, ravel agents, hotels, shops restaurants, and other tourist facilities. The direct, indirect and induced impacts of tourism in Singapore, calculated using a reverse matrix, were 11.9% of Singapore's GDP and 13.4% of Singaporean employment. Every tourist dollar in Singapore generated almost $2 of impact on the economy, and one million dollar of spending generated about 25 jobs. In Singapore, shopping, food and recreation, and accommodations accounted for 60%, 11%, and 20%, respectively, of the total visitor expenditures (Khan, Phang, and Toh, 1995). New Zealand is another small Island nations that is attempting to develop its tourism industry. This sector in New Zealand accounted for $11.4 billion in 1999, and the sector provide direct employment to nearly 100,000 people, and indirect employment to another 200,000 (Gnoth and Anwar, 2000).

In smaller regions, evidence suggests that the economic impact of tourism can also be pronounced. For example, in the Pocono Mountains region of Pennsylvania, direct visitor spending totaled about $1.06 billion in 2000, while general sales generated by traveler spending were $1.49 billion (Northeast Pennsylvania Business Journal, 2002).

In the context of developing nations, Kweka, Morrissey and Blake (2003) examined the economic potential of tourism in a country in Africa, Tanzania. According to the authors, African nations have had few opportunities to gain exporting earnings, and tourism provides a powerful method for these nations to raise government revenues and to earn foreign exchange.

Tyrrell and Johnston (2001) developed a standard approach for assessing direct economic expenditures and impacts associated with tourist events. Their results suggest that the impact of tourism in regions dominated by other tourist sites and attractions, such as heavily visited coastal cities, will vary from location in which only one tourist event is measured.

Chase and Alon (2002) attempted to measure the economic impacts of cruise tourism on an island economy using a generalized Keynesian model. Their findings revealed that:

- Total tourist expenditures has a positive impact on government spending in Barbados,
- Cruise tourism has insignificant impact on government spending, not needing a large investment in social overhead capital,
- Cruise tourism has a significant negative impact on import, enlarging net exports and aggregate demand stimulating the domestic economy, and
- Cruise tourism has no impact on investment, while total and stopover tourism has a significant positive impact.

With respect to island economies, Garcia-Falcon and Medina-Munoz (1999) advocated tourism as a method of sustainable economic growth, and studied the specific case of Gran Canaria.

The gaming industry spending was estimated at about $90 billion (Awe, Keating and Schwartz, 2002). It is an industry that relies in part on tourism and which has generated both economic growth and social hardships on selected socio-economic types. Despite the social and political debates that were raised about the desirability of the gaming industry, the growth of the industry and its associated impacts on output and employment have prompted 48 states in the US to turn into gaming for economic growth (Awe, et al., 2002). Lee and Kwon (1997) investigated the economic impact of the casino industry in South Korea and found that it is comparable to other export industries in terms of output, employment, value added and taxes, and significant to the overall economy when direct, indirect and induced impacts are taken into account.

Event and Sport Tourism

Event tourism is a special kind of tourism which includes travel to festivals and gathering staged outside the normal program of activities and sports activities. Sports tourism consists of travel generated from attendance in ongoing and periodic sports events. Such tourism is a special kind of tourism that has peaked the interest of economic impact researchers. Gnoth and Anwar (2000) developed a strategy for maximizing the economic benefit of event tourism by encouraging a well-integrated destination-based approach. The authors acknowledge, however, that gains from event tourism may not be sustainable.

Crompton (1999) measured the economic impact of sports tournaments and events using 30 case studies in seven cities. In 2001, the same author and his colleagues tried to develop a general model for tourism measuring the economic impact of a festival on Ocean City, Maryland.

Upneja et al. (2001) estimated the economic impact of sport fishing in the commonwealth of Pennsylvania, including the annual value of sport fishing resources and annual impact from the use of these resources, using a mail survey to collect data on licensed Pennsylvania anglers' annual equipment and trip expenditures for sport fishing and wildlife watching. The results revealed that the annual values of the sport fishing resources and wildlife-watching resources accounted for $3.98 billion and $0.50 billion, respectively.

Wiliams and Riley (2003) suggested an economic impact study approach that is inexpensive and manageable in order to obtain support from local businesses for youth sport events. Such events, according to the authors, attract first-time visitors and increase visitation in slow parts of the year. Tourists generated from special youth sports events have a positive impact on the local economy and outspend the locals in almost every category for the time they stay in the area. Lodging places and restaurants in the host community particularly benefited from such local sports events.

Economic Impact Studies of University Towns

University-based economic impact studies are important to our study since the studied area is a university-based small city. Humphreys and

Damerschen (2001) empirically examined the economic impacts of higher education in Georgia using the state's 34 institutions. The institutions impacts were divided into (1) spending on salaries and fringe benefits, (2) spending by the institutions for capital projects and construction, (3) spending by the students who attend the institution. Woodward and Tell (2001) found that the economic impact of the University of South Carolina System amounts to nearly $4 billion, and consist of direct, indirect and induced impacts derived from the university itself, its students, and athletic events. According to the authors, the impact of university research on the state's economy far exceeds that of sports.

There are few studies (particularly ones employing input-output models) which examine the direct, indirect and induced impacts of universities on local economies. Some colleges and universities measure only the direct impacts on their communities. New Hampshire Higher Education, for example, publicizes the number of degrees awarded, direct employment, and the direct impact of its affiliated institutions on the New Hampshire economy. Direct economic impact is measured as the total value of volunteer hours, capital expenditures, institutional financial aid, student and family expenditures, salaries, wages and benefits, and annual operating budgets (NHCUC, 1999).

Other economic impact studies of universities abound. Arizona State University generates a total of 39,900 jobs and $2.2 billion in spending (Hill, 2000). Total spending, according to Hill, consists of employee spending, student spending, visitor spending, and university spending. These quantified economic impacts do not include the more qualitative contributions to training, technology, cooperation with industry, competitiveness to local industry, and local faculty resources. Terry College of Business (1999) on the economic impact of the University of Georgia on the Athens Area, showed a local output multiplier of 1.44 and an employment multiplier of 10.41. The University of Alabama's Center for Business and Economic Research estimated an expenditure multiplier for its county (Tuscaloosa) of 1.5 (Federal Reserve Bank of Atlanta, 2000).

While many benefits accrue to communities hosting colleges and universities, there are costs associated with these benefits. Colleges and universities may have an adverse impact on revenues because they require a heavy investment in infrastructure and higher spending on public goods, but they are tax exempt (Federal Reserve Bank of Atlanta, 2000). University students incur not only the costs of attending college but also the opportunity costs associated with lost earnings. Other negative externalities include increases in noise pollution, environmental pollution, and crime. As a whole, however, studies have shown a significant positive economic impact of colleges and universities on their surrounding communities (Federal Reserve Bank of Atlanta 2000).

METHODOLOGY: IMPLAN ECONOMETRIC MODEL

This section describes in detail what, why, and how IMPLAN works, and provides an overview for non-economists on the different kinds of economic multipliers.

What is IMPLAN?

IMPLAN is a licensed software program that can access proprietary data collected by a Minnesota group of economists for the purpose of evaluating the economic structure of a region. This chapter uses IMPLAN (Impact Analysis for Planning) regional impact analysis software to calculate the local and regional economic impacts of the industries in Oneonta. The original IMPLAN model was created by the US Bureau of Land Management to measure the economic benefits of alternative land management and development policies. A group of economists (the IMPLAN group) at the University of Minnesota took over the model and currently maintain it (see www.implan.com).

Why IMPLAN?

IMPLAN is a flexible economic impact modeling tool, which can measure the peculiar impacts of various industries on selected regions, and can provide a comparable framework for analysis. In addition, IMPLAN was used in this study for economic impact assessment modeling because:

1. It is designed to build economic models to estimate the impacts of economic changes in states, counties, or small communities (e.g., zip code level);
2. It accounts for economic leakages such as imports, taxes and savings;
3. It calculates direct, indirect and induced effects on the local and regional economies; and
4. It adjusts for industry-specific variations in purchasing patterns.

IMPLAN is a fundamentally sound methodology for estimating the economic impact of spending in a particular industry on the local and regional economies (Goodman and Feser, 2000). The input-output models used in IMPLAN allow a researcher to create detailed descriptions of how money entering a region in a particular industry travels through the local economy creating additional output, employment and tax (Vogelsong and Graefe, 2001).

Applications of IMPLAN include studies of the impacts of watershed projects, wetland reservation programs, plant materials programs, forestry incentives programs, justification for local cost sharing, conservation policy, resource policy analysis, and state and regional planning (NRCS, 2000).

IMPLAN overcomes the deficiencies of some input-output economic models because it captures industry-level linkages (e.g., local purchases of labor, supplies, materials), as well as economic leakages (i.e., loss of dollars out of the local economy) due to imports, taxes and savings. This is particularly important when examining an institution like the College at Oneonta that operates in a rural area. This is because small rural communities typically lack a sufficiently diversified economy to retain income from economic activity. This situation can be altered as the community expands retail opportunities, promotes growth in business services, and encourages local public and private sector organizations to purchase goods and services locally.

A close contender to IMPLAN is the BEA's Regional Industrial Multiplier System (RIMS). Both models are based on input-output matrices, but slight variations exist in terms of the output, access, data sources, turnaround time, price, reports and other features. The main advantages of IMPLAN over RIMS are: (1) it is more flexible, allowing the user to adjust the regional purchase coefficients, specify the multiplier type, and internalize any number of institutions, (2) it is more practical and interactive, allowing the user to reconfigure regional data and run multiple variations of the same study during the same day, with a marginal cost of zero, (3) it offers additional features such as a complete set of social accounting matrices and user-specified varying levels of sector aggregation. From a practical standpoint, the program is cheaper, faster and more flexible (IMPLAN 2000b). The disadvantage of IMPLAN from an organizational standpoint is that some in-house knowledge of and experience with input-output models are necessary.

What is the theoretical underpinning of IMPLAN?

Economists know that aggregate income equals aggregate spending. That is, if we add up the incomes of entrepreneurs, landowners, capital holders, and workers, they will equal the total spending of consumers, businesses, government and foreigners. For this reason, there is a symbiotic relationship between producers and consumers. For example, households provide the labor input to firms in exchange for wages. These wages, in turn, fuel the demand for goods and services produced by these firms. Economic leakages occur because of savings, imports and taxes, while injections occur through investment, exports, and government spending. The economy is in balance when leakages equal injections.

Input-output models trace the flow of purchases and expenditures on goods and services. According to these models, income receipts (such as sales) equal expenditures (such as payroll and taxes). Profits balance expenditures with receipts. In other words, whatever is not spent on the factors of production is profit.

The IMPLAN study is grounded in input-output (I/O) analysis and its purpose is to analyze the impact of Institutional spending on the regional economy. The seminal work on the topic of I/O was developed by Wassily Leontief (1953) who won a Nobel Prize in Economics for developing the system into a formal set of equations, which determines the multipliers and describes the complex economic relationships among industries, government, and households.

Where does IMPLAN data come from?

Data used by IMPLAN are taken from a wide variety of local, regional and national data sources. Data files contain information on 528 potential industries (3 or 4 level SIC code breakdown), governmental transfers and taxes, regional exports and imports, factors of production, commodity trade, and household spending patterns. The output of the program includes information on the output and employment multipliers at various levels of analysis, tax receipts, and value added by employees, proprietors, and corporations. The Social Accounting Matrix (SAM) multiplier, which will be discussed later, primarily uses information from the Bureau of Economic Analysis (BEA), the Regional Economic Information System (REIS), the Bureau of Labor Statistics (BLS), and Consumer Expenditure Survey (CES) (For more on the data IMPLAN uses see Minnesota IMPLAN Group, 1999).

How does IMPLAN work?

Constructing a model using IMPLAN involves a number of steps. First, one needs to develop a study area. Data matrices for individual counties and cities are purchased from IMPLAN. More than one county or city, at the zip code level, can be integrated into a defined region. Once the study area is defined, the program generates statistics on the population, employment, number of households, area in square miles, number of industries, income per household, total personal income, and the year the data was collected. We used a matrix that was last updated on 9/23/1999.

Information is also available on the number of households for differing income ranges, regional output, value added by factors of production, employment by industry, institutional commodity demand, household commodity demand, government commodity demand, institutional sales, and IMPLAN to SIC classification bridge. The program also allows the user to custom design the aggregation of industries he/she wants to analyze, including 1-digit and 2-digit SIC codes.

After the study area is constructed, the analyst focuses on developing the regional economic impact model. The program develops social matrix accounts (SAM) to calculate a wide range of industry-specific impacts on various institutions and industries within the study area. The social accounts contain information on the local economic interactions in terms of the flow of dollars from purchaser to producers within the region.

Various advanced options are available for the researcher, who can edit the production model (commodities purchased by an industry required to produce its output), the by-products of industries (primary and secondary commodities produced by an industry), the trade flows (the transfer of goods between the region and the rest of the world) and institutional transfers (non-market monetary flows including taxes, government transfers, and savings).

Only after one builds a study area and an industry model can he/she proceed to evaluate the impact of an economic event, e.g. the impact of a capital project. The researcher can identify one or more economic events along with the specified industry within which the event will take place and choose the bases for analysis, i.e., commodity vs. industry. IMPLAN multipliers are sensitive to the characteristics of the industry, but not to the unique characteristics of individual firms within a particular industry. This is because industry averages of employment, production, imports and exports are used to generate the economic multipliers. Once the industry specific data is collected, the program is ready to analyze the economic impacts of a firm's spending on the value added to labor income, other property income, and indirect business taxes, as well as employment and output impacts. The multipliers obtained from IMPLAN are specific to the area being studied as well as the chosen industry.

What are economic multipliers?

The multiplier used in this study, which is referred to as the social accounting matrix or SAM multiplier, measures direct, indirect, and induced effects on output and employment in various industries. The SAM multiplier was used to calculate the impact of an industry on the local and regional economies because this multiplier includes information on (1) flow of dollars from purchasers to producers within the region, (2) flow of dollars between the region and the outside world, and (3) non-industrial transactions such as payment of taxes and government transfers. For households, the SAM multiplier accounts for job commuting, social security tax payments, household income, taxes, and savings. For a complete discussion of SAM see IMPLAN (2000a).

The multiplier shows how industry output is changed by a given change in Institutional expenditure. Three types of multipliers are calculated:

1. Type I multiplier – measures direct and indirect effects inter-industry effects only.
2. Type II multiplier – measures direct and indirect effect internalizing household expenditures as an industry.
3. Type III SAM multiplier – measures direct, indirect and induced effects including all information on payments to factors and institutions, including households and government.

Three effects are examined:

1. Direct effect – changes in industry in which final demand changed
2. Indirect effect – changes in inter-industry purchases derived from final demand
3. Induced effect – changes in household spending due to earnings from increased or decreased Institutional spending.

What are IMPLAN's Key Assumptions?

A discussion of a model will be incomplete without some references to its assumptions. There are several key assumptions that are made when calculating the direct and derived demand of an industry on the local economy.

1. Constant returns to scale – production function is linear and an increase in output will result in demand for inputs increasing proportionately.
2. No supply constraints – supply is unlimited and access to inputs is only limited by the demand for the final product.
3. Fixed commodity input structure – price changes do not cause firms to substitute their inputs and changes in the economy will affect an industry's output but not its input mix.
4. Homogeneous sector output – proportion of commodities produced by an industry is constant regardless of total output.
5. Industry constant technology – the same technology is used by all production in an industry and each industry has a primary product, and all other products are byproducts   (For more about the assumptions see Minnesota IMPLAN Group, 1999).

CASE STUDY: THE CITY OF ONEONTA, NY

Oneonta, New York, is located about half way between Binghamton and Albany New York. The city has a local population of about 17,739 and an area of about 90 square kilometers. The income per household is about

50,996 and there are about 5,947 households in the city. The area is generally economically depressed since the city is remote from any major metropolitan area and the local population can not support large industrial projects. Thus, economic development is a vexing priority for the city. Currently, the college of SUNY Oneonta is the largest employer in the City and the second largest employer in Otsego County (Alon et al., 2001).

The unique economies of university towns offer a diverse retail environment, sporting events, and a multitude of socio-cultural functions. These economies exhibit strong seasonal fluctuations, due to shifting student populations, but milder cyclical fluctuations created by the macroeconomy (Federal Reserve Bank of Atlanta 2000). This is because cutbacks in university funding tend to lag the business cycle and a surge in college demand can occur at the beginning of a recession when cyclical unemployment begins to increase. Because colleges and universities are labor-intensive industries they have a strong multiplier effect, particularly because of the induced effect. Academic institutions that are located in small cities fuel their local economies, provide a cushion against recessions, generate jobs, and often increase the future tax base of a region by absorbing graduates into their local economies.

Clearly, however, small university towns cannot only rely on one institution for economic growth and need to diversify their economic base to sustain long-term development. Franchising may offer a partial solution to this problem by providing a complete business support system to its owners and by infusing sorely-needed economic diversity to a region. Michael (1999) found that the elasticity of demand for restaurant franchising was 0.252, similar to previous studies on advertised consumer products. His result suggest that franchise systems provide product differentiation to at least some franchisees and are, thus, likely to be superior alternatives to mom-and-pop stores from an economic standpoint.

RESULTS

Economic output is the value of all final goods and services and is equal to the sum of payments to workers, interest payments, taxes, and profits. For the purposes of this study direct effects can be defined as the expenditures made in the study area by the industry concerned; the indirect effects represent the jobs and production located within the study area which are used to produce the direct effects; and the induced effects are the jobs and production required to fulfill the demands for goods and services of people employed by the studied industry.

As mentioned earlier, this chapter attempts to capture the economic impacts that result from spending in three industries associated with franchising. For the purpose of comparison, we assume that the initial expenditure in each of the industries is $100,000. While great variations exist in the start-up costs of a franchising firm, this figure was used as a basis for the initial comparison for measuring the multipliers: direct, indirect, induced and total. Table 4.1 shows the output impacts, while Table 4.2 shows the employment impacts for the three industries.

Table 4.1: Output Multipliers for the Three Industries

	Management Consulting	Eating and Drinking	Hotel
Direct	100,000	100,000	100,000
Indirect	21,759	24,746	22,568
Induced	21,469	17,193	18,502
Total	143,228	141,939	141,070
Output Multiplier	1.143	1.142	1.141

Table 4.2: Employment Impact for the Three Industries

	Management Consulting	Eating and Drinking	Hotel
Direct	1.7	3.1	1.8
Indirect	0.3	0.3	0.3
Induced	0.4	0.3	0.4
Total	2.4	3.8	2.5
Local Employment Multiplier per million of spending	24	38	25

As can be gleaned from tables 4.1 and 4.2, the overall output multiplier for all three industries is very similar ranging from 1.141 for the hotel sector to 1.143 for the management consulting sector. This means that for every $100,000 of spending in each of the industries, an additional of over $14,000 is generated in the economy through indirect and induced spending.

A closer examination of Table 4.1 reveals that eating and drinking places generate a greater level of indirect spending, but a lower level of induced spending. Eating and drinking places seem to be economically linked to the local economy. Furthermore, from Table 4.1, the reader can see that eating and drinking places have the highest level of direct and total employment per $100,000 spending. For every $100,000 spending, 3.8 jobs are generated. Taken together, what this means is that eating and drinking places, while generating higher level of employment, create jobs that in comparison to the other industries, are lower paying. This is inferred because the induced spending is lower, despite higher level of employment.

A question that arises from the above analysis is what are the linkages in the various industries analyzed? In other words, how do the industries differ in terms of their impact on sub-sectors of the local economy? Table 4.3 examines the total impact (direct, indirect and induced) on output for each of the industries by sub-sector of the economy.

Table 4.3: Total Output Impact by Industry by Sector

	Management Consulting	Eating and Drinking	Hotels
Agriculture	2	1	1
Mining	0	0	0
Construction	717	1,305	2,843
Manufacturing	1,768	5,870	2,255
TCPU	4,880	6,094	8,061
Wholesale and Retail Trade	8,667	111,513	7,190
FIRE	4,588	4,110	6,502
Services	122,086	12,765	113,810
Government	443	219	340
Other	78	62	67

TCPU = Transportation, Communications, and Public Utilities (Electric, Gas and Sanitary Services)
FIRE = Finance, Insurance, and Real Estate

The high economic impact in services for management consulting and hotels and in wholesale and retail trade for eating and drinking places is to a large extent accounted for by the original $100,000 initial investment. After discounting the $100,000 of direct spending in the industry, one can observe that management consulting has the greatest indirect and induced impact on the service sector locally, followed by wholesale and retail trade and TCPU and FIRE. Eating and drinking places have the greatest total impact on services followed by wholesale and retail trade and TCPU. Interestingly, eating and drinking places have a much stronger impact on manufacturing compared to the other two industries. Finally, hotels seem to have the greatest total output impact on the service sector, followed by TCPU and wholesale and retail trade.

All three industries have a significant impact on the service sector, wholesale and retail trade, TCPU, and FIRE. Franchising has long been acknowledged for stimulating the service sector, where it belongs. This chapter finds that it also has a significant economic impact on the development of transportation, communications, public utilities, finance, insurance, real estate and even manufacturing at the local level.

CONCLUSION

The present study proposes a methodology for measuring the economic impact of franchising investment on a given locality and uses Oneonta New York as a case study. Local economies wishing to develop economically should seriously consider franchising as a method of development because franchising enables entrepreneurs to take investment in the analyzed industries. One way to encourage franchising investment is to make information available to residents and entrepreneurs about franchising opportunities in the area. If the region is seeking the development of specific projects or sectors of the economy, it may want to emphasize those franchises that offer the greatest potential economic links to the industries concerned. For example, if Upstate New York wants to become a tourist attraction, it may want to encourage those franchises that support tourist-based infrastructure such as hotels, restaurants, and other consumer services. Policy makers can make loans available to entrepreneurs wishing to be involved in franchising to stimulate these sectors.

Second, we assumed an initial investment of $100,000 for each of the industries/franchises. This is clearly not the case. Franchises vary greatly in terms of the initial investment. Alon (1999) studied the professional business services, retailing, and hotel industries from 1990 to 1997 and reported that the average startup costs are $138,000 for the retailing sector, 1,904,000 for the hotel sector, and about 20,000 for the professional business service sector (in which management consulting resides). Table 4.4 calculates the total economic impact in dollar amount using the above estimates for the three industries.

Table 4.4: Estimates of Total Economic Impact in Dollar Amount for the Three Industries Using Average Start-up Costs

	Management Consulting	Eating and Drinking	Hotel
Startup Costs	20,000	138,000	1,904,000
Total Output Impact	22,860	157,596	2,171,464
Total Employment Impact	Less than 1 full time job	5.24 jobs	47.6 jobs
Output Multiplier	1.143	1.142	1.141
Local employment multiplier per million of spending	24	38	25

Each sector may have a different appeal to local entrepreneurs and varying levels of demand depending on the location-specific environmental factors. Nonetheless, taking these numbers at face value, the economic impact of the hotel sector may be a lot higher just on account of the fact that the initial spending is so much greater. Using the multipliers derived in this study, the hotel sector will have a much larger impact on every sector of the local economy, compared to the other sectors. On the other hand, there is more room for multiple units of eating and drinking places, as compared to hotels, and perhaps a larger pool of would-be entrepreneurs who would be willing to take the new venture.

In comparison to these three industries, Alon et al. (2001) empirically examined the impact of the State University of New York at Oneonta on its community using IMPLAN and found an output multiplier of 1.33 and an employment multiplier of 24.6 for every million spent. James Madison University (1999) investigated the impact of a university on the local and regional economies using IMPLAN. The study found a regional output multiplier 1.59 and a state output multiplier of 2.17. It also found that for each million dollars of additional institutional spending by the university, 23 jobs are created in the county and 33 jobs are created in the state. Universities in university towns seem to have a larger output multiplier, but a similar employment multiplier as compared to our analyzed industries.

FUTURE RESEARCH

Researchers are advised to continue to empirically examine the economic impact of franchising using other methodologies and models. Such triangulation of methods and data can help test the robustness of different approaches and to better evaluate the "real" impact of franchising on a community. Vogelsong and Graefe (2001) advocated multiple approaches to the study of economic impacts as they concern the hospitality sector, and the empirical approach of IMPLAN is one of them. Charney and Leones (1997) suggested fine tuning the matrices in IMPLAN by decomposing the direct and indirect effects from the induced effects by relative wage and regional distribution to provide more comparable impact results. Such analysis, however, requires strong econometric background.

Alternatively, other empirical approaches are also available and can be used in future studies to examine the economic impacts of franchising-related industries. The Federal Highway Administration (FHWA) designed the Surface Transportation Efficiency Analysis Model (STEAM) which may be used to measure econometric parameters of travel demand, which may be useful for the hospitality sector. Similarly, the economic impact analysis of Cambridge Systematics can help empirically evaluate major transportation infrastructure investments and adapted to evaluate other investments' cost-benefit.

This study should be viewed with caution because it is specific to the locality of Oneonta New York and because certain limiting assumptions are made. First, different economic linkages are present in other locations in the US and abroad. IMPLAN sells data for almost every region in the US and, thus, this study can be replicated for other locations.

We acknowledge that franchising is not the only way to invest in the industries we examined. We chose franchising as our focus of investigation because it enables individuals to invest in these industries without much prior knowledge. This is important to small and remote cities that don't have the skill base to support diverse industrial development. A study examining the differential empirical impacts of franchising versus non-franchising businesses in the same industry is warranted and will add to the almost non-existent literature in the area. Differences may exist because of the way money flows through the region under a franchising system that may, on the one hand, require the franchisee to outsource its inputs and pay franchising fees and royalties and, on the other hand, receive specialized know-how and a local advertising budget unavailable otherwise.

We hope that this study will stimulate interest in the economic impact of franchising since this field is largely unexplored. The International Franchising Association recently issued a call for proposals for an economic firm to take up this subject, indicating that the industry is very interested in understanding its impact on people and the environment both domestically and abroad. We call on our colleagues to take the challenge to produce additional research in this area.

REFERENCES

Alon, Ilan (1999), *The Internationalization of U.S. Franchising Systems (Transnational Business and Corporate Culture Problems and Opportunities)*, New York: Garland Publishing.

Alon, Ilan, Barry P. Warren, and Jeramie Barber (2001), "The Economic Impact of a College: A Regional Analysis of SUNY Oneonta," *New York Economic Review*, 32, 46-60.

Alon, Ilan (2004), "Global Franchising and Development in Emerging and Transitioning Markets," *Journal of Macromarketing*, Forthcoming.

Awe, Susan C., Kathleen Keating, David G. Schwartz (2002), "Studies in Chance: A Selective Guide to Gaming Industry," *Reference Services Review*, 30 (2), 169-175.

Bowling Green State University (1996), Ohio's Education Portolio, Columbus: Inter-University Council of Ohio, Unpublished Paper.

Bradshaw, Ted K. (1999), "Communities Not Fazed: Why Military Base Closures May Not Be Catastrophic," *Journal of the American Planning Association*, 65 (2), 193-206.

Charney, Alberta H., and Julie Leones (1997), "IMPLAN's Induced Effects Identified Through Multiplier Decomposition," *Journal of Regional Sciences*, 37 (3), 503-518.

Chase, Gregory and Ilan Alon (2002), "Evaluating the Economic Impact of Cruise Tourism: A Case Study of Barbados," *Anatolia: An International Journal of Tourism and Hospitality Research*, 13 (1), 5-18.

Crompton, John L. (1999), "The Economic Impact of Sports Tournaments and Events," *Parks and Recreation*, 34 (9), 142-150.

Crompton, John L., Seokho Lee, and Thomas J. Shuster (2001), "A Guide for Undertaking Economic Impact Studies: The Springfest Example," *Journal of Travel Research*, 40 (1), 79-87.

Federal Reserve Bank of Atlanta (2000), "Higher Education Translates Into Big Business: The Unique Economies of University Towns," *EconSouth*, (Second Quarter), 8-13.

Garcia-Falcon, Juan Manuel, and Diego Medina-Munoz (1999), "Sustainable Tourism Development in Islands: A Case Study of Gran Canaria," *Business Strategy and the Environment*, 8, 336-357.

Gnoth, Juergen and Syed Aziz Anwar (2000), "New Zealand Bets on Event Tourism," *Cornell hotel and Restaurant Administration Quarterly*, 41 (4), 72-83.

Goodman, Robert and Edward Feser (2000), "Understanding the Economic Impact of Casinos I Missouri," retrieved 3-18-2000, www.usgri.org/miss.html.

Hill, Kent (2000), "The Economic Impact of Arizona State University," *AZB Arizona Business*, 47 (2), 6-8.

Hudson, Ian (2001), "The Use and Misuse of Economic Impact Analysis: The Case of Professional Sports," *Journal of Sport and Social Issues*, 25 (1), 20-39.

Humphreys, Jeffrey M. and David R. Damerschen (2001), "The Economic Impact of Higher Education: A Case Study in Georgia," *The Mid-Atlantic Journal of Business*, 37 (4), 205-217.

IMPLAN (2000a), "Elements of the Social Accounting Matrix," Technical Report TR-98002, retrieved 3-18-2000, www.implan.com/reports.

IMPLAN (2000b), "BEA / RIMS data versus IMPLAN," retrieved 3-15-2000, www.implan.com/reports.

IMPLAN (1997), "Why Are County Multipliers Larger Than State Multipliers," KBID # 20029, (October 31), retrieved 2-11-2000, www.imlan.com/knowledgeBase/DisplayArticle.asp?KBID=20029

James Madison University (1999), "The Economic Impact of James Madison University on the Harrisonburg/Rockingham County Area and the Commonwealth of Virginia," retrieved 9-20-1999, www.jmu.edu/instresrch/resrchstud/economic/econimpt.htm.

Khan, Habibullah, Sock-Yong Phang, and Rex S. Toh (1995), "The Multiplier Effect: Singapore's Hospitality Industry," *Cornell Hotel and Restaurant Administration*

Quarterly, 36 (1), 64-69.

Kweka, Josaphat, Oliver Morrissey, Adam Blake (2003), "The Economic Impact of Tourism in Tanzania," *Journal of International Development*, 15 (3), 335.

Lee, Choong-Ki, and Kyung-Sang Kwon (1997), "The Economic Impact of the Casino Industry in South Korea," *Journal of Travel Research*, 36 (1), 52-59.

Leontief, Wassily (1953), *Studies in the Structure of the American Economy*. New York: Oxford University Press.

Michael, Steven C. (1999), "The Elasticity of Franchising," *Small Business Economics*, 12 (4), 313-320.

Minnesota IMPLAN Group (1999). IMPLAN Professional Version 2: Social Accounting & Impact Analysis Software, Stillwater: MIG.

Nexus Associates, Inc. (October 13, 1995). The Impact of Tufts University School of Veterinary Medicine on the Massachusetts Economy. Belmont, MA.

NHCUC (1999), "Economic Impact '99: New Hampshire Higher Education Creates $2.25 billion Economic Base," retrieved 3-18-2000, www.nhcuc.org/economic.htm.

North East Pennsylvania Business Journal (2002), "Travel Expenditures for the Poconos Total 1.06 Billion," (June, 02), 17 (8), 19.

NRCS (2000), "Current NRCS IMPLAN case studies," retrieved 3-18-2000, http://waterhome.brc.tamus.edu/NRCSdata/implan/

Shay, Matthew (2002), "IFA's government relations focus intensifies, grassroots action key to success," *Franchising World*, 34 (3), 39-40.

Terry College of Business (1999), "Economic Impact of the University of Georgia on the Athens Area," Georgia Business and Economic Conditions, Selig Center for Economic Growth, University of Georgia, Unpublished paper.

Tyrrell, Timothy J. and Robert J. Johnston (2001), "A Framework for Assessing Direct Economic Impacts of Tourist Events: Distinguishing Origins, Destinations, and Causes of Expenditures," *Journal of Travel Research*, 40 (1), 94-100.

Upneja, Arun, Elwood L Shafer, WonSeok Seo, and Jihwan Yoon (2001), "Economic Benefits of Sport Fishing and Angler Wildlife Watching in Pennsylvavnia," *Journal of Travel Research*, 40 (1), 68-78.

Vogelson, Hans and Alan R. Graefe (2001), "Economic Impact Analysis: A Look at Useful Methods," *Parks & Recreation*, 36 (3), 28-36.

Williams, Wayne and Kevin Riley (2003), "Using Economic Impact Studies to Gain Support for Youth Sports from Local Businesses," *Journal of Physical Education, Recreation, & Dance*, 74 (6), 49-57.

Woller, Gary and Robert Parsons (2002), "Assesing the Community Economic Impact of Microfinance Institutions," *Journal of Developmental Entrepreneurship*, 7 (2), 133-150.

Woodward, Douglas P. and Sandra J. Teel (2001), "The Economic Impact of the University of South Carolina System," *Business & Economic Review*, 47 (2), 3-10.

World Tourism Organization (1998) What We Offer, 23 December 2000, <http://www.world-tourism.org/omt/offer.htm>.

II. Franchising Strategies and Types

Chapter 5
Does Franchising Provide Superior Financial Returns?

Ilan Alon
Crummer Graduate School of Business, Rollins College

Ralph Drtina
Crummer Graduate School of Business, Rollins College

James Gilbert
Crummer Graduate School of Business, Rollins College

INTRODUCTION

Franchising -- a method of distribution in which the franchisor (the principal) passes along to the franchisee (the agent) business-specific information in return for a consideration usually in the form of fees and royalties – has been hailed as one of the most important innovation of the 21st century (Welsh and Alon, 2002). Trends and demographic changes taking place in the global arena have favorably influenced the development of franchising:

- The transition from a manufacturing-based to a service-based economy,
- Consumer desire for convenience,
- Workforce specialization,
- Increased participation by women in the workforce,
- The growth of minority segments of the population, and
- Global marketing (Reynolds, 2002:9).

The success and failure of franchising firms has been a topic of investigation that has increasingly drawn the attention of franchisors, franchisees, governmental agencies, the International Franchising Association, and franchising researchers. Overseas Private Investment Corporation (OPIC), a development agency of the US government, for example, provides funding for US franchisors and their affiliates to ensure global franchising success. According to the agency, OPIC has supported $138 billion worth of investment, generating over ¼ of a million US jobs, about $64 billion in US exports, $10 billion in host-government revenues, and

668,000 host-country jobs (OPIC, 2001). Franchising is one of the agencies new foci.

Most of the academic research to date on the success and failure of franchisors has focused on failure (Price, 1993; Kirby and Watson, 1999; Boyle, 2002; Stanworth et al., 1998). Furthermore, research on franchisors' financial performance and, in particular, the ROE is mostly absent. Elango and Fried (1997) synthesized the franchising literature and have called on the expanded use of different performance measures. To this extent, this chapter fulfills their call.

We focus on the restaurant industry for several reasons. First, the restaurant industry uses franchising to a large extent providing a sample large enough for empirical analysis. Second, by concentrating on a single industry we eliminate the cross-industry variations in franchising practices. Dant et al. (1996), Elango and Fried (1997), and Alon (1999) suggested that franchising researchers focus on particular industries because industry effects in franchising may confound investigated relationships, and each franchising industry may have its own distinctive correlations. Finally, the restaurant industry has been the focus of much research in the franchising literature (Parsa, 1996; Hadjimarcou and Barnes, 1998; Lee and Ulgado, 1997). Cultivating additional research on restaurant franchising has the potential to further our knowledge in the hospitality sector, the marketing discipline, and the franchising method of doing business.

We use the DuPont model --a highly established system of ratio analysis developed at DuPont by F. Donaldson Brown over 70 years ago -- for analyzing the financial performance of the firm. This model is pertinent because:

- Return on Equity (ROE) is a single measure that summarizes the overall financial health of the companies.
- It consists of three underlying factors which depict the profitability, efficiency and leverage of the firms (this point will be expanded upon in the methodology section).
- It is a standardized relational variable that can be used for comparison across companies. Thus it does not require the data to be segmented by asset size or revenues.
- It is a starting point for further financial analysis of the companies.

FRANCHISING SUCCESS/FAILURE LITERATURE

Franchising was shown to exert a powerful force in the US economy. Recent estimates by the International Franchise Association (IFA) suggest that franchising sales are around $1.5 trillion. This number is about 1/10 the US GDP and 1/7 the size of the service sector, where franchising prevails.

The sheer size of the franchising sector is a testimony for its success in the United States market.

Franchising is viewed as a hybrid organization form that has element of markets and hierarchies because the franchisor retains some ownership and control, but gives up the operations of the units. Firms attempt to balance the proportion of franchising outlets in relation to the total system's size in order to balance ownership, control, and profitability (Pizanti and Lerner, 2003; Dant, Paswan, and Kaufmann, 1996).

Two popular approaches to explaining the use of franchising have been resource-scarcity and agency theories (e.g., Oxenfeldt and Kelly, 1969; Combs and Castrogiovanni 1994; Combs and Ketchen, 1999; Alon, 2001; Pizanti and Lerner, 2003). Most studies using these theories have tried to explain the factors associated with the proportion of franchising. The theory of resource scarcity suggests that firms initially franchise because they lack the resources for expansion. Such resources are not merely financial (capital scarcity), but may also be managerial, knowledge-based, or organizational.

The agency perspective, on the other hand, focuses on the monitoring skills of the franchisor. According to the agency perspective, firms franchise because they are unable to monitor their managers efficiently. Because franchisees have a residual claim on sales, they are less likely to shirk, that is, avoid or neglect their responsibilities. Hence, the need for monitoring is diminished because franchisee profits and success depend on maintaining a close relationship with the franchisor. It is in franchisee self interest to adhere closely to standard operating procedures (Shane 1996). A number of recent studies have shown that resource scarcity and agency theory are complementary (Combs and Castrogiovanni 1994; Combs and Ketchen 1999; Alon 2001; Pizanti and Lerner, 2003).

There is growing, but contrasting, evidence on the success and failure of franchisors. Studies sponsored by franchising associations, most notably the International Franchise Association and the British Franchise Association, have found that franchising is a highly successful method of doing business (IFA 1998). According to the British Franchise Association, franchisees are five times more likely to succeed compared with independently owned outlets (Stanworth et al., 1998). Fulop and Forward (1997) wrote that the issue of franchising failure rate is contentious, the implicit assumption on the superiority of franchising is unconfirmed, and that franchising failure statistics remain inconclusive and unreliable. In the balance of this section, we present both sides.

An IFA survey of 1,001 franchisees selected randomly from 4,000 registered franchisors conducted by the Gallup Organization between September and October 1997 and released in March 1998 found that:

- 92 percent of franchisees considered themselves very or somewhat successful,
- 8 out of 10 were small businesses with only one franchise,

- The majority of franchise owners were satisfied with their business,
- 65 percent say they would purchase the franchise again if given the opportunity,
- 93 percent believe that being associated with the franchise gives them a competitive advantage,
- 72 percent said their expectations were met, and
- On average, gross earnings ranged from $76,000 for a single unit franchisee to $142,000 for a multiple-unit franchisee.

From this information, franchising emerges as a highly successful method of doing business which provides sustainable competitive advantage and reasonable standards of living for its owners.

On the other side of the debate, there is a scant and growing literature that challenges the superiority of franchising as a method of distribution and growth. Popular business magazines have started to alert their readers to the risks of franchising. Fortune magazine (1995), for example, reported that since the mid-1980s, franchising growth either matched or lagged behind GDP growth. Inc. magazine (2001) reported that (1) most franchising firms are small (less than 50 units), (2) the risk of failure is significant, (3) about 75% of franchising systems do not last 10 years, and (4) yearly turnover rates among franchisees is about 11%.

A number of franchising researchers have begun investigating the robustness of franchising systems, discovering significant weaknesses. Examining Tatler's Z-scores in exploring the effects of franchising on economic performance of fast-food companies, Price (1993) contended that franchising success is overrated and that failure rates in the British franchising industry may be under-monitored and misrepresented. Bates (1995) discovered that young franchise firms are both more likely to discontinue their operations and exhibit lower mean profitability than cohort independent businesses in the retailing sector. Market saturation in the retailing sector may have been a reason for lower rates of success among franchisors.

On a broader basis, a number of franchising researchers examined the overall trends in franchising. Stanworth et al. (1997) found that US franchising growth has kept pace with US economy, while in the UK, the franchise industry experienced negative real growth. The authors noted that in the UK, franchisee survival rate is no different from other start-up firms over a five-year period. Lafontaine and Shaw (1998) examined franchising data from the beginning of 1980s and found that within 11-12 years of startup less than 30% of franchisors survived. In a similar fashion, Shane (1996a) traced the survival of 138 US franchising systems and found that only about 25% survived after 10 years.

Some researchers attempted to offer explanations to failures in franchising. Stanworth et al. (1998) suggested that business failure rates in conventional and franchising companies are very similar and, in fact, franchising firms may be even more risky due to additional franchise specific risks such as franchisee selection risk, market saturation, high fees and royalties, fraud, intra-system conflict, and insufficient franchisee support. Kirby and Watson (1999) suggested that failures in franchising may be partly due to franchising specific reasons and partly attributable to general reasons of business failure. When small businesses attempt to franchise, the problems of smallness are magnified by the pressures of franchising. Franchising specific reasons include franchising regulatory pressures, underestimation of start-up costs, and lack of experience with franchising.

Frazer (2001) advanced that notion that some franchisors may purposefully stop using franchising due to both organizational and environmental reasons. Among the environmental reasons may be a slowdown in the industry or an increased regulatory burden, while among the organizational factors are personality conflicts, shirking, disputes and experience. Boyle (2002) provided a case study of Shell retail forecourts to examine the case of a failed franchising concept by a major multinational firm. Despite tremendous popularity of the retail concept, Shell experienced problems with the franchisees because of high start-up costs and insufficient profitability at the franchisee level.

In sum, the evidence of franchising success/failure is mixed. Accepted notions of lower level of risk or higher level of success have been challenged by multiple authors and franchising seems far from being a sure way of making money and surviving in a competitive and changing environment. Some authors went a step further to claim that franchising may actually worsen the chance of survival due to additional business and legal difficulties that need to be surmounted (Bates, 1995; Stanworth et al., 1998; Kirby and Watson, 1999). Our study contributes to the franchising literature by adding another piece to the franchising puzzle. In the next section, we explain our methodology in more detail.

METHODOLOGY

We ran several statistical tests to find if there are significant differences in financial performance between franchising and non-franchising firms in the restaurant industry. The basis for our study is the DuPont model. It is calculated as follows:

ROE = Net Income/Sales X Sales/Assets X Assets/Stockholders' Equity

The model relies on four measures of financial performance: ROE, Profitability Ratio, Efficiency Ratio, and Leverage Ratio, where:

- ROE – dollars earned on each invested dollar.
- Profitability ratio – net income dollars generated from each dollar of sales.

- Efficiency ratio – dollars earned by each dollar of assets.
- Leverage ratio – dollars of assets acquired by each dollar invested by stockholders.

The first measure, ROE, is a multiplicative function of the other measures. It is the most prominent test of profitability for purposes of this chapter. If the model is reduced, ROE equals Net Income/Stockholders' Equity since the other terms cancel out. ROE is the primary performance measure, but is explained by the other components of the model. Of the three industry leaders in terms of sales dollars, McDonald's reported an ROE of 8.7%, Darden 21.1%, and Starbuck's 12.5%.

DESCRIPTION OF THE DATA

The chapter is based on data of US restaurant chains taken from COMPUSTAT, a popular software containing up-to-date financial information on US publicly traded firms[1]. The criterion for selection was the restaurant industry code. In all, there were 124 firms included in the original data set. Firms were then separated into those that had franchise operations and those that had none. We did not identify the propensity of franchising, but rather only whether the firm did or did not franchise. This determination was made by analysis of company documents and public reports.

Several firms were dropped from the original data set because of problems with data. In some cases, COMPUSTAT did not report data needed to complete the DuPont model. Other firms reported ROE percentages (+/- 600%) that were extreme outliers. Still other firms reported positive ROE amounts that were mathematical anomalies, resulting from negative net income and owners' equities. That is, since both numerator and denominator were negative, the resulting ROE became a positive percent. Firms exhibiting any of these characteristics were dropped from the data set, resulting in a sample size of 92.

Figure 5.1 offers a scattergram showing the distribution of ROE results for 92 firm samples. Most percentages are clustered within a range of plus or minus 50%. We then created a smaller sample set to include only those firms falling within this smaller range. Figure 5.2 offer a scattergram for the outcome, based on 76 firms. In our opinion, this smaller data set enables a better view of dispersion, and it falls within a more likely range of ROE outcomes for stable firms. Companies that have ROE results that are more than plus or minus 50% reflect unusual circumstances, such as startup operations, financial distress, or bankruptcy. There are 8 franchised restaurants with return on investments of more than ±50 and 8 non-franchised restaurants with greater than ±50 return on investments. Throughout this chapter, statistical tests revealed similar outcomes on both the larger sample size of 92 firms and the smaller sample of 76 firms. However, we limit our reported data to the smaller sample with the idea that these firms better indicate how ongoing franchise entities are likely to perform.

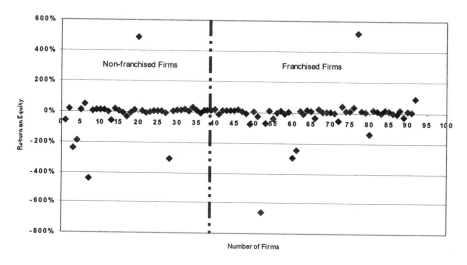

Figure 5.1: Return on Equity for all Firms (n=82)

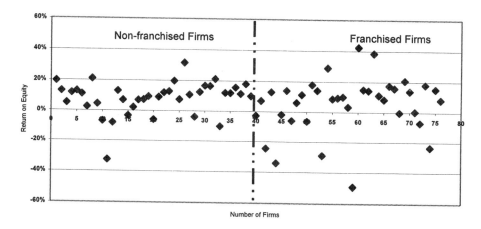

Figure 5.2: Return on Equity for Firms with No More than +- 50 ROE (n = 76)

DESCRIPTIVE STATISTICS

Information about the nine variables used in the chapter is given in Table 5.1. The left side of the table lists these variables, with the next two columns reporting their means and standard deviations. The first variable listed, Franchise, categorizes each firm as either being franchise or not franchise. All other variables are taken from the firm's financial statements. Sales, Net Income, Assets, and (Stockholders') Equity are reported as thousand dollar amounts. Thus average sales are $709.82. The standard deviation for sales is large, $1,893.83, suggesting there is much variation in size of firms. One end of the spectrum is McDonalds at $15,405.7 and Darden Restaurants at $4,368.7. The other includes lesser known brands, such as Ultimate Franchise System, $3.03 and Noble Romans at $6.7. Size however does not matter in deriving ROE comparisons, since the data are normalized. The last four variables in Table 5.1 exhibit these normalized relationships. The first derived variable, Net Income/Sales, reports a mean of 0.030 and a standard deviation of 0.050. On average, a firm earns $.03 on each dollar in sales revenue, but 68% of firms within one standard deviation, would fall within a range of minus $.02 to plus $.08 of profit per sales dollar. ROE, the criterion of profit, is 7.0% with a standard deviation of 15%.

Table 5.1 also provides a correlation matrix. The same variables reported along the left side of the table are reported along the top. Consider the results from the perspective of determining whether franchising helps explain differences in firm profitability. The franchise variable reports low correlations with the other eight variables in the model. The implication is that a firm's franchise activity does little to explain any other variable under study.

Compare these results with results for other variables in the model. (Stockholders') Equity is highly correlated with the results of other financial data, like Sales (0.97), Net Income (0.97), and Assets (0.99). That is, Equity tends to move predictably higher with increases in sales, net income, and assets. Further, consider variables with low correlations, like the profitability ratio, NI/Sales. This ratio does not move in close tandem with Sales (0.14), Net Income (0.22) or Assets (0.10), although it is positively correlated with all three. It is likely that the percent of NI/Sales is driven by other factors, such as the firm's ability to reduce expenses.

RESULTS

We conducted a series of t-tests to determine whether firm profitability differed between franchise firms and non-franchised firms. Results are reported in Table 5.2.

Table 5.1: Correlations Matrix (n = 76), Return on Equity Limited to ±50%

	Mean	SD	Franchise	Sales	Net Income	Total Assets	Equity	NI/Sales	Sales/Assets	Assets/Stockholders Equity	ROE
Franchise	0.61	0.49	1.00	0.05	0.08	0.08	0.06	0.12	-0.16	0.03	-0.02
Sales	709.82	1893.83		1.00	0.99	0.96	0.97	0.14	-0.14	-0.66	0.11
Net Income	38.38	112.37			1.00	0.95	0.97	0.22	-0.15	-0.08	0.16
Total Assets	680.79	2764.06				1.00	0.99	0.10	-0.17	-0.02	0.05
Equity	332.89	1204.65					1.00	0.12	-0.18	-0.02	0.08
NI/Sales	0.03	0.05						1.00	-0.18	-0.19	0.67
Sales/Assets	1.56	0.73							1.00	-0.04	0.10
Assets/Stockholders Equity	2.23	1.82								1.00	0.16
ROE	0.07	0.15									1.00

Note: Bold values are significant at the 0.05 level. Correlations were developed with a "dummy" variable. A "0" representing non-franchised restaurants and a "1" representing franchised restaurants.

Table 5.2: Two Sample T-Test Results 9n = 76); Return on Equity Limited to ±50%

Descriptive Statistics					t-test Analysis Summary			
Variable	Franchise	Mean	Std. Dev.	Std. Error	Mean Diff.	Std. Error	t score	p-value
Return on Equity	No	0.07	0.12	0.21	0.01	0.04	0.19	0.85
	Yes	0.07	0.17	0.03				
NI/Sales	No	0.02	0.04	0.02	-0.01	0.01	-1.09	0.28
	Yes	0.04	0.06	0.03				
Sales/ Assets	No	1.70	0.83	0.15	0.24	0.17	1.40	0.17
	Yes	1.46	0.65	0.10				
Assets/ St. Equity	No	2.15	1.42	0.26	-0.12	0.43	-0.28	0.78
	Yes	2.27	2.04	0.30				

Note: Franchised firms in sample = 30; non-franchised firms in sample = 46.

We created a stepwise regression model to determine which variables best explained the company's ROE. The results for variables that remain in the model are reported in Table 5.3. The variables that were excluded from the model were: Sales, Net Income, and Franchise. The fact that the franchising variable was dropped is significant to this chapter since it is the focus of our investigation and confirms no impact on the ROE. As shown in Table 5.3, the remaining variables explain 63.6% of the variation in ROE. Each variable that was kept in the model met the p-value cutoff of 5%. This model supports the conclusion reached in Table 5.2 – a firm that is franchised does not contribute firm profitability.

The first variable reported is Return on Equity (ROE), the percent of earnings that the firm generates per dollar of shareholder investment. The mean of non-franchise firm ROE, 7.29% was actually more than that of franchise firm, 6.61%. A t-test was conducted on the difference between these means, 0.68%. The test reports a p-value of 0.849. At a 5% cutoff level, the difference is not significant. We find similar results when the three component ratios of ROE are tested.

The mean difference for NI/Sales is 1.38%, which has a p-value of .281. For Sales/Assets, the mean difference is 23.79% with a p-value of .167. For Assets/Stockholders' Equity, the mean difference is 12.05% with a p-value of .779. The implications are consistent for this sample. There is no evidence to suggest that franchise firms generate better financial performance than non-franchise firms.

Table 5.3: Stepwise Regression Summary Output (n = 76), Return on Equity Limited to ±50%

Regression Statistics				
Multiple R	0.80			
R Square	0.64			
Adjusted R Square	0.61			
Standard Error	0.10			
Observations	76			
ANOVA				
	df	*SS*	*MS*	*F*	*Significant F*
Regression	5	1.11	0.22	24.43	0.00
Residual	70	0.63	0.01		
Total	75	1.74			
Regression				
	Coefficients	*Std. Error*	*t Stat*	*P-value*
Intercept	-0.16	0.03	-4.77	0.00
Total Assets	0.00	0.00	-2.21	0.03
Equity	0.00	0.00	2.27	0.03
NI/Sales	2.10	0.22	9.68	0.00
Sales/Assets	0.06	0.02	3.71	0.00
Assets/Stockholders Equity	0.03	0.01	4.51	0.00

CONCLUSION

Despite the growth and apparent success of franchise firms, the findings of this study fail to uncover any sustainable profit advantage for franchised firms in the restaurant industry. Financial performance, measured by various elements of return on equity, did not differ between the franchise and non-franchise networks. Our analysis concludes that franchising is neither a negative nor a positive in the financial performance of a restaurant chain as far as the DuPont model is concerned. Perhaps the positive factors balance the negative factors of franchising in the restaurant sector.

It is reasonable to assume that franchise firms need fewer assets to generate sales, since they generate franchise fees and royalties from their franchisees. The business of franchising is thought to be less capital intensive because the franchisee is most often responsible for constructing the plant and purchasing equipment. The second component of the ROE equation, Sales/Assets, gets at this relationship. However the assumption was not supported by the results of this study. It may also be reasonable to assume that a franchise firm requires less leverage. Since a firm is not building capital assets, it would not have a need to take out construction debt. Again, the study failed to support this assumption. The third term of the model, Assets/Stockholders' Equity, measures a firm's leverage. The two types of firms did not differ.

Admittedly, this study is narrow in scope. We believe that this narrowness allowed us to focus on an important dimension of franchising financial success and to keep many of the environmental and contextual industry differences to a minimum. The use of franchising does not seem to alter profitability in any big way at least as far as the restaurant industry is concerned. Additional research into other industrial sectors of franchising is advisable to see whether the same results will hold. Secondly, our research is cross sectional examining the latest available public information. A longitudinal study or a multi-year comparison may further elucidate the impact of franchising on profitability. Third, applying other financial measures of success, such as return on assets, may reveal new patterns. Finally, an examination of franchising systems in countries other than the US and the UK may help explain how context and environment may impact the success of franchising systems. Clearly, franchising success/failure is a fruitful area of research about which little is conclusive. We hope that this study can provide the impetus for future research on the financial viability of franchising vs. non-franchising firms.

NOTES

[1] At the time of our investigation, financial data available were last updated on August 31, 2003.

REFERENCES

Alon, Ilan and Dianne Welsh, eds. (2003), *International Franchising in Industrialized Markets: Western and Northern Europe*, Chicago IL: CCH Inc. Publishing.

Alon, Ilan (2001), "The Use of Franchising by US-Based Retailers," *Journal of Small Business Management*, 39 (2), 111-22.

Alon, Ilan (1999), *The Internationalization of U.S. Franchising Systems*, New York: Garland Publishing.

Bates, T. (1995), "Analysis of Survival Rates Among Franchise and Independent Small Business Startups," *Journal of Small Business Management*, 33 (2), 26-36.

Block, Z., and MacMillan, I. (1993), *Corporate Venturing*. Boston: Harvard Business School Press.

Boyle, Emily (2002), "The Failure of Business Format Franchising in British Forecourt Retailing: A Case Study of the Re-branding of Shell Retail's Forecourts," *International Journal of Retail and Distribution Management*, 30 (5), 251-63.

Castrogiovanni, G. J., Justis, R. T., and Julian, S. D. (1993), "Franchise Failure Rates: An Assessment of Magnitude and Influencing Factor," *Journal of Small Business Management*, 16, 105-14.

Combs, James G., and Gary J. Castrogiovanni (1994), "Franchisor Strategy: A Proposed Model and Empirical Test of Franchise versus Company Ownership," *Journal of Small Business Management*, 32 (2), 37-48.

Combs, James G. and David J. Ketchen (1999), "Can Capital Scarcity Help Agency Theory Explain Franchising? Revisiting the Capital," *Academy of Management Journal*, 42 (2), 196-207.

Dant Rajiv P., Audhesh K. Paswan, and John Stanworth (1996), "Ownership Redirection Trends in Franchising: A Cross-Sectoral Investigation," *International Journal of Entrepreneurial Behavior and Research*, 2 (3), 48-67.

Dant, Rajiv P., Audhesh K. Paswan, and Patrick J. Kaufmann (1996), "What We Know About Ownership Redirection in Franchising: A Meta-Analysis," *Journal of Retailing*, 72 (4), 429-44.

Elango, B. and Vance H. Fried (1997), "Franchising Research: A Literature Review and Synthesis," *Journal of Small Business Management*, 35 (3), 68-81.

Falbe, Cecilia M., Thomas C. Dnadridge, and Ajith Kumar (1998), "The Effect of Organizational Context on Entrepreneurial Strategies in Franchising," *Journal of Business Venturing*, 14, 125-40.

Falbe, Cecilia M. and Dianne H. B. Welsh (1998), "NAFTA and Franchising: A Comparison of Franchisor Perceptions of Characteristics Associated with Franchisee Success and Failure in Canada, Mexico, and the United States," *Journal of Business Venturing*, 13, 151-71.

Fortune (1995), "Trouble in Franchise Nation," 131 (4), 115-17.

Frazer, Lorelle (2001), "Why Franchisors Discontinue Franchising But Continue Operating," *International Small Business Journal*, 19 (3), 29-38.

Fulop, Christina and Jim Forward (1997), "Insights into Franchising: A Review of Empirical and Theoretical Perspectives," *The Service Industries Journal*, 17 (4), 603-25.

Hadjimarcou, John and John W. Barnes (1998), "Case Study: Strategic Alliances in International Franchising –the Entry of Silver Streak Restaurant Corporation into Mexico," *Journal of Consumer Marketing*, 15 (6), 598-607.

Inc. (2001), "McBusiness," 23 (7), p. 34-36.

International Franchise Association (1998), "IFA Educational Foundation Survey of Franchise owners, Conducted by the Gallup Organization, Finds 92 Percent Successful, Majority Would Do It Again," Washington D.C., 1-2.

Kirby, David and Anna Watson (1999), "Franchising as a Small Business Development Strategy: A Qualitative Study of Operational and Failed Franchisors in the UK," *Journal of Small Business and Enterprise Development*, 6 (4), 341-49.

Lafontaine, E. and K. Shaw (1998), "Franchising Growth and Franchisor Entry and Exit in the U.S. Market: Myth and Reality," *Journal of Business Venturing*, 13 (2), 95-113.

Lee, Moonkyu and Francis M. Ulgado (1997), "Consumer Evaluations of Fast-Food Services: A Cross-National Comparison," *The Journal of Services Marketing*, 11 (1), 39-52.

Mehta, Sanjay S., Dawn Luza, Carey Counsil, and Balasundram Maniam (1999), "Analysis of Franchising Data: A Comparative Evaluation of Leading Secondary Sources," in *Proceedings of the 13th Annual International Society of Franchising Conference*, Miami, (March).

Oxenfeldt, Alferd R., and Anthony O. Kelly (1969), "Will Successful Franchise Systems Ultimately Become Wholly-Owned Chains?" *Journal of Retailing*, 44, 69-87.

Overseas Private Investment Corporation (OPIC) (2001), "OPIC Finances Mail Boxes Etc. Franchise," www.opic.gov/pressreleases/2001/1-08.htm (retrieved Dec. 25, 2003).

Parsa, H.G. (1996), "Franchisor-Franchisee Relationships in Quick-Service-Restaurant Systems," *Cornell Hotel and Restaurant Administration Quarterly*, 37 (3), 42-50.

Pizanti, Inbar, and Miri Lerner (2003), "Examining Control and Autonomy in the Franchisor-Franchisee Relationship," *International Small Business Journal*, 21 (2), 131-59.

Price, Stuart (1993), "Performance of Fast-Food Franchises in Britain," *International Journal of Contemporary Hospitality Management*, 5 (3), 10-15.

Reynolds, John R. (2002), "Foreword," in *International Franchising in Industrialized Markets: North America, the Pacific Rim, and Other Countries*, D.H.B. Welsh and I. Alon, eds., CCH Inc., 9-10.

Sen, Kabir C. (1998), "The Use of Franchising as a Growth Strategy by US Restaurant Franchisors, *Journal of Consumer Marketing*, 15 (4) 397-407.

Shane, Scott A. (1996a), "Hybrid Organizational Arrangements and Their Implications for Firm Growth and Survival: A Study of New Franchisors, *Academy of Management Journal*, 39 (1), 216-34.

Shane, Scott A. (1996b), "Why Franchise Companies Expand Overseas," *Journal of Business Venturing*, 11 (2), 73-88.

Stanworth, John, David Purdy, Stuart Price, and Nicos Zafiris (1998), "Franchise Versus Conventional Small Business Failure Rates in the US and UK: More Similarities than Differences," *International Small Business Journal*, 16 (3), 56-69.

Stanworth, John, David Purdy, and Stuart Price (1997), "Franchise Growth and Failure in the USA and the UK: A Troubled Dreamworld Revisited," *Franchising Research: An International Journal*, 2 (2), 75-94.

Swartz, L. N. (2001), "Franchising Successfully Circles the Globe," in *International Franchising in Emerging Markets: Central and Eastern Europe and Latin America*, D.H.B. Welsh and I. Alon, eds., Chicago, IL: CCH Inc.

Welsh, Dianne and Ilan Alon, eds. (2002), *International Franchising in Industrialized Markets: North America, Pacific Rim, and Other Developed Countries*, Chicago IL: CCH Inc. Publishing.

Chapter 6:
How Do Franchisors Evaluate Foreign Markets?

Ilan Alon
Crummer Graduate School of Business, Rollins College

David McKee
Graduate School of Business, Kent State University

INTRODUCTION

Despite the rapid expansion of US international franchisors into foreign markets, little is known about the country factors influencing this behavior. The recency of the internationalization of US franchise systems coupled with the scant theoretical attention given to the subject provide the need for an explanatory model of US international franchising. It is the objective of this chapter to develop a macro environmental model for international franchising that would be useful to academics wishing to construct empirical models as well as to franchisors wishing to establish ventures in international markets.

Franchising is a growing method of doing business both domestically and internationally. It started in the United States in the early 1900s, but did not gain acceptance worldwide until the 1960s. The recent growth in international franchising was fueled by both push factors, such as saturation, competition, and diminishing profits in the domestic market, and pull factors, such as the liberalization of the Eastern block countries, the formation of regional trading blocks, and the emergence of some newly industrialized countries in the international market place.

The initial internationalization efforts of US based franchisors were directed toward Canada, Britain, and Australia, countries that are culturally, politically, and economically similar to the United States. As franchising systems matured in these countries, profit potential decreased because of increasing domestic and international competition (Welch, 1992). Therefore, US based franchisors had to seek growth avenues in less developed, culturally dissimilar or politically unstable countries. These environments presented a new set of challenges which often required changes in the product/service mix, contractual arrangements or methods of operation.

With the increased diversity of countries in which franchisors sought potential outlets came the need to develop a systematic way to evaluate potential host countries. The standardized nature of franchising necessitates a high degree of cooperation and control by the franchisor, which is complicated in a multicultural context. This article develops a model that judges the investment climate of a host country from an international franchising perspective and provides a starting point for comparative analysis of competing locations around the globe. This model considers four factors important to country analysis including (1) economic, (2) demographic, (3) distance, and (4) political variables. These categories were used to group the environmental variables that were discussed in the literature of international franchising. Information from governmental (Kostecka, 1988), conceptual (Eroglu, 1992), survey (Arthur Andersen, 1996), and empirical (Yavas, 1988) studies was used to build the model.

The focus of this chapter is on business format franchising because it was shown to provide faster growth than product name franchising in the domestic market (Kostecka, 1988) and was the source of most of the successful international franchising ventures (Burton and Cross, 1995). Burton and Cross (1995, p. 36) defined international franchising as "a foreign market entry mode that involves a relationship between the entrant (the franchisor) and a host country entity, in which the former transfers, under contract, a business package (or format), which it has developed and owns, to the latter." This host country entity can be either a domestic franchisee, a foreign franchisee, a master franchisor, or an entity which is partly owned by the franchisor itself.

International franchising is a unique method of entry which differs from licensing, exporting, and foreign direct investment. International franchising is a unique mode of entry because (1) the characteristics of the business stay the same regardless of who is the owner and (2) the ownership can be transformed with relative ease, even after operations have been established, without any noticeable difference (Burton and Cross, 1995). Shane (1996, p. 86) concluded that "the use of franchise contracts appears to be an important long-term strategic choice in its own right for international service firms."

MODEL DEVELOPMENT

The research on international franchising falls into two categories: (I) internal and (2) external explanations. Internal explanations have focused on the company characteristics leading a franchising firm to internationalize, while external explanations focus on the macro environmental factors leading to either a choice of country or a choice of entry strategy.

In the context of internal explanations of international franchising, Eroglu (1992) suggested that the firm size, operating experience, top management's tolerance for risk, and top management's perceptions of the firm's competitive advantage impact the decision of franchisors to internationalize. Using resourcebased and agency theories, it was shown that the resources (Fladmoe-Lindquist 1996), emanating from the firm's size, growth rates, brand equity and managerial talent, and monitoring capacity, including the price structure of the franchise and the physical dispersion, influence the decision of franchisors to internationalize (Shane 1996).

The external factors of international franchising include the environmental determinants for selecting and evaluating a host country. Research has shown that in recent years the greatest growth in international franchising occurred in Asia, South America, Central America and Mexico (Arthur Andersen, 1996). This is because the markets of most of the developed countries became increasingly saturated and competitive. As more and more franchisors expand to diverse countries, the importance of host country selection and evaluation will increase. The model presented in the next section borrows on the literature of empirical, conceptual, survey and governmental studies.

The model developed in this article lies in the realm of external explanations of international franchising because it focuses on the macro environmental factors responsible for the expansion into a host country. It consists of 10 variables which are assigned a value from -2 to 2, where a -2 represents a negative score on the factor evaluated (See Table 6.1). The zero point represents a neutral point which reflects no problem with the proposed variable. A simple sum of the assigned scores will result is a country rating which falls between -20 and 20, where 20 represents the best score. Macro environmental scores for countries that fall above zero are generally favorable while those that fall below zero are generally unfavorable. The scores are ordinal measures that can be used as a starting point for analyzing the host country and comparing the relative climate of different nations. A weight can be assigned to each variable to control for its relative importance to the franchisor. The model can be used to evaluate and compare the environments of a host country from the standpoint of an international franchisor. However, the scores that are obtained from this model are only as good as the people evaluating them. Analysts should be familiar with the franchise concept, the host country's culture and language, and business practices in the host country. This model does not attempt to answer the question of what should be the entry strategy once a country has been evaluated, although it provides a good base for this decision. Countries that score low using the evaluation instrument provided should be entered via a low risk mode, such as master franchising, to limit the financial exposure of failure.

Although past research shows that the desire to internationalize was often motivated by a third party, such as a franchisee or a foreign national

(Welch, 1992), franchisors should analyze the environments of a host country in order to evaluate the receptivity of the franchise system. Furthermore, a wrong decision about a host country can be embarrassing, at best, and harmful to both the profitability and the brand name of the franchisor, at worst.

International franchising researchers, practitioners, and consulting firms have begun to chart the country variables that are important to international franchisors. These variables fall into four categories: (1) economic, (2) demographic, (3) distance, and (4) political factors. Eroglu (1992) proposed that the perceived favorability of the external environment is negatively related to the perceived risk and positively related to the perceived benefits. This means that stability in the host country's economic, cultural, and political factors will increase the likelihood that an international franchisor will seek expansion in the host country.

The Economic Dimension

Among the economic factors alluded to in the literature of international franchising and included in Table 6.1 were (1) the individual income, (2) economic growth (Arthur Andersen, 1996), and (3) the level of urbanization (Yavas, 1988). The income of the citizenry, in particular disposable income, determines whether the average person can frequent the proposed franchise and suggests whether an adequate market potential exists. A readily available measure which can be used as a proxy for individuals' incomes is the per capita GDP. Using pooled cross section (6 countries) and time series (10 years) regression, Yavas (1988) found that per capita income was positively related to the number of international restaurant franchises. In Table 6.1 per capita GDP is used as a proxy of individual income.

The level of economic growth was ranked as the third most important factor in determining whether a foreign country is likely to be receptive to a franchise system. Eighty-five percent of international franchisors rated economic growth as either important or the most important consideration in host country evaluation (Arthur Andersen, 1996). This construct can be measured using the rate of GDP growth over a specified number of years. In Table 6.1 a period of 7 years was selected with an eye to suppress short-term fluctuations.

The level of urbanization was ranked as the fifth most important factor of the acceptance of the franchise system in a foreign market with 73 percent of respondents reporting it as either important or very important (Arthur Andersen, 1996). Several factors may have contributed to this result. First, as a shift in the population from rural to urban life occurs, the opportunity cost of time will increase for the city dwellers and they will wish to buy some of the services previously produced at home. Second, even in developing and less developed countries, large cities have an adequate number of affluent consumers, providing fertile ground for international franchising expansion. Finally, inputs of the franchise service, such as unskilled as well as skilled labor, are relatively abundant in densely populated areas.

Table 6.1: A Normative Macro Environmental Model of International Franchising

Economic Dimension
1. GDP per capita
-2 (Very Low) __ __ __ __ __ +2 (Very High)

2. 7 year average GDP growth
-2 (Very Low) __ __ __ __ __ +2 (Very High)

3. Level of urbanization
-2 (Very Low) __ __ __ __ __ +2 (Very High)

Demographic Dimension
1. Extent of the middle class
-2 (Very Low) __ __ __ __ __ +2 (Very High)

2. Population growth
-2 (Very Low) __ __ __ __ __ +2 (Very High)

3. Proportion of female labor participation
-2 (Very Low) __ __ __ __ __ +2 (Very High)

Distance Dimension
1. Physical distance
-2 (Very Big) __ __ __ __ __ +2 (Very Small)

2. Cultural distance
-2 (Very Big) __ __ __ __ __ +2 (Very Small)

Political-Related
1. Internal political risk
-2 (Very High) __ __ __ __ __ +2 (Very Low)

2. External political risk
-2 (Very High) __ __ __ __ __ +2 (Very Low)

The Demographic Dimension

Among the demographic variables are (1) the size of the middle class (Arthur Andersen, 1996), (2) population growth (Arthur Andersen, 1996), and female labor force participation (Yavas, 1988). Arthur Andersen (1996) found the existence of a substantial middle class as the most important factor in determining whether a host country will be suitable to the US franchising system. A substantial middle class has the potential to support most US based franchises which ordinarily tailor their services to that segment of the population. Even in countries with small populations, but with a substantial middle class, such as Israel and Kuwait, franchises have a viable market in many service industries.

Arthur Andersen (1996) also reported that 62 percent of the responding franchisors considered population growth an important or very important determinant for choosing a host country. A high level of population growth means that there is a future potential to the franchise system.

In the past decades, women in developed countries have moved from their traditional roles as housewives into labor markets. Franchisors who tailored their services to the time constraints and household services, such as fast food restaurants and cleaning services, have thus proliferated. In many developing countries, women are currently entering labor markets in increasing numbers creating the same type of demand for services. Yavas (1988) supported the hypothesis that the proportion of females in the labor force is positively associated with the number of international restaurant franchises. Therefore, the greater the proportion of female labor force participation, the more attractive the host country will be to foreign based franchisors.

The Distance Dimension

The distance dimension consists of (1) physical distance (Kostecka, 1988) and (2) cultural distance (Eroglu, 1992). Physical distance was one of the most mentioned factors in US international franchising expansion (Kostecka, 1988). This is why most US based franchisors planning international franchises chose Canada as the first site of international expansion followed by Mexico (Arthur Andersen, 1996). Fladmoe-Lindquist (1996) posed the problem of physical distance from the standpoint of administrative efficiency theory. Physical distance makes monitoring difficult and expensive. Communications technology is not perfectly standardized across and among countries because of software, hardware, connectivity, and regulations regarding transmission (Fladmoe-Lindquist, 1996). Furthermore, physical distance makes logistical support more difficult especially when inputs have to be imported from the home country. Arthur Andersen (1996) reported that 38 percent of franchisors planning international franchises and 21 percent of franchisors with existing international franchises rated proximity to the United States as the primary reason for choosing a host country. Physical distance can be measured in either absolute term or using travel time. The present study favors the latter because travel time relates to the transportation and delivery time of human and nonhuman resources.

Cultural distance refers to the difference in the culture and language of the host and home countries (Eroglu, 1992). Differences in values and methods including the use of language influence the success of US international franchisors. Culture impacts the negotiation of contracts, the daily operations, the hiring of personnel, as well as the format of the franchise (Fladmoe-Lindquist, 1996; Justis and Judd, 1989). "The transferability of the [franchising] system becomes a function of cultural distance between the foreign and domestic cultures. The very strength of a franchising format, its standardization, makes its successful replication in foreign markets difficult" (Fladmoe-Lindquist 1996, p. 425). Cultural distance affects internal managerial and operational business practices, communication and performance evaluations, as well as providing an attractive service to local consumers (Eroglu, 1992). The greater the cultural distance the less the perceived benefits and the greater the increased costs of internationalization.

Cultural distance can be measured by Hofstede's four measures of (1) power distance, (2) individualism/collectivism, (3) uncertainty avoidance, and (4) masculinity. These measure are available for 40 countries and have been highly cited in the management literature. Another readily available measure that can be adopted by US based franchisors is the use of English in the host country. The use of English has prompted many US based franchisors to choose Australia, England, and Canada as the initial sites for international expansion. The wide spread use of English has been noted as either very important or important in determining the success of franchises in a host country by 39 percent of franchisors (Arthur Andersen, 1996).

The Political Dimension

The political dimension consists of political risk factors that can be divided into external and internal components. Political risk refers to the internal or external events emanating from government or society that negatively affect the business environment. Internal causes are induced by the host country, while external causes are generated by the home country, a third country, or the global environment.

Among the internally generated political risk factors relevant to franchisors are (1) governmental regulations and red tape (Kostecka, 1988), (2) political stability, (3) the proliferation of bribery, and (4) ownership restrictions (Justis and Judd, 1989). The external environment of political risk directly influencing international franchisors includes (1) foreign exchange controls and (2) import restrictions (Justis and Judd, 1989).

Burton and Cross (1995, p. 45) wrote "firms employing franchising contracts in their internationalization process can and frequently do, invest significant amounts of equity in host country franchise subsystems." Furthermore, Arthur Andersen (1996) revealed that the average investment in a foreign franchise is $ 680,000. McDonald's invested over $50 million in its Russian venture before even opening the first store (Love 1995). Therefore, the assumption inherent in early definitions of international franchising that international franchising is a mode of entry that involves no capital outlay and, therefore, no political risk may be erroneous.

Political risk may affect import restrictions or the remittance of royalties to the home country, significantly influencing the profitability of the foreign operation. Many franchisors require their franchisees to purchase their operating supplies from them (Fladmoe-Lindquist, 1996), therefore increasing their exposure to exchange rate risk and import restrictions. Although foreign franchisees often use local sources of supply, initially foreign franchisees are frequently required to import supplies and capital equipment, and this relationship often continues throughout the life of the franchise system. Royalties may also be adversely influenced by foreign exchange fluctuations caused by political risk. Given the effect of political risk on international franchising, Fladmoe-Lindquist (1996) wrote that a host country policy evaluation and exchange rate management are two key skills a global franchisor must possess.

Franchisors can analyze the political risk factors affecting their franchise themselves or obtain political risks measures from commercially available sources. Even if the macro political risk is obtained through an outside vendor, companies will also need to analyze the micro political risk associated with their industry or company. Past research on international franchising has shown that different industries face varying level of political risk exposure. This micro risk is akin to the unsystematic political risk and, therefore, beyond the scope of this article.

CONCLUSION

This article has suggested a macro environmental model of international franchising which divides the host country factors into economic, demographic, distance and political dimensions. By specifying the macro environmental variables that are responsible for choosing a host country for a franchise concept, this article can help international franchising researchers build empirical models. Furthermore, the resulting model can help franchisors evaluate and rate international locations and can produce cumulative scores that can be used as references for comparing and contrasting competing environments.

The scores achieved by this model can suggest an entry strategy into the host country. Host countries with relatively unfavorable environments can be entered via low risk low involvement methods, such as master franchising. The master franchisor has responsibilities to sell the franchises in the host country, identify and qualify potential franchisees, collect franchise and royalty fees, train the franchisees, and provide supplies and support services (Justis and Judd, 1986). The entrance of many US franchisors into unfavorable or even hostile environments was often through low cost and low involvement strategies. The increased involvement of US franchisors in diverse economic, cultural and political environments has influenced their entry strategies. Consequently, most of the international franchising expansion to these countries was associated with master franchising (Arthur Andersen, 1996).

REFERENCES

Arthur Andersen (1996). *International Expansion by US. Franchisors.* Washington, DC: Arthur Anderson LLP Chicago, Illinois in cooperation with the International Franchise Association.

Burton, F. N., & A. R. Cross (1995). *Franchising and Foreign Market Entry.* In International Marketing Reader, S. J. Paliwoda and J. K. Ryans, eds., London: Routledge, 35-48.

Eroglu, Sevgin (1992). The Internationalization Process of Franchise Systems: AConceptual Model. *International Marketing Review,* 9: 19-30.

Fladmoe-Lindquist (1996). International Franchising: Capabilities and Development. *Journal of Business Venturing,* 11: 419-438.

Justis R. and R. Judd (1989). *Franchising.* Cincinnati: South-Western publishing Co.

Kostecka, Andrew. 1988. Franchising in the Economy. Washington DC: US Department of Commerce.

Love, John F. (1995). *McDonald's Behind the Arches.* New York: Bantam Books.

Shane, S. 1996. Why Franchise Companies Expand Overseas Journal of Business Venturing, 11: 73-88.

Welch, Lawrence S. (1992). Developments in International Franchising. *Journal of Global Marketing,* 6: 81-96.

Yavas, Burhan F. (1988). The Role of EconomicDemographic Factors in US International Restaurant Franchising: An Empirical Investigation. *Journal of Global Marketing,* 2: 57-72.

Chapter 7
When is Master International Franchising a Preferred Mode of Entry?

Ilan Alon
Crummer Graduate School of Business, Rollins College

INTRODUCTION

The 1990s have seen an increase in the number of international franchisors and foreign franchised units. Since the rapid rate of international franchising growth is expected to continue, franchising scholars have predicted that within less than a decade the majority of U.S.-based franchisors will have international outlets (Justis and Judd 1998; Alon 1999a).

International franchising consists of "a foreign-market entry mode that involves a relationship between the entrant (the franchisor) and a host country entity, in which the former transfers, under contract, a business package (or format), which it has developed and owns, to the latter" (Burton and Cross 1995, p. 36). This host-country entity can be a domestic franchisee, a foreign franchisee, a master franchisor, or an entity which is partly owned by the franchisor itself. International franchising, therefore, encompasses multiple forms of international franchising, including master international franchising, direct international franchising, and joint ventures.

Increasingly, the mode of entry used by franchisors has been master international franchising. Hackett (1976) observed the use of master franchising in a global setting, observing that 20.7 percent of the firms surveyed used this form of organizational structure in their international operations. A more recent study conducted by Arthur Andersen (1996) found that 81 percent of the reporting firms used master franchising in 1996, up from 59 percent in 1989. This study revealed that master franchising was the most popular franchising mode of entry, used by 14 percent more franchisors than direct international franchising. To many franchisors, master international franchising has been a "short-cut" to globalization, sometimes allowing them to develop outlets overseas before they even have outlets in a neighboring state (Ryans, et al. 1999).

There are three factors outside the control of the organization that account for the increased use of master international franchising: (1) the increase in United States franchisors' entry into distant and culturally dissimilar countries, (2) the increase in the number of small and young companies entering international markets, and (3) the increase in the number of available master franchisees who are eager to develop a U.S.-based franchising system abroad. Between 1989 and 1996, there was a significant increase in the number of franchise units in emerging markets in Asia, South America, the Caribbean and the Middle East (Arthur Andersen 1996).

Younger franchising firms are seeking foreign markets to expand their presence, but much of the international expansion is in response to inquiries from abroad. According to the International Franchising Association, many franchising systems that are 10 years or younger are already franchising abroad or are planning on doing so in the near future. Alon (1999a) found that for the retailing industry, age was negatively related to the franchisor's decision to internationalize, and suggested that younger retailers are seeking international markets early in their life cycles because of domestic market saturation.

Ryans, et al. (1999) suggested that the prevalence of unsolicited offers to franchisors from foreign partners helps to explain the increasing use of master international franchising abroad. Often, other companies, large financial investors, government officials, or industry representatives make these offers.

Master franchising has been chosen as the focus of analysis because (1) it is the most popular mode of entry by U.S.-based franchisors overseas, (2) compared to the other modes of entry, it has experienced the highest growth in use by franchisors overseas, (3) it is the mode with least risk, commitment and control[1], and (4) it is a mode of entry unique to franchising firms, one that has not been the focus of the mode-of-entry literature.

MASTER INTERNATIONAL FRANCHISING TRADE-OFFS

Master franchising has been defined by Kaufmann and Kim (1995, p. 50) as "a form of umbrella licensing agreement which differs from the standard unit or location-level franchise in two ways: (1) it provides for the granting of an exclusive territory extending beyond the trade area of a single unit, and (2) it envisions from the outset the introduction of an additional layer of control between store level management and the franchisor." Master international franchising refers to the contractual agreement between the franchisor and an independently owned sub-franchisor to develop a specified number of franchises in a given country in exchange for the exclusive right to use the business format for a specified amount of time. The master is an intermediate party between the franchisor and the franchisee that has the responsibility to sell the franchises, qualify franchisees, collect part of the royalties and the majority of the franchise fee, and train franchisees in the host country. The master pays a fee for the territory based on the perceived strength of the area, often measured by the level of population (Justice and Judd 1986).

Kaufmann and Kim (1995) identified two basic types of master franchising: sub-franchising and area development. The difference between the two types of master franchising is that sub-franchisors are allowed to sell the franchising rights within their territory to sub-franchisees. Within their territory, sub-franchisors essentially assume most of the franchisor's duties with respect to developing, training, and monitoring the sub-franchisees.

Master international franchising offers franchisors a number of benefits, but at a cost. Justice and Judd (1986) proposed that the major advantages of using master international franchising in foreign market entries are (1) increased speed of development, (2) little capital outlay, and (3) knowledge of local markets. In line with these advantages, Kaufmann and Kim (1995) found a positive correlation between the use of master franchising and system growth rate. Since much of the local investment is born by the master franchisee, the franchisor's capital investment in the host country is nil. Franchisors often seek "masters" who are familiar with the local culture. Knowledge of the foreign market decreases the risk of failure because necessary adjustments to the franchise mix can be made *a priori*. Master international franchisees can provide the home franchisor with relevant foreign-market information about the environment, the industry, the consumer, and the fit between the franchisor's concept and the potential market. The master international franchisees can help the franchisor by raising money for the foreign operation, sharing the risk of failure, reducing costs of operation, providing market-specific know-how, combating local competitors, securing vertical and horizontal linkages, gaining location-specific assets, and overcoming legal constraints.

The franchisor assumes very little political and market risks because it receives the initial fees up front and a small percentage of sales over time without making a significant capital investment. Alon (1999b) identified and discussed the trade-offs associated with five basic modes of international franchising expansion: (1) master international franchising, (2) direct international franchising, (3) direct international franchising with a subsidiary, (4) joint ventures, and (5) sole venture. There is an appreciable variation among these types consistent with their varying levels of commitment, assumed risk and parent company control (see figure 7.1). Master international franchising is a mode of entry that requires the least amount of equity investment and level of control. It is a mode of entry that is low in both risk and control because it involves an arm's length transaction with a host-country independent entity: the franchisor makes no significant financial commitment. The franchisor delegates most of the responsibilities of monitoring and control to the master who, in turn, keeps a portion of the franchise royalties.

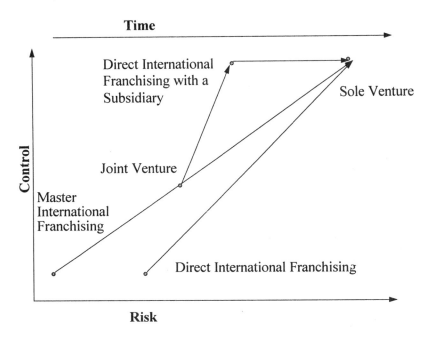

Figure 7.1: The Evolution of Franchising Entry Strategy

Master international franchising offers the franchisor geographical diversification. Using master franchisees, franchisors may end up entering countries they would not otherwise consider. Even large multinational firms may prefer to enter risky foreign markets through a master if market potential exists. Master international franchising can provide companies with a presence in remote locations around the world, establishing a beachhead that can be used as a starting point for launching more aggressive market-expansion plans when markets stabilize.

Master franchisees can also provide the franchisor with access to key resources in the foreign market. One of Pizza Hut's first master franchisees in Sao Paulo, Brazil -- United Food Companies (UFC) -- was also a cheese producer, allowing the company access to cheese products (Daniels and Radebaugh 1998). McDonald's chose to partner with the city of Moscow officials to help them with obtaining advantageous locations and cutting through the bureaucracy. Red tape and bureaucracy have been major obstacles to the internationalization of franchisors. A well-connected master can help a franchisor locate key resources and smooth out business transactions in the foreign market.

There are also a number of disadvantages associated with master international franchising as a mode of entry. The prolonged nature of the franchising contract (usually 10-20 years) exposes the franchisor to problems associated with choosing the wrong master, ensuring quality, and being sued by the master's constituents (Justice and Judd 1986). Selecting an inappropriate master franchisee can lead to less than optimal market expansion, brand-name deterioration, expropriation of expertise and expensive legal disputes. In case of a dispute between the franchisor and the master, Burton and Cross (1995) have observed that the master may keep the franchisees since they are used to working with the master and are reluctant to deal with the franchisor.

Monitoring the master franchisee becomes necessary to ensure that the market is being efficiently utilized and that company assets are not being misused. Whether the franchisor utilizes area franchising or sub-franchising in the master franchising agreement, some efficiencies will be lost. Area franchising reduces small-scale efficiencies because individual owners do not operate the franchised outlets, while sub-franchising reduces large-scale efficiencies because some of the franchisor's functions are redundant (Kaufmann and Kim 1995). The primary costs and involvements of primary operations with their respective master franchisees -- including recruiting, screening, training, and monitoring -- are considerable. The disadvantages associated with master franchising led McDonald's to abandon this method of doing business abroad (Flynn 1997).

EXPLAINING MASTER INTERNATIONAL FRANCHISING

International franchising is a hybrid organizational structure, which allows for multiple modes of international-market entry, with variable levels of equity ownership and overall control. Erramilli (1990, p. 51) proposed that "service firms could organize their business transactions through market contracting (no internalization), by internalizing these transactions within the organization (full internalization), or by some other mode reflecting an intermediate degree of internalization." International franchisors can use various entry methods, ranging from master international franchising (low internalization) to sole ventures (high internalization).

The mode of entry chosen by franchisors tends to depend upon both organizational and environmental conditions. In this section, the analysis focuses on the organizational determinants of master international franchising, the mode of entry with the least level of internalization. Environmental variables, such as economic potential and political risks, are excluded because they cannot explain why there is a considerable variation in the modes of entry used by different franchisors within the same foreign market. This section examines theories of franchising and master franchising in the domestic and international contexts, and develops propositions between select organizational variables and the use of master international franchising.

In the domestic context, two popular explanations for franchising are resource-based and agency theories. According to the resource-based explanation, companies use franchising to extend scarce resources. While most of the previous research emphasized financial-capital acquisition, companies are also able through franchising to acquire labor, human capital, entrepreneurial talent, local knowledge and distance-management skills (Alon 1999a).

The agency perspective proposes that franchising reduces agency costs including adverse selection – a condition in which agents misrepresent information regarding their skills – and moral hazard – a condition in which agents misrepresent information regarding their levels of effort. Since franchisors typically get a percentage of sales through royalties, shirking by franchisees using inflated expenses is less likely. Since franchisees are recipients of residual income in the business, they will typically put forth their best efforts. Monitoring of the franchisee can be reduced because the franchisee has a lot at stake if he/she does not conform to the strict franchising contract. Hence, one is more likely to see franchising in remote locations where direct monitoring costs can be expensive.

Because master international franchising is often a multi-unit franchising agreement, some of the agency benefits of franchising are reduced. Multi-unit franchising arrangements may decrease the likelihood of adverse selection if the master is a present franchisee, but does not solve the moral hazard problem at the micro level because the master needs to employ store managers to operate individual outlets (Kaufmann and Dant 1996).

The master supplants the major responsibilities of the franchisor in the host country, bridging the cultural and geographic distance between the host-market franchisees and the home-market franchisor. As a result, the monitoring of individual franchisees becomes more fluid. The foreign master can monitor the behavior of its franchisees for the franchisor ensuring that the foreign outlets are strictly adhering to the franchisor's standards and quality specifications. A new problem arises: who will monitor the master franchisee? The master, like the franchisee in the domestic context, can lose its franchise rights if it does not abide by the rules, limiting the monitoring needs of the franchisor. Master franchising, therefore, involves dual levels of franchising. The duplication of effort is less severe in the international context because the master franchisee provides much needed resources and market know-how that the franchisor lacks and that are important for success in the foreign market.

Since master franchisors provide significant funds to the parent firm, capital may overcome agency problems in promoting growth in the system (Kaufmann and Dant 1996). The resources that master international franchising brings to a franchisor go beyond mere financial capital, and can help a company succeed in a foreign market in which it has little or no experience. As mentioned before, the master can provide access to key resources such as real estate, raw materials, and equipment and facilitate contacts with governmental officials, consumer groups, and suppliers.

PROPOSITIONS

The organizational determinants of master international franchising divide into three general categories: (1) resource-based, (2) knowledge-based, and (3) strategy-based explanations. Among the resource-based explanations, it is proposed that size and age, as well as brand-name asset specificity will positively affect the desired level of control. The knowledge-based explanations include experience in managing foreign operations and know-how. Finally, strategy-based explanations consist of price, product and firm strategies.

Resource-Based Explanations

Size and Age

Size and age are two common proxies used for resources in the franchising literature (e.g., Alon 1999a). While they are rough proxies, they directly relate to both tangible and intangible firm assets. Size, measured as the number of outlets in the franchising system, affects many aspects of the franchisor's behavior and its position in the market. Size is positively related to the financial and non-financial resources of the firm. The bigger the firm, the greater are the (1) brand name recognition, (2) economies of scale, (3) ability to raise money in capital markets, and (4) ability to attract prospective franchisees. Borrowing from the competitive theory of the firm, Huszagh, et al. (1992) have suggested that increases in franchisor size lead to economies of scale in purchasing, promotion, R&D, quality assurance, and monitoring.

Large firms have the resources to expand via wholly owned subsidiaries, and excess money can be utilized more efficiently by investing in the company's line of business. Contractor and Kundu (1998) have theorized that smaller firms lack the resources and expertise for high levels of internalization and, thus, prefer shared-entry modes. When environmental conditions are conducive to a high level of internalization, big franchising firms may prefer large investment and high-risk modes of entry because the company does not need to share its profits with an agent. The British retailing giant Marks and Spencer, for example, entered the United States and Canada through acquisitions, but established franchising agreements in the Middle East and the Far East (Alon 2000). El Torito, a Mexican restaurant, owns all of its outlets in the U.S. market, but utilizes master international franchising abroad. Likewise, Choice Hotels only uses master international franchisees overseas.

Small franchising firms cannot afford to enter foreign markets, even large ones, via wholly owned outlets. Therefore, they have to rely on a foreign partner for capital and competitive information. Silver Streak Restaurant Corporation, a relatively new and small "hamburger" franchisor located in El Paso Texas, for example, partnered with a large Mexican firm in Mexico to provide capital, organizational structure, operational support, cross-cultural adaptation, political and business contacts, and host market information about the industry and the environment (Hadjimarcou and Barnes 1998). Master franchisors bring much needed resources to small firms in foreign markets.

P1a: The bigger the franchisor, the less likely it is to use master international franchising.
P1b: The older the franchisor, the less likely it is to use master international franchising

Brand Name Asset Specificity

According to Fladmoe-Lindquist and Jacque (1995, p. 1241), brand name "is perhaps the most important intangible asset to protect against potential hazard since service companies cannot depend upon patented proprietary technology or processes as a protection against close substitutes." Kentucky Fried Chicken (KFC) in Syria lost its distinctive marketing appeal, leading to the deterioration of its competitive advantage, after it was forced to rename itself as Kuwaiti Food Company (KFC) to avoid any suggestion of American cultural imperialism (*The Economist* 1998, August 15). A company may be justified in using a mode of entry that is high in equity investment and level of control when there is a risk that the brand name may be diluted by a third party.

The agent's use of intangible assets, such as a brand name, affects the perceptions of customers and, ultimately, the entire chain's success. Brand names are susceptible to free-riding -- a condition in which the franchisee benefits from the positive image of the brand without following the precise format of the franchise. To avoid free-riding, franchisors with high brand name asset specificity may prefer to own rather than franchise host country outlets, inducing internalization to guard proprietary technology (Erramilli 1990). Franchisors with well-known brand names are exposed to damage of their global reputations. Thus, they will be more likely to seek additional high-risk, high-control modes of entry, even in countries that are very unstable. In Russia, for example, McDonald's and Allied Domecq invested more than $40 million each, particularly in infrastructure and distribution systems, before opening their first stores. They chose to do so despite the potential hazards in the business environment there. Because of their recognizable brand names, McDonald's and Baskin Robins claimed a record number of customers during their first years of operation (Alon and Banai 2000). The ability of franchisors to control their brand names is a key motivator for increasing the level of equity investment and control in the foreign market. Franchisors with less recognizable brand names are more likely to use master international franchising because the potential damage to their reputations is less severe.

P2: The greater the franchisor's brand name asset specificity, the less likely the franchisor is to use master international franchising.

Knowledge-Based Explanations

Experience in Managing Foreign Operations

Firms new to internationalization try to avoid making costly mistakes; they tend to enter through low-equity modes of entry. As they become more confident of their ability to assess foreign markets, they are more likely to favor higher equity arrangements (Fladmoe-Lindquist 1995). Mudambi (1998) argued that experience captures virtually all the intangible benefits of a known environment because of (1) learning benefits, (2) the first-mover advantages of long experience, and (3) the path dependency of sunk/switching costs. By implication, firms with experience in a particular region of the world are more likely to invest there. Firms with less experience will be less likely to do so.

For example, Pizza Hut entered the Brazilian market through master franchisees who were given rights to develop sections of the country in 1988, a period characterized by inflation, political instability and exchange-rate fluctuations. The company looked for master franchisees with financial backing, experience in operating in an inflationary economy, preferably in the same or a related industry. After franchising in the Brazilian market for five years, Pizza Hut decided to buy back many of its outlets there in 1993, despite the potential volatility of this important emerging market (Daniels and Radebaugh 1998).

Contractor and Kundu (1998) have suggested that more internationally experienced firms will need less local help and will be more likely to use a partner-free mode of entry. These companies will build on their organizational capabilities through sequential experience in foreign markets, entering first through non-equity positions and later increasing equity investment levels as they gain experience in the host country. Familiarity with the host market reduces the uncertainty about the environment, reducing the discount rate and increasing the likelihood of equity investment. Master franchisees can facilitate easy entry into a foreign market when the franchisor is inexperienced by duplicating the franchisor's role in a multi-cultural context.

P3: The greater the franchisor's international experience, the less likely it is to use master international franchising.

Know-How

Firm-specific advantages are important in developing a competitive stance in the host country. Internationalization theory suggests that firms with much firm-specific know-how will prefer modes of entry that are high in risk and control because of the risk of dissemination: "Dissemination risk refers to the risk that firm specific advantages in know-how will be expropriated by a licensing or joint venture partner" (Hill, et al. 1990, p. 119). This same study divided know-how into tacit know-how and proprietary know-how. The category of tacit know-how includes informal operating procedures and routines and human capital that cannot be easily transferred via arm's length. The potential loss of royalties due to inefficient or ineffective operation of the franchise may lead the international franchisor to transfer its tacit know-how intra-organizationally by setting up a wholly-owned subsidiary or buying back existing franchised units.

The transfer of proprietary know-how refers to the transfer of the business-format franchise blueprint. While franchisors attempt to reduce the dissemination risk through the franchise contract, the drafting, negotiating, monitoring, and enforcing of the contract as well as the potential loss associated with unanticipated contingencies and subsequent opportunism by the agent increase the transaction costs and lower the advantages associated with using a contractual mode of entry (Hill et al. 1990). Fear of expropriation of proprietary knowledge has led firms to open their own outlets in otherwise risky countries. In Russia, for example, many franchisors have preferred to open company-owned outlets rather than to franchise. This is at least partly due to the uncertain legal and criminal environments, which make the enforcement of rules difficult (if not impossible) for a foreign firm (Alon and Banai 2000).

McDonald's initially granted a master franchise to Raymond Dayan to open 166 stores in France for a reduced fee because of expected lower demand for American style eateries. Together, they found the most desired locations in Paris for 14 stores, which Dayan operated successfully.

Ultimately, however, McDonald's revoked Dayan's rights because of substandard cleanliness standards, but they lost their rights to the superb Parisian locations, which were subsequently sold to a competitor -- Quick, the largest fast food chain in France (Daniels and Radebaugh 1998). Subway's experience in Moscow was similar: after a franchisee decided to opt out of the franchise and operate under his own brand name using Subway's operating knowledge, Subway lost not only its foothold, but its central location (Alon and Banai 2000). When the risk of dissemination or expropriation of proprietary knowledge is high and when tacit know-how is a key factor in the success of the franchise abroad, franchisors are more likely to prefer a non-sharing mode of entry, such as a wholly owned subsidiary.

P4a: The greater the franchisor's tacit know-how, the less likely it is to use master international franchising.
P4b: The greater the franchisor's proprietary know-how, the less likely it is to use master international franchising.

Strategy-Based Explanations

Price Bonding

Price bonding is a measure used in the franchising literature to quantify the *ex ante* agency costs associated with monitoring the franchising agent. Shane (1996) and Alon (1999a) showed that the greater the initial fee in relation to the royalties (price bonding), the more bonded the franchise agent is to the contract, and the more likely the franchisor is to internationalize. This relationship holds because much of the initial investment, often a substantial amount of money, is borne by the franchising agent. Violation of the contract by the agent can result in the franchisor's expropriation of the agent's franchise rights, leading to a significant loss to the agent. Thus, high price bonding reduces the monitoring costs as well as the foreign market risks. It suggests that the franchisor is internalizing less of the receipts associated with future income. Franchisors that utilize a high initial fee in relation to the royalty rate are, therefore, more risk averse. Ironically, a risk-averse strategy does not necessarily produce optimal results even in countries that are extremely volatile. In Russia, Allied Domecq', for example, waived the franchise fees for its initial Baskin Robins' investors, but did not waive the $40,000 fee for its Dunkin Donuts' shops. The result was that Baskin Robins developed rapidly through its network on franchisees, while Dunkin Donuts was forced to scale back operations because of deteriorating economic conditions and a lack of potential franchisees (Alon and Banai 2000).

When franchising firms use master international franchising agreement, the initial fee tends to be higher, while the royalty rate tends to be smaller. Master international franchising agreements restrict the future receipts of the franchisor from the foreign operation because the franchisor has to share its royalties with the master. High royalty payments suggest that that the value of the know-how transferred under contract is high. Consistent with the previous proposition, therefore, a high royalty rate will increase the possibility that the franchisor will internalize its foreign operations.

P5: The greater the price bonding, the more likely the franchisor is to use master international franchising.

Product/Service Standardization

Standardization reduces the need for entry modes with high internalization because the business system can be transferred via contractual means relatively easily. Firms that require a high degree of customization, such as advertising and consulting companies, often require a high level of internalization because the needs of customers are heterogeneous and often require a high degree of specialized know-how and professional skills that cannot be easily transferred. Firms with a high level of standardization, such as restaurants and retailers, can transfer their franchising systems more easily to a foreign agent (Erramilli 1990).

Since franchisors typically sell "soft" services – services in which consumption and production cannot be separated – the concept cannot be exported. The very strength of a franchising system resides in its ability to standardize its operations across heterogeneous locations. "The transferability of the [franchising] system becomes a function of cultural distance between the foreign and domestic cultures. The very strength of a franchising format, its standardization, makes its successful replication in foreign markets difficult" (Fladmoe-Lindquist 1996, p. 425).

Too much adaptation will diminish the value of the franchise in the eyes of consumers and potential franchisees, but too little can decrease acceptance. When McDonald's entered Holland for the first time it dropped the Quarter Pounder from the menu and added a number of Dutch favorites such as apple-sauce and deep-fried chicken croquettes. The departure from the basic McDonald's formula in Holland led to a deterioration of store performance, which served as a valuable learning experience for McDonald's (Love 1995). The success of some American concepts abroad was partly due to their ability to export American culture and introduce cultural change. The diffusion of U.S.-based franchises abroad is often related to the foreign society's desire to assimilate American way of life.

The level of possible standardization depends in part on the cultural, economic, and legal peculiarities associated with the foreign market. Many aspects of the franchising systems, such as the production process, the service delivery, the communicated message, the product/s, the atmosphere, and the management are adaptable. The question is usually not whether to adapt or standardize, but rather how much to adapt. When the cultural and geographic gulfs between the host market and the home market are large, the level of necessary adaptation increases. Master international franchisees, who are typically nationals of the host market, can aid in deciding what elements of the franchising system need to be modified in the host country.

Even some of the most standardized franchises have needed to adapt their concepts to local market conditions. Kentucky Fried Chicken redesigned its equipment layout in Japan to save space -- which carried a high price tag – eliminated mashed potatoes and decreased the sugar level in its coleslaw to adapt to local tastes. Pizza Hut and Dominos change the toppings on their pizzas to adapt to local flavors and tastes. The pronunciation of McDonald's in Japan was altered to "MaKudonaldo." McDonald's needed to modify its core product – the Big Mac – when it entered India because cows are sacred animals there.

To the extent that adaptation is needed, franchisors are more likely externalize their foreign operations. Environmental differences between the host and the home market of the franchisor enlarge the information gap and limit the extent to which a franchisor can transfer its operational know-how. Experience in operating within the U.S. cannot be easily converted to operating in Eastern Europe, Latin America or Asia because of distinctions in the economic landscape, the cultural customs, the legal environment, and the geography of foreign markets. Modifications in strategy formulation, operating policy, and marketing program are often necessary. Master international franchisors can help the home company adapt its formula to local market conditions. Relying on its Mexican partner's advice, Silver Streak fast-food restaurants enlarged their patio eating areas to accommodate the eat-in lunch crowd, and developed a Mexican-like breakfast menu. These modifications proved to be advantageous in the Mexican market since 80 percent of sales were from within the restaurant (compared to 20 percent in the U.S.) and the Silver Burrito became the best selling item on the menu (Hadjimarcou and Barnes 1998).

P6a: The more standardized the franchisor's concept across heterogeneous locations, the more likely it is to use master international franchising.

P6b: The greater the franchisor's need for adaptation, the more likely it is to use master international franchising.

Strategic Orientation

The company's strategic orientation determines whether the company uses a multi-domestic strategy or a global strategy. A multi-domestic strategy assumes that countries are different and require unique marketing approaches, while the global approach assumes that market segments transcend national boundaries. Therefore, global firms tend to concentrate on providing lower-priced goods, more standardized distribution and promotion, and a global image, while multi-domestic firms concentrate on national distribution channels and product image, as well as a more customized product or concept.

The master often tailors the franchise concept and the management to the host country, selects, trains and monitors the franchisees, and adapts selected products, promotions and distribution components of the marketing mix. The master franchisee is often provided with some latitude in developing its own sources of supply, labor and franchisees. Since franchisors tend to delegate country-specific responsibilities to the master international franchisee, this mode of entry is more consistent with the multi-domestic strategy.

In contrast, global firms are more likely to use modes of entry with high level of internalization to increase the level of required coordination and control. It is from this level of coordination and control that global franchising firms derive the benefits of economies of scale in production and marketing, transfer of experience and know-how across countries, and a uniform global image. Firms using a global strategy focus on the coordination and rationalization of goods and services across countries, without regard to country-specific peculiarities. Such a strategy requires a configuration of the firm's global value chain with certain national subsidiaries specializing in the production of only part of the global line or a certain component of the end product (Hill et al. 1990). As an example of the global strategy, The Big Mac in the Ukraine is assembled using sesame seeds from Mexico, pickles from Germany, special sauce from Germany, buns from Russia, onions from the United States, beef patties from Hungary, cheese from Poland, and lettuce from Ukraine. Since master franchisors have leeway in designing only the national character of the franchise system, such a level of global synergy is more difficult to achieve.

P7: Franchisors that pursue a global strategy are less likely to favor master international franchising.

CONCLUSION

A franchising firm should evaluate its readiness for internationalization and the attractiveness of the host country before deciding on the level of risk and control it wants to assume in each of the targeted countries. On the practical side, this study suggests that practitioners should evaluate the firm's resource base, knowledge, and strategies prior to selecting a mode of entry in a foreign market. Large franchisors with much international experience, well-known brand names, sophisticated know-how, and highly customized business formats are more likely to use company-owned expansion in foreign countries. On the other hand, franchisors who are small, proffer unknown brand names, have little experience with international markets, possess a standardized franchise concept that can be easily transferred via arm's length, and delegate national development to an agent -- who may be more familiar with the market and who can tailor the franchise to local tastes -- are more likely to use low-commitment, low-risk modes of entry such as master international franchising. Firms that use master international franchising as a mode of entry are more likely to charge larger up-front fees and smaller royalties and pursue a multi-domestic strategy that allows for tailoring their concepts to individual foreign markets.

Master international franchising is among the fastest growing modes of international franchising expansion. Thus, more studies are needed to explain and predict the propensity of franchisors to opt for this important mode of entry. The present study has concentrated on developing propositions regarding the organizational determinants of master international franchising. Future studies can contribute by augmenting this theoretical framework – for example, by including environmental variables – and by testing the suggested propositions. It is likely that in countries that are culturally distant from the home market, economically volatile, politically unstable, or extremely competitive, franchisors are more likely to seek master international franchisees (Alon and McKee 1999).

NOTES

[1] Since much of international franchising is in "soft"-service industries -- those that require simultaneous production and consumption – exporting is often precluded from consideration. Ackerman et al. (1994) have equated international franchising to exporting because both are means of entering global markets with little investment and limited risk. Master international franchising is the closest equivalent of exporting for the international franchisor because it involves the least amount of risk and control. On the other hand, the experience of many franchisors reveals that entering a foreign market involves at least some investment by the international franchisor (Love 1995; Arthur Andersen 1996). Furthermore, unlike exporting, international franchising may require close attention to tracking down equipment, securing local raw materials that meet the franchisor's quality specifications, and protecting trademarks and trade secrets (Steinberg 1992).

REFERENCES

Ackerman, K., D. E. Bush, and R. T. Justis (1994), "Determinants of Internalization of Franchise Operations by US Franchisors," *International Marketing Review*, 11 (no. 4), 56-68.

Alon, Ilan and Moshe Banai (2000), "Franchising Opportunities and Threats in Russia," *Journal of International Marketing*, (Forthcoming).

Alon, Ilan (2000), "The Internationalization of Marks and Spencer," A case study with teaching notes, State University of New York, College at Oneonta.

Alon, Ilan (1999a), *The Internationalization of US Franchising Systems*, New York: Garland Publishing.

Alon, Ilan (1999b), "International Franchising Modes of Entry," in *Franchising Beyond the Millennium: Learning Lessons From the Past*, John Stanworth and David Purdy, eds., Society of Franchising 13th Annual Conference.

Alon, Ilan and David McKee (1999), "Towards a Macro Environmental Model of International Franchising," *Multinational Business Review*, 7 (1), 76-82.

Amos, James H. (1993), "Trends and Developments in International Franchising," in *The Franchising Handbook* (Endorsed by the International Franchise Association), Andrew J. Sherman, eds., New York: AMACOM, 458-465.

Arthur Andersen (1996), *International Expansion by U.S. Franchisors*. Arthur Andersen LLP Chicago, Illinois in cooperation with the International Franchise Association, Washington, DC.

Aydin, N. and M. Kacker (1990), "International Outlook on US-Based Franchisors," *International Marketing Review*, 7 (2), 206-219.

Boddewyn, J. J., B. M. Halbrich, and C. A. Perry (1986), "Service Multinationals: Conceptualization, Measurement and Theory," *Journal of International Business Studies*, (Fall), 41-57.

Burton, F. N., and A. R. Cross (1995), "Franchising and Foreign Market Entry," in *International Marketing Reader*, S. J. Paliwoda and J. K. Ryans, eds., London: Routledge, 35-48.

Contractor, Farok J., and Sumit K. Kundu (1998), "Model Choice in a World of Alliances: Analyzing Organization Forms in the International Hotel Sector," *Journal of International Business Studies*, 29 (2), 325-357.

Daniels, John D. and Lee H. Radebaugh (1998), *International Business Environments and Operations* (Eighth Edition), Massachusetts: Addison-Wesley.

The Economist, (1998), "The Road from Damascus," (August 15), 57.

Erramilli, Krishna M. (1990), "Entry Mode Choice in Service Industries," *International Marketing Review*, 7 (5), 50-62.

Falbe, Cecilia M., and Thomas C. Dandridge (1992), "Franchising as a Strategic Partnership: Issues of Cooperation and Conflict in a Global Market," *International Small Business Journal*, 10 (3), 40-52.

Fladmoe-Lindquist, Karin (1996), "International Franchising: Capabilities and Development, " *Journal of Business Venturing*, 11 (5), 419-435.

Fladmoe-Lindquist, Karin, and Laurent L. Jacque (1995), "Control Modes in International Service Operations: The Propensity to Franchise," *Management Science*, 41 (July), 1238-1249.

Flynn, Pat (1997), "Telephone interview with the Executive Vice President and Senior Operating Officer of McDonald's Corporation," (March 17).

Gatignon, H. and E. Anderson (1988), "The Multinational Corporation's Degree of Control Over Foreign Subsidiaries: An Empirical Test of a Transaction Cost Explanation," *Journal of Law, Economics and Organization*, (Fall), 305-366.

Hackett, D. W. (1976), The International Expansion of US Franchise Systems: Status and Strategies," *Journal of International Business Studies*, 7 (Spring), 66-75.

Hadjimarcou, John and John W. Barnes (1998), "Case Study: Strategic Alliances in International Franchising – The Entry of Silver Streak Restaurant Corporation into Mexico," *Journal of Consumer Marketing*, 15 (6), 598-607.

Harrigan, K. R. (1985), "Vertical Integration and Corporate Strategy," *Academy of Management Journal*, 28 (2), 397-425.

Hill, Charles W. G., Hwang Peter and W. Chan Kim (1990), "An Eclectic Theory of the Choice of International Entry Mode," *Strategic Management Journal*, 11, 117-128.

Hoffman, Richard C., John F. Preble (1991), "Franchising: Selecting a Strategy for Rapid Growth," *Long Range Planning*, 24(No 4), 74-85.

Justis R. and R. Judd (1986), "Master Franchising: A New Look," *Journal of Small Business Management*, 24 (3), 16-21.

Kaufmann, Patrick J. and Rajiv Dant (1996), "Multi-Unit Franchising: Growth and Management Issues," *Journal of Business Venturing*, 11 (5), 343-358.

Kogut, Bruce and Harbir Singh (1988), "The Effect of National Culture on the Choice of Entry Mode," *Journal of International Business Studies*, 19 (Fall), 411-432.

Kostecka, Andrew (1969 -1988), "Franchising in the Economy," US Department of Commerce, Washington DC.

Love, John F. (1995), *McDonald's Behind the Arches*, New York: Bantam Books.

McIntyre, Faye S., and Sandra M. Huszagh, "Internationalization of Franchise Systems," *Journal of International Marketing*, 3 (4), 39-46.

Mudambi, Ram (1998), "The Role of Duration in Multinational Investment Strategies," *Journal of International Business Studies*, 29 (2) 239-262.

Root, Franklin R. (1987), *Entry Strategies for International Markets*. Mass.: Lexington Books.

Ryans, John K., Sherry Lotz, and Robert Krampf (1999), "Do Master Franchisors Drive Global Franchising?" *Marketing Management*, (Summer), 33-37.

Shane, S. (1996), "Why Franchise Companies Expand Overseas," *Journal of Business Venturing*, 11 (2), 73-88.

Simon, J. D., (1982), "Political Risk Assessment: Past Trends and Future Prospects," *Columbia Journal of World Business*, (Fall), 62-71.

Stapenhurst, Fredrick (1992), *Political Risk Analysis Around the North Atlantic*, London: MacMillan Press.

Steinberg, Carol (1992), "International Franchising: Signs of the Times," *World Trade*, 5 (Aug/Sep), 110-113.

Toncar, Mark, Ilan Alon and David McKee (1999), "Cultural Determinants of International Franchising: An Empirical Analysis of Hofstede's Cultural Dimensions," in *Seventh Annual Cross-Cultural Research*, Scott Smith, ed., Cancun, Mexico.

Welch, Lawrence S. (1989), "Diffusion of Franchise Systems Use in International Operations," *International Marketing Review*, 6 (5), 7-19.

Chapter 8
How Do International Franchisors Cluster?

James Johnson
Crummer Graduate School of Business, Rollins College

Ilan Alon
Crummer Graduate School of Business, Rollins College

INTRODUCTION

While not an American idea by origin, franchising as a method of distribution became popularized in the United States of America in the 1950s and 1960s by the fast food and hotel industries. Today, franchising accounts for more than $1 trillion in sales, roughly 10% of the entire United States economy, and spans over 75 different industries (Welsh and Alon, 2002). In the 1960s and 1970s, early U.S. adopters of the franchising system, such as McDonald's and Hilton, started to venture abroad. The internationalization of franchising systems was a result of push and pull factors. Push factors included increasing domestic market saturation, competitive pressures, and ⸳⸳⸳ʳe regulations; pull factors included attractive environmental condiᴛᴵ⸳. overseas, such as increasing incomes, pent-up demand for American-style goods and services, and lack of strong competitors in market niches in which the franchisors were operating.

As more and more franchisors forayed abroad, the competitive conditions there intensified and franchisors sought foreign partners to guide and advise them in these foreign lands. Opportunities for simple extensions of the company's model through direct international franchising into culturally and economically similar countries, such as Canada and United Kingdom, have since diminished, and franchisors have started to seek franchisees in emerging and transitioning markets where economic, cultural and legal conditions are more challenging. The question facing many franchisors is less whether to franchise or not to franchise abroad, but rather how to franchise abroad (e.g., what mode of entry to use?). Indeed, the data we analyze in this chapter shows that most domestic franchisors already have a desire to extend their operations internationally.

As demonstrated in the literature review that follows, there have been many studies of the determinants of franchising in general, and international franchising in particular. However, concerns have been voiced about the validity of some of these studies, particularly empirically-based ones, since they may have suffered from sample heterogeneity that can mask the applicability of their findings. These concerns have led some franchising researchers to favor explanations of franchising that divide franchisors into different types (e.g., Carney and Gedajlovic, 1991; Castrogiovanni, Bennett, and Combs, 1995). Initial efforts were ad-hoc, utilizing descriptive statistical methods to differentiate among franchisors, and they focused mainly on domestic franchisors. Castrogiovanni and Justis (1998) were the first to provide a theoretical explanation for franchisor types by adapting Mintzberg's (1979) organizational typology to franchising organizations. It is on the basis of these authors that we build our hypotheses in this study. Our chapter uniquely extends their work by being the first to empirically examine the typologies of internationally-minded franchisors at the system level and to focus on the mode of franchise entry they are likely to use.

LITERATURE REVIEW

Market Entry Mode and Franchising

Anderson & Gatignon (1986) define the foreign market entry mode as the institutional arrangement chosen by a firm for the foreign market, which can range from non-equity forms of market entry, such as exporting and licensing, to equity forms, such as a joint venture and a wholly-owned subsidiary. Theoretical explanations for the choice of entry mode include the Scandinavian stages model of entry (Johanson and Vahlne, 1990), transaction-cost economics (Anderson and Gatignon 1986; Erramilli and Rao 1993) and the eclectic paradigm (Dunning 1988; Hill.Hwang & Kim, 1990), agency theory (Fladmoe-Lindquist and Jacque, 1995; Garg & Rasheed, 2003; Shane 1994, 1996), institutional theory (Davis, Desai & Francis, 2000, Brouthers 2000), and cultural distance (Brouthers, 2000; Kogut & Singh, 1988).

One way of categorizing entry modes is by the level of control that a particular entry mode permits, and the level of resource commitment that it requires. According to these criteria, international franchising is a medium-control mode, allowing balanced interests between partners (Anderson and Gatignon, 1986). International franchising consists of "a foreign market entry mode that involves a relationship between the entrant (franchisor) and a host country entity, in which the former transfers, under contract, a business package (or format), which it has developed and owns, to the latter" (Burton & Cross, 1995, p.36). The "host country entity" can take many forms, including direct franchising to a host-country or third-country franchisee, franchising to a master franchisor, or a joint venture that is partly owned by the franchisor itself. Although franchising may be used as an initial market entry mode prior to establishing a wholly-owned subsidiary, Shane (1996) argues that international franchising should be considered as a fully-fledged international mode of entry rather than a temporary business strategy.

The international franchising literature consists of two distinct streams, descriptive and conceptual. The descriptive stream focuses on issues such as the differences between domestic and international franchisors (e.g., Aydin & Kacker 1990; Kedia & Ackerman, 1994), the strategic behavior of international franchisors (Amos, 1993; Hackett, 1976; Huszagh, Huszagh & McIntyre, 1992; Shane, 1996), and barriers to internationalizing franchise systems (Aydin & Kacker 1990). While these descriptive studies explain what international franchisors do, they do not explain why firms choose franchising as a mode of entry, or what form of franchise they choose to use. The conceptual literature, in contrast, focuses on developing a theory of international franchising (Alon 1999a, 1999b; Ekeledo & Sivakumar, 1998; Eroglu 1992; Garg & Rasheed, 2003; Sashi & Karrupur, 2002; Shane 1996) that will predict the conditions under which a firm will elect to franchise its operations overseas, and what form of franchise the firm will use. In general, a firm's selection of entry mode is considered to be dependent on internal, organizational factors – such as the firm's size and age, brand-name specificity, experience in managing foreign operations, dependence on proprietary know-how – and external factors, such as the degree of political risk in the target country (Eroglu, 1992). However, in a Delphi study using industry experts, Duniach-Smith (2003) found that differences in the relative importance of internal and external variables thought to determine the decision to go international and those variables that determine the decision to enter a foreign market via franchising. For example, resourced-based factors (such as age and size) and agency related factors (such as price bonding and geographical dispersion) appeared to be important determinants of the franchisor's initial decision to internationalize, but of less importance in choice of franchise entry mode. She concluded that a specific conceptual framework is needed to explain the entry mode choice by international franchisors. Based on agency theory, transactions costs analysis, and studies of domestic franchising, Sashi and Karrupur (2002) developed such a framework. They posited that international franchising will be favored under the following conditions: positive firm-specific assets (a strong brand name, low level of technical knowledge required); internal uncertainty (cultural and geographic distance, positive global experience); external uncertainty (political and economic instability, currency fluctuation); and type of product (high initial investment and capital costs required, high degree of local added value).

Based on Mintzberg's (1979) typology of five configurations for business organizations, Castrogiovanni and Justis (1998) identified three common franchising configurations: *entrepreneurial, confederation,* and *carbon-copy.* The first is a "pure" organizational form, identified by Mintzberg (1979). Entrepreneurial organizations are driven by the need for survival and direction (Castrogiovanni & Justis, 1998; Mintzberg, 1979). They operate in an uncertain environment, so there is a need for strong direction from the franchisor but, since knowledge is imperfect, this is allied with the need to take calculated risks. This franchising form is more common when the organization is relatively young and small. When franchise units increase in number and geographic dispersion, the entrepreneurial form is no longer suitable and a transition to a more complex form is required. However, Castrogiovanni and Justis (1998) argue that the other "pure" forms are unlikely for several reasons: first, franchising occurs over geographically dispersed markets; second, franchised goods and services must be produced locally; third, replication of business operations is possible through standardization across units; fourth, standardization and the extension of a reputable brand name can bring economic benefits. Consequently, franchise organizations switch to one of two hybrid configurations, which offer greater organizational complexity than the entrepreneurial form. The confederation form is a hybrid of Mintzberg's *diversified* and *adhocracy* configurations. It is characterized by a loosely-coupled organizational network in which each franchisee has considerable autonomy; market opportunities are abundant, so each unit can experiment with new approaches without harming the operations of others. Knowledge is communicated to others in the network through an emphasis on cooperation among units. According to Castrogiovanni and Justis (1998), this organizational form is best suited to franchising operations that involve licensing a brand name that is associated with certain products or services – such as Coldwell Banker Real Estate or Pearle Vision – and leaving the day-to-day operations to the franchisee. In contrast, the second hybrid form, carbon-copy, has characteristics of Mintzberg's (1979) *machine* and *diversified* configurations. It is commonly found among fast-food restaurants and retail stores, such as "McDonald's" and "7-11", where each unit operates as a "carbon-copy" of the other and there is a need for very tight financial and operational controls. Franchisees have very little, if any, autonomy; customers tend to purchase on a repeat basis and the product offerings from one franchise outlet to the next are standardized.

To date, the three franchising configurations conceptualized by Castrogiovanni and Justis (1998) have not been empirically identified in the international business literature. In the following section, we discuss the concept of master franchising and its use in foreign market entry. We then return to examine the relationship between and develop hypotheses about the three franchising configurations and international master franchising.

Master Franchising

The decision to franchise or not to franchise is just one stage in the foreign market entry process. Assuming that a firm opts to franchise its operations, it must then choose among different forms of franchising. Alon (1999a) notes that, in a global context, master franchising has increasingly become the entry mode of choice. Master international franchising refers to "the contractual agreement between the franchisor and an independently owned sub-franchisor to develop a specified number of franchises in a given country in exchange for the exclusive right to use the business format for a specified amount of time" (Alon, 2000, p. 3). The master franchisee assumes responsibility for qualifying local franchisees, selling franchises, training the franchisees, and collecting the royalty payments and franchise fees. There are essentially two types of master franchising: sub-franchising and area development. In the former, the master franchisee acts as a franchisor, selling sub-franchises within a defined territory; in the latter, the area developer assumes responsibility for a defined territory in which he commits to opening and operating a set number of outlets within an agreed timeframe. Kaufmann and Dant (1996), however, view area development as a special case of master franchising, so for the purposes of this study the two types will be treated as one.

Alon (2000) examines the organizational determinants of master franchising and suggests that firms with modest resources, brand names without an international reputation, limited experience in overseas markets, and easily-transferable know-how are more likely to prefer master franchising to single-unit franchising. The use of a master franchisee in an overseas market also reduces the firm's costs of coordination and communication. Garg and Rasheed (2003) argue that in the international context, master franchising addresses agency problems, such as bonding, adverse selection, information flow, shirking, inefficient risk-bearing, free-riding, and quasi-rent appropriation, more effectively than does single-unit franchising. Similarly, Sashi and Karrapur (2002) posit that firms are more likely to use master franchising when reliable information for evaluating potential franchisees – such as credit worthiness -- is not available, or where the legal system does not permit the firm to impose penalties on franchisees for violating the franchise agreement. By selecting a reliable and trustworthy master franchisee, the firm shares the risks of conducting business, and reduces adverse selection, franchisee moral hazard, and opportunistic behavior. Also, where political uncertainty is high, the use of a master franchisee who is familiar with the local environment can provide the franchisor with some immunity from political risk.

The advantages to the firm of using international master franchising are many (Alon, 2000), in addition to addressing the agency problems listed above. They include speed to market, a faster system growth rate, little capital outlay, and the master franchisee's knowledge of the foreign market environment. Furthermore, the master franchisee may be able to provide market-specific know-how and assist the franchisor in raising funds for further development of the foreign market and/or locating key resources. There are also disadvantages associated with international master franchising. They include problems associated with a po or choice of master franchisee, such as brand-name deterioration, appropriation of expertise, less than optimal market expansion, and legal entanglements, and the costs of monitoring the master franchisee from afar (Alon, 2000).

HYPOTHESES

Castrogiovanni and Justis (1998) identified three franchising configurations: *entrepreneurial, confederation,* and *carbon-copy*. We would expect to find all three configurations among domestic franchisors that are have internationalized or are intending to internationalize their operations. The age and size of franchisors is an important variable in determining the most appropriate organizational configuration. The entrepreneurial form is associated with franchisors that are relatively young. Furthermore, this configuration tends to be transitory (Castrogiovanni and Justis, 1998), since the franchisor typically switches to a more complex organizational form as it gains experience, and franchisors with a large number of outlets are associated with the confederation and carbon-copy forms. Confederation and carbon-copy forms of franchising are differentiated by the need for autonomy and loose coupling in the case of the former, and by the need for tight financial and operational controls by the latter. Thus, hypothesis 1 states that analysis of the internal variables (size, age, dispersion, etc) of franchisors will yield three discrete groupings.

The entrepreneurial form is associated with franchisors that are relatively young; we would expect that the entrepreneur category has the smallest number of total franchise outlets thus hypothesis 2 states that one grouping of franchisors will, on average, be younger and will have a smaller number of units than other types of franchisors: this group will correspond to entrepreneurial franchisors.

In contrast, the carbon-copy form is associated with franchisors that have developed a highly repetitive, standardized product or service and seek economies of scale and scope by replicating franchise units in new markets (Castrogiovanni & Justis, 1998). In order to minimize costs and capture economies of scale, they maintain tight control over all aspects of the operation from the selection of franchise location to the design of facilities and training of staff. Typically, the business model has been tried and tested, so high start-up costs can be expected so that the franchisee can replicate every aspect of the business. In order to maximize growth in new markets, franchisors using this configuration are more likely to offer financial incentives to franchisees, such as preferential financing of start-up costs. Thus, hypothesis 3 states that one grouping will have the largest number of outlets and the highest start-up costs, and will provide more financial support to franchisees than the other groupings. This grouping will represent the carbon copy franchisors.

Use of Master Franchising

Alon (1999) argues that franchisors with modest resources, brand names without an international reputation, limited experience in overseas markets, and easily transferable know-how are more likely to use master franchising: it is also more likely to be used where the costs of coordination and communication are high. Using a master franchise overseas offers the franchisor a single point of contact in the foreign market thus, geographical distance notwithstanding, satisfying the franchisor's need for tight direction while simultaneously deferring to the master franchisee's greater knowledge of local market conditions. These factors appear to apply most to entrepreneurial franchisors, since master franchising allows them to quickly enter the uncertain environment of a foreign market with little immediate financial risk, and it addresses agency problems more effectively than does single-unit franchising. Entrepreneurial franchisors, because of their small size and relatively short time in the market, are also more likely to lack an international reputation for their brand. Thus hypothesis 4a states that entrepreneurial franchisors are more likely to enter a new market via master franchising than are other types of franchisors.

The documented advantages of master franchising -- speed to market, a faster system growth rate, little capital outlay, and the master franchisee's knowledge of the foreign market environment – suit the entrepreneurial franchisor's need for rapid growth in order to ensure survival. However, this does not imply that the other forms of franchisors avoid master franchising, since this mode of market entry is appropriate for any type of franchisor that seeks fast growth. Therefore, those franchisors that adopt master franchising are likely to experience faster growth than those that choose other forms of expansion thus hypothesis 4b states that franchisors that use master franchising will experience faster growth than franchisors that do not use master franchising.

METHODOLOGY

We tested the typology of international franchisors by using cluster analysis on a sample of franchising firms domiciled in the United States of

America. *Entrepreneur* magazine (2001) listed US-based franchisors that had expressed an interest in expanding overseas; Shane (1996) indicated that franchisors' "intention to internationalize" is a good proxy for actual internationalization. Data from *Entrepreneur* magazine has been used previously in both domestic franchising research (e.g., Castrogiovanni, et al., 1995) and international franchising research (e.g., Alon, 1999a). Of the 640 franchisors featured in the annual list, 403 (63%) sought international franchisees. Among these 403 internationally-bound franchisors, 25% focused on Canada exclusively, and 33% only wished to use master franchising as a mode of entry into the foreign country. Observations that contained missing data were deleted. The resulting sample included 261 franchisors which were seeking international franchisees. The following variables were included in our analysis: the age of the company, the age of the franchise system, the number of years it took the company to begin franchising, whether it used master franchising exclusively, the number of franchises, the number of company owned outlets, the startup costs, the franchising fee, the percentage of royalties, and whether the company financed accounts receivables, equipment, the franchising fee, the inventory, the lease, the payroll, the startup fee, and/or the working capital (see Table 8.1).

Carney and Gedajlovic (1991) asserted that franchising data suffers from sample heterogeneity and limited generalizability and thus advocated the use of grouping techniques. According to Castrogiovanni et al. (1995), Carney and Gedajlovic (1991) were the first to suggest that franchisors fell into various groupings and, as a result, criticized the conclusions of previous research that failed to account for the various franchising types. Castrogiovanni et al. (1995) called for additional research on franchising classifications. Therefore, we utilized cluster analysis to determine whether international franchisors fall into the categories suggested by Castrogiovanni and Justis (1998). Cluster analysis is an appropriate multivariate technique when variables are interdependent and metric in nature and when the researcher wants to classify the data by maximizing Euclidean internal (within-cluster) homogeneity and external (between-cluster) heterogeneity. We use two-step cluster analysis because it allows for categorical variables in formulating clusters and suggests an optimal number of clusters.

RESULTS AND DISCUSSION

Many of the variables were found to be multicollinear, further underscoring the merit of using cluster analysis. Table 8.1 reveals the results of our 2-step cluster analysis. It confirms the three configurations identified by Castrogiovanni and Justis (1998), showing three clusters roughly equivalent to the confederation form (cluster 1), carbon copy form (cluster 2), and entrepreneurial form (cluster3) organizations, thus supporting H1. Our discussion will start with the entrepreneurial firm since it is a starting point for most franchising organizations, consisting of the youngest and smallest firms and is featured in our second hypothesis.

Table 8.1: Results of Cluster Analysis

Variable	Cluster 1 Confederation	Cluster 2 Carbon Copy Form	Cluster 3 Entrepreneurial
Observations	135	28	98
Year the company began	1979	1948	1981
Year the franchise began	1984	1966	1987
Dispersion (number of regions in the US-up to 7)	6.75	7.00	6.69
Number of years before it began franchising	5.6	17.1	5.9
Total outlets	369	4,592	254
Company owned outlets	23	907	29
Franchise owned outlets	346	3,685	225
Startup costs (000)	347	3,167	232
Franchise fee (000)	27	27	25
Royalties (%)	5	26	5
Use of master franchising (%)	43.7	28.6	24.5
Financing accounts receivables (%)	29.6	7.1	1.8
Financing equipment (%)	98.5	57.1	8.1
Financing franchise fee (%)	77.7	42.8	23.4
Financing inventory (%)	80.0	14.3	0
Financing lease (%)	0.7	3.5	0
Financing payroll (%)	29.6	2.0	0
Financing startup fee (%)	88.9	32.1	2.0
Financing working capital (%)	0	3.5	1.0
Average financing (%)	50.6	20.3	4.5

The Confederation Franchising Type

The confederated franchising organization is the largest group of internationally-minded franchising firms, consisting of more than half of our sample. These represent the next stage in the evolution of franchising firms and tend to be older and bigger than the entrepreneurial type. In our sample, the confederated type was established on average in 1979 and has 369 outlets (45% larger than the entrepreneurial type). Like the entrepreneurial type, it is widely dispersed and takes a short time to start franchising (5.6 years). The confederation type is the most active in franchising and the outlets are 94% franchised. The franchising start-up costs are slightly larger than for the entrepreneurial type, but significantly less than the carbon copy form. However, they are the most prepared to offer financing to franchisees, with most franchisors providing financing for equipment (98.5%), the start-up fee (88.9%), inventory (80%), and the franchise fee (80%). This suggests that these franchisors need to offer greater financial incentives to prospective franchisees than do the other categories of franchisors.

Another feature that differentiates the confederation form is their use of master franchising in their international expansion strategies. As described by Castrogiovanni and Justis (1998), the confederated expansion into heterogeneous geographical locations limits the use of direct supervision as a controlling mechanism, makes direct business format franchising less feasible and licensing more practical, and encourages multi-unit experimentation and cross-communication. The need for geographical concentration and decentralization increases with this form. Master international franchising is most akin to licensing, geographical concentration and decentralization, and organizational learning on a global basis. According to Castrogiovanni and Justis (1998), the confederated form is transitory, however, since the franchisor ultimately wants to exert more control over the dispersed franchisees.

To support the rapid international expansion of this type, financing is a key according to our data, which explains why this type of franchising organization is most likely to help its franchisees in practically every way. It appears that resource scarcity is less of an issue and that agency costs may be more of a problem given the increased decentralization and expansion.

Carbon Copy Franchising Type

The carbon copy franchising type is the oldest group among our clusters and it is also the largest, supporting H3. On average, this type was established in 1948 and took the longest to become franchising-bound (17.1 years). The total number of outlets of this form exceeds by a large margin both the entrepreneurial type and the confederated type with an average of 4,592 outlets. Interestingly, it represents the smallest number of franchisors who seek international franchisees. A number of reasons may account for this result. First, this type of franchisor is resource-rich and may not need franchising to expand overseas, preferring to control operations, quality and expansion in the foreign market via company-owned outlets. McDonald's and KFC, for example, belong to this group of franchisors. In the case of their expansion to China, Russia, India and other large emerging markets, the companies preferred not to use franchising at first due to legal complications, the desire to develop an entrenched system in the country, and the need to control the operations and vertically integrate. The second reason for less interest in expanding internationally is that these mature franchising systems may be less willing to venture abroad and to take risks. Alon (1999a) found that in the retailing sector, younger and smaller franchisors were more likely to internationalize since they were born into a more competitive domestic environment, needed to develop scale rapidly, and were more globally minded and less risk averse.

According to Castrogiovanni and Justis (1998), the carbon copy franchising system is a more standardized, vertically integrated, and rigidly controlled organization. Organizational size, a standard business format, and work process simplification typify this form of organization, allowing it to maintain a consistent image across heterogeneous locations. The carbon copy franchisor is the least franchised among the clusters with an average franchising rate among its outlets of 80.2%. It uses the company-owned outlets to test market new concepts, products and processes, rather than letting the franchisees experiment as in the case of the confederated form.

The carbon copy form of franchising is similar in organizational characteristics to the "mature franchisors" identified by Carney and Gedajlovic (1991). These "mature franchisors" in Québec have been in existence for a long time, have been franchising for 19.2 years, are relatively larger, experience market saturation, and are more likely to "buy back" some of their franchisees. The last point may account for the lower percentage of franchising in the overall ownership of outlets.

The costs of franchise ownership vary significantly for the carbon copy franchise system. At an average of over $3 million per unit, the startup costs are more expensive by a factor of 9 compared with the confederated form and by a factor of 16 compared with the entrepreneurial type. The royalty percentage is also significantly higher at 27% as compared to an average of 5% for a confederated or entrepreneurial type. The higher cost invested in standardizing a system proven across multiple and diverse locations, as well as the brand name capital available through a large and entrenched system, justify the added price that a franchisee may need to pay.

H3 predicted that, because of the size of their operations and high start-up costs, carbon-copy franchisors will provide more financial support to their franchisees. The data do not support this. In terms of financing, the carbon copy form is situated between the entrepreneurial type, which provides very little help to franchisees, and the confederated which offers many incentives to potential franchisee. Most of the help is given in financing the necessary equipment, followed by financing the franchise fee. Unlike the confederated form, the franchise startup costs are much less likely to be financed even though they are much more expensive. Nevertheless, the high number of franchised outlets along with reduced financial support for franchisees suggests that carbon-copy franchisors have little need to offer financial inducements to prospective franchisees.

Our final hypotheses dealt with the use of master franchising. H4a predicted that entrepreneurial franchisors will be more likely to enter new markets via master franchising as compared to confederation and carbon-copy franchisors. Our results show that in fact they are the least likely to use master franchising in foreign markets, and that the confederation form is more likely to use master-franchising. Figure 8.1 shows the use of master franchising as a method of expansion.

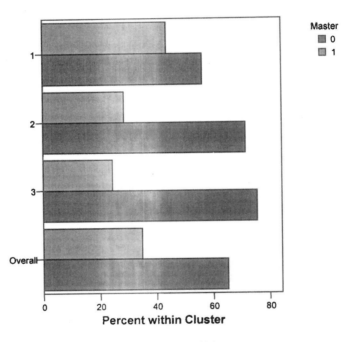

Percentage of Master Franchisors by Cluster

0 = No Master Franchising; 1 = Master Franchising
Cluster 1 = Confederation; Cluster 2 = Carbon-Copy; Cluster 3: Entrepreneurial
Figure 8.1: Use of Master Franchising

We also hypothesized that franchisors using master franchising will grow more rapidly because this form of franchising provides a quick entry at low cost that leverages local expertise and capital outlay. Tables 8.2 and 8.3 show the differences in system growth rate between those franchisors that use master franchising and those that do not. Our results here are surprising. In fact, master international franchisors show no significant difference in their growth rates, suggesting that the drawbacks of master franchising equal their benefits from a system-wide growth-rate perspective. What is surprising is that master-franchising-only international franchisors have grown their franchising outlets at a slower pace and their company-owned outlets at a higher pace than their non-master-franchising-only international franchisors.

As Table 8.4 shows, however, the difference in the change of the proportion of franchising between master franchising and non-master franchising was not significant in the two year study period under examination.

Table 8.2: *Master Franchising Growth*

Average Annual Growth Rate From 1997 to 1999			
	Franchised	*Company-Owned*	*All*
Non-Master	28.9%	11.7%	23.2%
Master	19.9%	20.4%	19.8%
All	25.9%	14.7%	22.1%

Table 8.3: *Difference in Growth Rates between Master and Non-Master Franchisors*

Two-sample analysis for Total growth rate from 97 to 99_0 minus Total growth rate from 97 to 99_1		
	Total growth rate from 1997 to 1999_0	Total growth rate from 1997 to 1999_1
Summary stats for two samples		
Sample sizes	206	101
Sample means	0.232	0.198
Sample standard deviations	0.465	0.588
T-Test of difference=0 versus two-tailed alternative		
Hypothesized mean difference	0.000	
Sample mean difference	0.034	
Pooled standard deviation	0.509	NA
Std error of difference	0.062	0.067
Degrees of freedom	305	163
t-test statistic	0.553	0.511
p-value	0.580	0.610
T-Test of equality of variances		
Ratio of sample variances	1.594	
p-value	0.003	

Table 8.4: *Difference in Franchising Change between Master and Non-Master Franchisors*

Two-sample analysis for % Change of proportion from 97 to 99_0 minus % Change of proportion from 97 to 99_1		
	% Change of proportion from 1997 to 1999_0	% Change of proportion from 1997 to 1999_1
Summary stats for two samples		
Sample sizes	201	99
Sample means	0.055	0.023
Sample standard deviations	0.342	0.167

Two-sample analysis for % Change of proportion from 97 to 99_0 minus % Change of proportion from 97 to 99_1		
	% Change of proportion from 1997 to 1999_0	% Change of proportion from 1997 to 1999_1
T-Test of difference=0 versus two-tailed alternative		
Hypothesized mean difference	0.000	
Sample mean difference	0.032	
Pooled standard deviation	0.296	NA
Std error of difference	0.036	0.029
Degrees of freedom	298	298
t-test statistic	0.873	1.080
p-value	0.383	0.281
T-Test of equality of variances		
Ratio of sample variances	4.182	
p-value	0.000	

The Entrepreneurial Franchising Type

The entrepreneurial franchising organizations began operations, on average, in 1981 and started to franchise within the first six years of their existence; they are the youngest of the three clusters, thus supporting H2. They have the smallest number of outlets (on average 254), which also supports H2, and on average they franchise about 88.6% of them. The entrepreneurial franchising type has the lowest operational costs, which include start-up costs, franchise fee, and royalties. This is logical since they have the least proven systems and thus present the most uncertainty to potential franchisees. The entrepreneurial franchising firm is least likely to expand internationally via master franchising only. The entrepreneur may want to exert strong control over the international operation and, thus, may be unwilling to wield power to a potential master franchisee. One explanation suggested by Castrogiovanni and Justis (1998) is that entrepreneurial franchising firms are leader-dependent, relying on the owner's intimate knowledge of the business and decision-making skills. As far as financing is concerned, this organizational type is resource-constrained and is least likely to provide financing to its franchisees; when financing is provided, the franchise fee is the most likely to be financed. This cluster is the second largest among our internationally-bound franchisors in terms of sample size.

The entrepreneurial type is similar to Carney and Gedagjlovic's (1991) "rapid growers" type found in a sample of franchisors in Québec. According to these researchers, the "rapid grower" has franchised for the least amount of time (4.1 years), has a relatively large network (157 units), waits a short time before beginning franchising (1.3 years), has a lower franchising cost (125K start-up fee), is geographically dispersed beyond the Québec province, and consists of mainly franchising outlets (92.7%). While there is no perfect correspondence between "rapid growers" in Québec and "entrepreneurial type" in the United States, the reader can observe the many similarities in their characteristics. Differences may be attributed to the differing environment of Canada and the smaller scale of Québec. Québec is culturally distinct from the rest of the English-speaking Canada and entrepreneurial firms in this area may be smaller and more aggressive in their local franchising expansion.

CONCLUSION

In this study, we examined the typologies of internationally-minded franchisors at the system level, focusing on the modes of entry they are likely to use when expanding overseas. Analysis of the organizational variables of international-bound franchisors yielded three groupings as Hypothesis 1 suggests, and these groupings roughly follow those theorized by Castrogiovanni and Justis (1998). Though we used the insight provided by Carney and Gedajlovic's(1991) franchising clusters, we did not find exact correspondence with their clusters; neither could Castrogiovanni, et al. (1995) replicate Carney and Gedajlovic's typologies. It is possible that the difference in regions (Québec vs. USA) accounts for this difference. Jones and Wong (2002) describe the franchising conditions in Canada as distinct from those in the USA.

We also found that the entrepreneur type and confederated types franchising organizations are younger and have a smaller number of units compared with the carbon copy type. Figure 8.1 shows the 95% confidence intervals for means in age and size for the three types. As can be seen from these confidence intervals, the entrepreneurial and confederated types are more similar to one another and highly distinct from the carbon copy type as far as their age and size are concerned. As predicted by H3, carbon-copy franchisors were the largest in terms of the total number of units; however, in contrast to H3, our findings show that carbon-copy franchisors were not the most likely to offer incentives to franchisees. This accolade went to confederated franchisors, followed by the carbon copy type and the entrepreneurial type.

Our predictions about the use of master franchising by internationally-minded franchisors were not supported by the data. Although we had hypothesized that master-franchising would be favored most by entrepreneurial franchisors, the data showed that these were the least likely to use this type of entry mode and that instead master-franchising was the preferred entry mode for the confederation form of franchisors. The reasons for this are likely to be twofold: first, although we had assumed that master franchising offers the entrepreneurial franchisor a compromise between the need for tight control of operations and the difficulty of exerting control over geographically dispersed units in a foreign environment, it appears from the data that the need for control overrides other factors, thus making master franchising a sub-optimal mode of entry for entrepreneurial franchisors. Second, the types of services that tend to be offered by confederated franchisees, such as real estate, tax preparation, hairdressing, etc. are generally based on professional skills that require licensing by domestic authorities (Castrogiovanni and Justis, 1998). Because of the franchisor's lack of knowledge about the local market and regulatory requirements, it makes sense to rely on a master-franchisor whose duties will include ensuring that individual franchisees are properly licensed to provide professional services.

Similarly, our prediction that master-franchisors will experience a faster system-wide growth rate was not supported by the data. Despite the stated advantage of master franchising for rapid market development, it seems as though those franchisors that use master franchising may have had agency problems that have limited their expansion efforts at the system level. What is more interesting is that those who used master franchising exclusively grew their company-owned outlets at a faster rate than their own franchise network and at a faster rate than their non-master franchising peer group. More research on the impact of the use of master franchising on growth is needed in light of these peculiar results.

Finally, this study provides evidence to support the earlier research of Castrogiovanni and Justis (1998) and Carney and Gedajlovic's(1991) that franchise groupings exist and may help explain variance in franchising strategies. Our sample consisted of American franchisors that are internationally-bound, using data collected by Entrepreneur magazine. In order to extend the geographical scope of the research, future studies that wish to expand on our efforts should use franchise data from non-US based sources as well as primary data collected for the specific purpose of the investigation. The anomalous results described here may be explained by insufficient data on organizational variables, so future studies should aim to capture data on additional internal variables such as access to resources, desire to grow quickly, previous international experience, degree of control over franchised operations, and the strength of the franchise's brand name. In addition, given the propensity for master franchising to address agency problems, researchers should also examine franchisors' concerns about issues such as bonding, adverse selection, information flow, shirking, inefficient risk-bearing, free-riding, and quasi-rent appropriation. Such variables may better illuminate the franchisor's decision whether or not to use master-franchising in international expansion.

REFERENCES

Aydin, N. and Kacker, M. (1990) "International outlook on US-based franchisors." *International Marketing* Review, 7 (2): 206-219.

Alon I. (1999a) *The Internationalization of U.S. Franchising Systems*, New York: Garland Publishing Inc.

Alon I. (1999b) "Organizational determinants of international franchising in the hotel sector." *Journal of Global Business*, 10(18): 55-62.

Alon I. (2000) "The organizational determinants of master international franchising." *Journal of Business and Entrepreneurship*, 12 (2): 1-18.

Amos, J.H. (1993). "Trends and development in international franchising." In A. J. Sherman (ed.) *The Franchising Handbook*, pp. 458-465, NY: AMACOM.

Brouthers K.D. (2002) "Institutional, cultural and transaction cost influences on entry mode choice and performance." *Journal of International Business Studies*, 33(2), 203-221.

Burton, F.N. and Cross, A.R. (1995) "Franchising and foreign market entry." In S.J. Paliwoda and J.K. Ryans (eds.), *International Marketing Reader*, pp. 35-48. London: Routledge.

Carney, M. and Gedajlovic, E. (1991) "Vertical integration in franchise systems: Agency theory and resource explanations," *Strategic Management Journal*, 12: 607-629.

Castrogiovanni, G. J., Bennett, N. and Combs, J.G. (1995) "Franchisor types: Reexamination and clarification." *Journal of Small Business Management*, 33 (1), 45-55.

Castrogiovanni, G. J. and Justis, R.T. (1998) "Franchising configurations and transitions." *The Journal of Consumer Marketing*, 15 (2), 170-187.

Davis P.S., Desai, A.B. and Francis, J.D. (2000) "Mode of international entry: An isomorphism perspective." *Journal of International Business Studies*, 31 (2), 239-258.

Duniach-Smith, K. (2003) "International entry mode choice in a franchise setting." Presented at Economics and Management of Franchising Networks conference, Vienna, Austria.

Dunning, John H.. (1988) "The eclectic paradigm of international production: A restatement and possible extensions." *Journal of International Business Studies*, 19: 1-32.

Ekelado, I. and Sivakumar, K. (1998) "Foreign market entry mode choice of service firms: A contingency perspective." *Journal of the Academy of Marketing Science*, 26 (4): 274-292.

Entrepreneur Magazine (2001) 22nd Annual Franchise 500, 173-269.

Eroglu S. (1992) "The internationalization process of franchise systems: A conceptual model." *International Marketing Review*, 9(5), 19-30.

Fladmoe-Lindquist K. and Jacque, L.L. (1995) "Control modes in international service operations: The propensity to franchise." *Management Science*, 41(7), 1238-1249.

Garg, V.K. and Rasheed, A.A. (2003) "International multi-unit franchising: an agency theoretic explanation." *International Business Review* 12 (3): 329-348.

Hackett, D.W. (1976). "The international expansion of US franchise systems: Status and strategies." *Journal of International Business Studies* 7 (Spring): 66-75.

Hill, C. W., Hwang, P. and Kim, W. C. (1990) "An eclectic theory of the choice of international entry mode." *Strategic Management Journal* 11 (2): 117-128.

Huszagh S.M., Huszagh, F.W. and McIntyre, F.S. (1992) "International franchising in the context of competitive strategy and the theory of the firm." *International Marketing Review*, 9(5): 5-18.

Jones, P. and Wong, M. (2002) "Franchising in Canada/La franchise au Canada," in Dianne Welsh and Ilan Alon, (eds.), *International Franchising in Industrialized Markets: North America, Pacific Rim, and Other Developed Countries*, pp.233-248. Chicago, IL: CCH Inc.,

Kaufmann, P. J., and Dant, R. P. (1996) "Multi-unit franchising: Growth and management issues." *Journal of Business Venturing, 11*: 343–358.

Kedia, B.L. and Ackerman, D.J. (1994) "Determinants of internationalization of franchise operations by US franchisors." *International Marketing Review*, 11 (4): 56-68.

Kogut B. and Singh, H. (1988) "The effect of national culture on the choice of entry mode." *Journal of International Business Studies*,19(3), 411-432.

Mintzberg, H. (1979) *Structuring of Organizations*, Prentice-Hall, Englewood Cliffs, NJ.

Sashi, C.M. and Karuppur, D.P. (2002) "Franchising in global markets: Towards a conceptual framework." *International Marketing Review*, 19 (5): 499-524.

Shane S.A. (1996) "Why franchise companies expand overseas." *Journal of Business Venturing*,11: 73-88.

Welsh, D. and Alon, I. (eds.) (2002) *International Franchising in Industrialized Markets: North America, Pacific Rim, and Other Developed Countries*. Chicago IL: CCH Inc. Publishing.

III. Franchising in Emerging Markets

Chapter 9
Franchising in Russia

Noora Anttonen
University of Jyväskylä, School of Business and Economics

Mika Tuunanen
University of Jyväskylä, School of Business and Economics

Ilan Alon
Crummer Graduate School of Business, Rollins College

INTRODUCTION

The Russian market has generally been considered as a highly unpredictable and unfavorable business environment (Mendelshon, 1996; Alon and Banai, 2000). However, recent economic stabilization programs and government reforms have made the appearance of Russia more appealing in the eyes of foreign investors. The aim of the chapter is to provide a general environmental framework for analyzing the international franchising environments in Russia, contributing to franchising practitioners' ability to enter the market successfully.

The U.S. Commercial Service in Russia has identified franchising as a sector possessing a significant potential for development and offering vast opportunities for U.S. franchisors (Sarkisov 2002). The conditions for franchising in the country are becoming more attractive as the economy has shown remarkable stabilization since the economic crisis in 1998. The demand for high quality Western products is prevailing. Russia's effort to join the *World Trade Organization, WTO* affects positively the business and economic environment. The Russian government is making an effort to build an efficient market and to raise the country's standard of living. Substantial progress has been achieved in improving legislation governing economic, business and investment activity. The state is consolidating its control functions and implementing structural reforms such as moderating the tax burden of enterprises.

The chapter aims to analyze Russia as a target market for international franchisors. First, past research and literature on franchising in Russia is reviewed. The country analysis includes five parts, (1) demographics, (2) economy, (3) social and political environment, (4) culture, and (5) legislation.

LITERATURE REVIEW: INTERNATIONAL FRANCHISING IN EMERGING MARKETS

In recent years, franchising has experienced phenomenal growth both in the U.S. and abroad. The success factors are well documented (e.g., Shane and Spell, 1998; Alon, 2004). Past research describes three primary motivations for franchising (Dant, 1995). First, the resource constraint perspective suggests that franchising is an efficient way to collect three fundamental resources a growth-oriented company needs: financial capital, market knowledge and human capital. Second, the efficiency perspective emphasizes that franchising is a vehicle to achieve a variety of scale economies, especially in production, promotion and coordination. Finally, agency theory perceives franchising as an effective answer to the classical principal-agent problem, because franchising eliminates the shirking problem often related to principal-agent relationships.

Alon (1999) investigated the effect of five company-specific independent variables on the decision of professional business service franchisors to internationalize their operations. A model using resource-based theories and agency theories for its theoretical foundation was developed and tested. The results indicate that internal characteristics of the franchising system, especially the number of outlets, significantly influence the intention of domestic franchisors to seek franchisees overseas. This confirms that resource-based explanations and, perhaps, agency explanations may help explain the internationalization of the franchise system in addition to the use of franchising in any one country's context.

Doherty and Quinn (1999) examined international retailing and franchise research in the context of agency theory to explain major elements of international franchise activity and internationalization. The same authors, Quinn and Doherty (2000), examined the mechanisms used to control and co-ordinate the international franchise network and reported the findings from an in-depth, ethnographic study of the internationalization activity of one retail franchise company.

Pizanti and Lerner (2003) examined the franchisor-franchisee relationship from two theoretical perspectives - agency theory and exchange theory, and tested their ideas on a domestic firm and two international firms in the restaurant industry - McDonald's and Burger King. Their research indicates that domestic and international franchisors are distinguishable in some respects showing varying forms of integration of control and autonomy among the three chains.

Since the markets of developed countries are becoming more saturated and competition is diminishing profit potential, more and more franchisors are looking to emerging market economies (Alon and Toncar 1999). While in the U.S., Canada, and parts of Western Europe franchising has reached domestic market saturation, emerging markets remain relatively untapped. Emerging markets, accounting for 80% of the world's population, are among the fastest growing target markets for international franchisors (Welsh and Alon 2001). Franchising has been advocated as a method of growth for developing countries, providing know-how, and advanced marketing and management practices that are of high importance in the post-communist countries (Alon and Toncar 1999). Because business format franchising focuses on the transfer of retail know-how rather than on product distribution, it is the form of international franchising most likely to have a direct effect on the economic development of developing countries (Kaufmann and Leibenstein 1988).

A number of authors have identified emerging markets as a topic that needs further investigation (e.g., Welsh and Alon 2001; Kaufmann and Leibenstein 1988). This chapter provides an overview of franchising conditions and opportunities in one of the biggest and fastest growing markets, Russia. Even though the business conditions are similar to those in other emerging economies, the high quality of human resources and patterns of consumption come close to those in developed countries (Alon and Toncar 1999). Previous studies and analyses on franchising in Russia can be divided into four steams of research described below.

Firstly, investigations have focused on case studies of franchise systems penetrated into Russia. These include for instance *Pizza Hut* (Christy and Haftel 1993), *Baskin Robbins* and *Subway* (Gorovaia 2003). The first case study focused on *Pizza Hut's* rationale for entry into the country describing the company's objectives and plans, whereas the latter paper addressed the performance of *Baskin Robbins* and *Subway*.

Secondly, prior examinations have concentrated also on specific industries. Swerdlow and Welsh investigated the Russian hospitality industry in several papers. They conducted a cross-cultural research by a series of in-depth interviews of Russian and US hospitality firms 1992 - 1994. Their studies focused on job satisfaction, and organizational commitment and training (Swerdlow and Welsh 1992; Swerdlow, Cummings and Welsh 1997; Roehl, Swerdlow and Welsh 1999).

Thirdly, the majority of the articles describe the franchising environment in Russia by analyzing the opportunities and/or threats it offers to foreign franchisors. The macro environmental approaches have concentrated on either specific environmental issues, such as legal aspects (Kellman 1989), or on a more comprehensive overview of the economy (Christy and Haftel 1992; Alon and Toncar 1999; Swerdlow, Roehl and

Welsh 2001). According to the authors' own acknowledgement, the first empirical study concerning franchising in Russia was a survey conducted by Welsh and Swerdlow in 1990. The focal point of the inspection was the opinions of the Soviet university students about the future prospects of franchising in Russia[1]. The conclusion of the study was that franchising has a promising future in the country, but at the same time the results pointed out confusion about what franchising means.

Finally, some articles have pursued a more general perspective. In 1996 *Russian Franchise Association (RFA)*, together with a U.S. franchise consulting firm, *Sibley International*, carried out a survey among Western franchisors operating in the markets. The results suggested that financing was the biggest operational challenge for foreign franchisors. Alon and Banai (2000) examined the environmental factors, the four Ps (i.e. product, price, place, promotion), and entry strategies available for prospective franchisors offering a normative framework of franchising entry into Russia. *The U.S. and Foreign Commercial Service* and *U.S. Department of State* have published two general reports analyzing franchising in Russia. The reports discuss market highlights and best prospects, a competitive situation, consumer markets, and market access (Kuzmina 1997; Sarkisov 2002).

Environmental factors have been shown to be useful for international franchisors in evaluating a host country for expansion (Alon and McKee 1999). The present analysis provides an up-to-dated overview of Russian franchise environment, integrating research on the topic and collecting some primary information on the ground in Russia. The section that follows analyses the macro environmental conditions of franchising in Russia focusing previously-established franchising-specific influential variables relating to the demographic, the economic, the financial, the social, the political, and the regulatory environments. It should be noted that while we contribute to the literature by updating previously published information on the international business environments of franchising in Russia, Russia's fast changing and sometimes chaotic environment is hard to predict, and rapid changes can ultimately change the favorability of the environment for franchising, or any other business type.

ENVIRONMENTAL ANALYSIS OF FRANCHISING IN RUSSIA

The Demographic Environment of Franchising

Population size, the level of urbanization and female labor participation (Alon, Toncar and McKee 2000) together with the size of the middle class (Alon and McKee 1999) are regarded as the main host country demographic factors from a franchisor perspective.

Russia is geographically a vast country with 143.4 million inhabitants. In spite of a negative population growth, there is a great market demand. Female labor participation is nearly half (49.1%) of the total labor force (World Bank 2003). According to Alon, Toncar and McKee (2000) high female labor force participation is a positive factor from the franchising point of view. The fact that rather highly educated labor in Russia is plentiful and inexpensive is also a positive sign for an international investor wishing to mobilize the labor force (Alon and Banai 2000). Table 9.1 presents a comparison of key demographic information of Russia and the USA to give the reader a reference point for key demographic variables.

Table 9.1: A Comparison between Russia and the USA

Demographics	Russia	USA
Population (Million)	143,4	290,4
Population Growth Rate (Annual %)	-0.5	0.7
Surface Area (Million sq. km)	17.1	9.6
Population Density (Inhabitants/ sq. km)	8	30
Urbanization (%)	73	78
Life Expectancy, Male/Female (Years)	64/73	74/80
Female Labor Force Participation (%)	49	46
Poverty Rate (% of population below 2 USD per day)	7.5	-

Source: World Bank 2003, World Bank 2005a

The size of the middle class is a disputable indicator depending greatly on how the definition is understood. According to one definition and survey, middle class includes people with a monthly income of more than 150 USD in the regions, and 200 USD in Moscow. In this respect, middle class represents one fifth (20%) of the Russian population (or approximately 10 million families), and accounts for more than half of the consumption. The average annual income of the middle class in Russia is approximately 3,900 USD with an annual growth rate of 8-10% between 1999 and 2001. ("Expert" No. 45, Dec. 3, 2001; in Sarkisov 2002) The income rate is even more favorable when examining central cities in Russia. Seven out of ten Russians live in cities. Traditionally Moscow and St. Petersburg have attracted most of foreign investments but improving infrastructure has increased opportunities in the regions. However, there are thirteen cities with a population of more than one million, ten of which are underlined in the map of Russia (See Figure 9.1).

Figure 9.1: Map of Russia - Cities with more than 1 million inhabitants include Moscow (10.1 mil inhabitants), St. Petersburg (4.67), Novosibirsk (1.43), Nizhni Novgorod (1.31), Yekaterinburg (1.29), Samara (1.16), Omsk (1.13), Kazan (1.1), Chelyabinsk (1.08), Rostov (1.07), Ufa (1.04), Volgograd (1.01) and Perm (1.0).

The Economic Environment of Franchising

Current Russian economy is rather modest with GDP of 582.4 USD billion. The GDP per capita is only 4,044 USD, which accounts for less than ten percent of the corresponding number in the USA and European Union countries on the average[2]. On a purchasing power parity basis, however, the average annual income for all income classes reaches about 9,900 USD (The Economist 2005). The purchasing power parity income per capita is a lot higher in Russia than the one calculated using exchange rates because the cost of living in Russia is in general much lower than the one in the United States of America for example.

In 1998, the Russian economy dived into a serious recession. The crisis later referred as the Russian Crisis resulted in a major devaluation of the Russian currency, ruble and reduction of disposable income of Russian citizens. Also, the prices of input and the level of economic uncertainty increased (Alon and Banai 2000; Swerdlow, Roehl and Welsh, 2001).

At least three main reasons can be found to account for the lag of the economy. First, bartering is still common in Russia. A number of transactions involve no money. Second, the black economy is rather prevalent, but naturally not included in the official statistics. Third explanation for the small GDP is the low-income rate of the citizens. Nevertheless, the Russian economy continues to grow at a rapid pace, and in 2004 Russia's GDP growth (7.1%) exceeded the most optimistic expectations. (World Bank 2003, 2005b).

In addition to GDP growth, monetary and exchange rate stability is important because it affects royalty repatriation, payments of imported goods, and consumer income. The Russian business life suffers from high exchange rates and inflation. (Alon and Banai 2000) However, after the major devaluation of the ruble in August 1998, the exchange rates have been stabilizing. Inflation has gradually been declining although still remaining high (11.7%) from a western point of view. The key macro environmental factors of the Russian economy are presented in Table 9.2.

Russia has had the image of a country with highly unpredictable and unfavorable business environment and naturally, the Russian Crisis had a negative effect onto the development of foreign investments. (Sarkisov 2002) Nevertheless, in 2004 inflows of foreign direct investment reached record levels (9.4 USD). In general, the Russian economy has seen an upturn, and since 1999 the main economic trend in Russia has been stabilization (Sarkisov 2002). Three relevant economic indicators can point out stabilization: GDP, inflation and exchange rates (See Table 9.2).

The growing income rate has lead to an increase in the volume of the consumer market. Overall, the (per capita) real cash income has been gradually growing during the 21st century, although it still remains rather low. (See Table 9.2). Despite of the general income growth, poverty remains a severe problem in the country where 7.5 percent of the population survives with less than two dollars a day.

Given an unequal distribution of wealth in Russia, a segment of the population exists that is very wealthy and can lead international franchising development. Such individuals, also known as "new Russians," often have local ties and knowledge, access to large sums of money, and other related businesses and are, thus, ideal candidates for buying multi-unit franchising outlets. The efforts of these individuals can promote local entrepreneurship and stave off capital flight. Multi-unit franchising is an important source of entrepreneurship globally (Grunhagen and Mittelstaedt 2002). Multi-unit franchising in Russia gained popularity in the 1990s, but given the low level of control that it entails, the contractual arrangement sometimes failed because master franchisees have acted opportunistically or failed to abide by the rules of the franchisor (Alon and Banai 2000).

The infrastructure in Russia varies, and in this way is similar to other developing countries. The level of development in both traditional transportation and telecommunications changes by location. Poor infrastructure can restrict franchisors′ activities and reduce the desired control, which franchisors may wish to have (Alon and Banai 2000).

Table 9.2: Main Macro Economic Indicators in Russia from 1997 to 2004

Indicator	1997	1998	1999	2000	2001	2002	2003	2004
GDP	436.0	277.8	184.6	246.9	302.2	346.5	432.9	582.4
GDP Growth Rate (%)	+0.9	-4.9	+5.4	+8.3	+4.9	+4.0	+7.3	+7.1
GDP Per Capita (USD)	3,047	1,840	1,249	1,697	2,140	2,390	2,970	4,040
Inflation (CPI, %)	11.3	84.5	36.5	20.2	18.6	15.1	12.0	11.7
Unemployment (%)	11.2	11.8	12.4	9.9	8.7	7.1	8.4	8.3
Average Exchange Rate*	5,875	9.7	24.6	28.16	29.19	31.39	29.45	27.75
Real Personal Cash Income	106.4	84.0	88.1	113.4	110	110.3	114.0	107.8
Foreign Direct Investment	3.90	3.36	4.26	4.43	3.98	4.00	6.8	9.4
Foreign Portfolio Investment	3.3	0.191	0.031	0.145	0.451	0.472	0.401	0.333
Total Exports	86.9	74.4	75.6	105.0	101.6	106.9	135.9	183.4
Total Imports	72.0	58.0	39.5	44.9	53.8	60.5	76.1	96.2

Notes: Figures in USD billions if not mentioned otherwise; * RUB/USD;
Source: U.S. Department of Commerce 2002; The Central Bank of the Russian Federation 2003; World Bank 2005a, b

Russia's competitiveness is found to be rather low. The *World Economic Forum* (2005) has investigated nations' competitiveness worldwide and ranked countries accordingly. Recently Russia's ranking has been rather low. In 2005 Russia's ranking was 70, whereas Mexico, for example, took the 48th position (See Table 8.3).

Table 9.3: Growth Competitiveness Index for Selected Countries in 2004

Russia	NAFTA	European Union (5/2005)
Russia 70. (70.)	USA 2. (2.)	Highest: Finland 1. (1.)
	Canada 15. (16.)	Median: Luxembourg 26. (21.)
	Mexico 48. (47.)	Lowest: Poland 60. (45.)

Note: 2003 rankings in brackets   Source: World Economic Forum 2004

Several scholars (e.g. Hanson 1995; Mendelsohn 1996; Alon and Banai 2000) have stated that one of the main franchising related impediments in Russia is the poor availability of financing. Funding a business in Russia is both limited and expensive (Alon and Toncar 1999). Anyway, political and institutional stability, coupled with declining inflation and real ruble appreciation over the last years, has significantly increased the availability of financing for small businesses. A number of Russian commercial banks offer micro and mini loans to start-ups. For example, *Sberbank* offers micro loans of up to 30,000 USD and small loans of up to 200,000 USD, with maturity of one year and two years respectively. The loan application process is relatively simple and the banks generally decide within one week from application. Financing is thus becoming more available, but estimates indicate that less than 50% of small businesses have even considered applying for loans. (Sarkisov 2002)

The initial investments required to set up a franchise business can be rather considerable for small Russian businesses. One way to attract new franchisees is to establish financial arrangements with banks in order to increase the inflow of new requests for franchise agreements with them. For example, *Rostic International* has signed an agreement with *Small Business Credit Bank*, which opens two-year credit lines for *Rostics'* franchisees. Investments required to buy a western franchise are usually higher than a domestic one. Therefore, franchisors willing to expand through franchising in Russia should consider similar arrangements with reliable financial institutions. (Sarkisov 2002)

The Cultural Environment of Franchising

The unique Russian culture creates conditions, which have to be taken into account in doing business. One of the biggest challenges is the Russian language, the role of which should not be underestimated in the business life. Thus, one needs to consider, for example, whether or not to translate the trade name into the Cyrillic alphabet.

Cultural variables affect the feasibility and acceptance of a franchise system (Alon and McKee 1999). Cross-cultural research has often employed the work of Hofstede who divides cultures along four dimensions: (1) individualism/collectivism, (2) power distance, (3) uncertainty avoidance, and (4) sex role differentiation (masculine/feminine). Alon, Toncar and McKee (2000) have argued that particularly high levels in masculinity and individualism are preferable franchising country-related factors. Considering this, Russia is not among the most appealing host country alternatives, because the culture is very feminine. In the individualism/collectivism dimension the countries score is somewhat average. Furthermore, power distance and uncertainty avoidance (both of which are considered as negative features) are high in the Russian culture.

Franchising is a relatively new phenomenon in Russia. The word franchising does not exist in the Russian language, but efforts are being made to educate the public, business and governmental audiences (Alon and Toncar 1999). There are several associations in Russia promoting franchising. *The Russian Franchise Association,* RFA was established in 1997 as a non-profit organization. The RFA promotes franchising as a business concept and lobbies for the amendment of the Civil Code. Association members include franchisors, franchisees, and government agencies, business support organizations, non-government funds, banks, accounting firms and consultants. (Sarkisov 2002).

A related business development organization is the *Russian Association for the Development of Franchising* (RADF) which started around 1997 and whose primary functions are to train businesses, educators, and consultants and to hold tradeshows, seminars and publications encouraging the use of franchising (Mendelsohn 1996). The RADF and the RFA organized the first International Conference and Exhibition "Franchising in Russia" in November 2002. The International Conference and Exhibition aims at becoming a center of franchising business activity and establishing contacts between both local and foreign franchisors and franchisees.

Another association, *Center for Franchise in Small Business,* is established through the *State Committee for the Promotion of Small Business.* Its main task is to promote franchising in the regions of the Russian Federation and to help local businesses identify business opportunities and establish contacts between potential franchisees and franchisors. Association also provides counseling, information support, and organizes conferences on franchising topics. (Sarkisov 2002)

Franchising in Russia is becoming more attractive because of the high demand for Western products, the establishment of a local franchising community and educational directives (Zeidman 1995). Demand for Western products is healthy in Russia, fueling the growth in foreign investments (Alon and Toncar 1999). According to Sarkisov (2002), the U.S. franchisors are more popular than other foreign brands, because of the perception that USA is the "motherland of franchising". Besides the increase in local consumption, the growing tourist sector creates opportunities for franchisors especially in the hotel and motel sector (Alon and Toncar 1999).

The Political Environment of Franchising

Host country's political instability is important for a franchisor, because country politics directly affects the business environment. The political risk remains high despite the government's efforts to stabilize the economy. Governmental instability, corruption and organized crime are still omnipresent in Russia (Alon and Toncar 1999). The democracy is somewhat different in Russia than in the Western countries.

Transparency International has measured corruption rates in several countries worldwide. The indicator is *Corruption Perception Index (CPI)* score, which ranges between 10 (highly clean) and 0 (highly corrupt). In 2004 Russia's score was 2.8. Russia's CPI has been gradually increasing since 2000 when the score was as low as 2.1. Although Russia has passed laws that resist corruption, their effective implementation remains uncertain. For example, a reform enacted in 2001 aimed at cutting down courtroom bribery by introducing a fivefold increase in judges' salaries. (Transparency International 2005) Further results are presented in Table 9.4.

Table 9.4: Corruption Index for Selected Countries in 2004

Russia	NAFTA	European Union (5/2005)
Russia 2.8	Canada 8.5	Maximum (Finland) 9.7
	USA 7.5	Median (Malta) 6.8
	Mexico 3.6	Minimum (Poland) 3.5

Source: Transparency International 2005

The Regulatory Environment of Franchising

Russian legislation is under a constant change. Some of the laws are new, whereas others derive from the Soviet times. Legislative reforms are needed to revise confusing, insufficient and partially contradictory laws. The problem is that sometimes the reforms are difficult to manage and the outcomes can be unpredictable.

The Civil Code in its treatment of competition law, intellectual property law and general contract law contains provisions that clearly permit franchising practices and normal contractual arrangements (Mendelsohn 1996). In addition to the general contract law, a code of laws for franchising was established. The law referred as "*Law on Contract of Commercial Concession*" is included in the Chapter 54 of the Russian Civil Code, which became effective in 1997. Mendelsohn (1996) considered the creation of the law difficult to understand, because at the time franchising was barely known in Russia. Apparently the law was created for educational purposes, although a code of law seems a very strange method to choose for education purposes. Further, a law that clearly takes positions on issues, many of which are difficult for franchisors to live with, does not encourage franchising development in Russia. (Mendelsohn 1996) In the countries, where franchise is regulated with special legislative acts, the main attention is paid to the obligation for the franchisor to make full disclosure of information about his business to potential franchisees planning to invest into a new business. And exactly this important theme finds no reflection in the Chapter 54. (Mailer 2003)

One of the main weaknesses of economy is the complex tax structure. The number of taxes targeted on firms' profits is numerous. As a consequence, firms try to avoid taxes by various accounting methods. The Russian government has been working on a simplified tax structure to cut off the black economy. One of the latest tax reforms is the simplification of small business taxation. Since the beginning of 2003, small businesses are given a choice of paying either a unified tax rate of six percent of turnover or fifteen percent of income[3]. (Sarkisov 2002)

The head of the RFA, Mr. Alexander Mailer, has gathered a comprehensive list of the main shortcomings of the law. The key elements of his analysis are compiled and presented in Appendix 1. His analysis shows that the existence of the Chapter 54 of the Civil Code has a negative influence on the development of franchising in Russia. The most radical solution would be to stop enactment of this chapter, or to exclude it from the Civil Code. Other chapters of the Civil Code, concerning contract relations between the legal bodies such as the Trade Mark Law and antimonopoly legislation create necessary legislative basis for successful development of franchising in Russia. (Mailer 2003) The RFA also adapts the Code of Ethics created by *The European Franchise Federation*. Even though law does not enforce the Code, the members of the RFA are obliged to comply with the Code.

CURRENT STATE OF FRANCHISING IN RUSSIA

Most franchisors entered Russia right after the fall of the Soviet Union and the opening of the market economy. However, franchising as a business method did not start to flourish until the mid 1990's. Sarkisov (2002) listed the main impediments that have constrained the development of franchising in Russia as follows:

- Legal environment was lacking clarity that would boost the development of the sector.

- Local businesses had very limited knowledge of the mechanisms and advantages of franchising.

- Until recently, the state did not undertake any significant efforts to support SME development.

- Cultural and psychological particularities of local business ethics made the idea of purchasing intellectual capital unattractive.

- There was a high degree of mistrust among businesses, and inadequate protection of ownership rights.

The development of franchising in Russia is difficult to estimate, because no reliable statistics are available. The franchisors and franchisees prefer to register franchise agreements under various legal forms such as licensing agreements or sales contracts making the compilation of statistics impossible. (Sarkisov 2002) The franchise agreements used to be registered in the *State Registration Board of the Russian Ministry of Justice*. In 2002 the responsibility was transferred to the *Russian Federation Ministry of Taxes*. (Ernst and Young 2003) Still, if the agreements are not registered as franchise agreements, no statistics can be prepared. The *Russian Association for Franchise Development* is making an effort to create a "Franchise in Russia" database. The database includes the basic information on franchise companies operating in Russia as well as on companies planning to enter franchise operation. (Russian Association for Franchise Development 2003).

It is estimated that franchising accounts for one percent of the retail in Russia (Picot-Coupet and Cliquet 2003), whereas in the USA the comparable percentage is over forty. In 1997, *Sibley International* reported that there were thirty-three franchise systems operating in Russia. According to the data provided by *the Franchising Center for Small Businesses*, there were approximately forty companies that had franchise agreements in 2000. In 2001, the number exceeded fifty, and by the mid 2002, more than 100 franchisors were present on the local market (Sarkisov 2002). Moreover, Kamins (2002) estimated that there are 75-100 franchise chains operating in Russia. On the other hand, Kuzmina stated already in 1997 that according to experts, there were 200 franchising firms at the time. Furthermore, Picot-Coupet and Cliquet (2003) reported that the number of franchise networks is 200. However, it should be noted that these figures might contain also franchisors that do not have any franchised outlets in their channel of distribution. For example, McDonald's runs only company-owned outlets in the country.

Both foreign and local franchisors are present in the Russian market. Table 9.5 shows information on selected franchising chains in Russia. The number of foreign franchisors is estimated to be one third of all market players. The primary entry modes used by international franchisors include sole ventures, joint ventures, direct franchising, and master franchising (Alon and Banai 2000). Currently, the main stream of potential franchisees is seeking agreements with franchisors in the following business sectors: fast food, printing and copying services, photo-shops, auto repair and maintenance services, body and health care services, and retail sale. (Sarkisov 2002)

CONCLUSION

Russian society can be rather contradictory. The recent economic stabilization presents Russia as an attractive investment target for international franchisors. A large consumer market with growing income rate is an appealing target market for any company searching for growth. Furthermore, the market is still relatively untapped, the demand for western products is evident and the population is rather concentrated. In addition, several organizations are promoting and supporting the growth of franchising.

The macro environmental analysis suggests that most problems are related, not necessarily to franchising, but to all business in general. Alon and Banai (2000) listed the unfavorable business environment features as follows: (1) very high political risk, (2) monetary instability, (3) underdeveloped infrastructure, (4) crime and corruption, and (5) limited amount of capital, especially foreign currency. From these features, it can be noted that actually only the monetary instability has become more favorable, if compared to the situation three years ago. Other problems still remain.

The political and economic risk is omnipresent in the country. Legal, political and economic institutions are inter-linked and corruption is rather common. Many Russian citizens are unhappy with the way national wealth was distributed during the privatization of national conglomerates. The gap between the rich and the poor is widening. The rich, oligarchs, are hated and government actions are mistrusted. Social differences and instabilities will affect the entrepreneurial atmosphere in Russia.

Table 9.5: Selected Franchisors in Russia

Company (home country)	Industry	Entry year in Russia	Company-owned/franchised outlets	Initial investment (USD)	Initial franchise fee (USD)	Royalty (USD)	Marketing fee (USD)	Term of the agreement (years)
ABK (Russia)	Retail (consumer goods)	1997	17/1	na	2,000	1,5 %	-	na
AMD Lab (Russia)	Retail (cosmetics)	1995	0/24	na	5,000-10,000	-	300/year	5
Chemdry (USA)	Service (cleaning)	1994	0/3	20,000-	-	100-300/year	-	3
EF English First (Sweden)	Service (language school)	1995	na	160,000	30,000	10 %	10 %	10
Enton (Russia)	Retail (clothing)	1990	3/3	100,000-120,000	-	-	5 %	1 +*
Grillmaster (Germany)	Fast food	1978	0/5	70,000 +	25,000	5 %	-	5
Kodak (USA)	Retail (Photography)	1992	0/1300	40,000-120,000	-	200/year	-	1
Masterfibre (Australia)	Retail (Recycled rubber products)	2001	1/1	na	15,000	-	-	5
Rostiks (Russia)	Fast food	1990	12/23	250,000-350,000	25,000	6 %	2-5 %	na
Лавка Жизни (Russia)	Retail (consumer goods)	1995	0/2600	na	-	0-5 %	-	1 +*

(Source: Russian Association for Franchise Development 2003)
N.B. The percentages from net sales
*Minimum term one year.

The parliamentary election held in December 2003 delivered a victory to the allies of President Vladimir Putin. The two parties, which would be recognized in the West as liberal, supporting democracy and western market economy, the SPS and Yabloko, both failed to reach the 5% barrier. After nearly four years in the Kremlin, Mr. Putin still appears to have genuine support. The hard line, which his administration has taken against corruption and oligarchs, has gone down well with many voters. However, there is a fear that Russia is taking steps towards a monarchy and nationalism rather than a democracy. Mr. Putin's re-election in April 2004 seems obvious.

Further, the *Organization for Security and Co-operation in Europe,* OSCE which had about 400 observers in Russia, said the elections called into question Moscow's commitment to Western standards of democracy. The OSCE claimed that the government used resources and control of the media to dominate the election, and criticized the biased use of taxpayers money (BBC 2003). Many people in Russia and abroad have raised alarms over the steady erosion of democratic freedoms, but voters have clearly embraced political stability and economic development that Mr. Putin and his party promise to nurture (New York Times 2003). It is believed that the election result and Mr. Putin's growing power will positively affect the economic stabilization and support the growth of the economy. President Putin will apparently go on with the economic reforms and international co-operation. Finally, Mr. Putin has been generally positive in relation to international investments into the country, and perhaps he will enable Russia to get the membership in the WTO.

In addition to the instability of the society, there are certain impediments, which are specifically related to franchising in Russia. In spite of the legislation concerning the protection of intellectual property rights, the practice has shown that franchisors face it as a challenge. Russian legislative bodies are rather corrupted and there is no guarantee that court decisions will be enforced in real business life. Also, the law on commercial concession is regarded as an entry barrier for foreign franchisors. The code includes parts that clearly restrict franchise practices. Especially the article that allows the franchisee to renew the franchise agreement under the same terms is very restricting and unjustified from a franchisor point of view. Another major shortcoming of the law is the part that sets the franchisor subsidiarily liable for claims filed against the franchisee. This statement contradicts the main principle of the franchise system, the independence of franchisee as an entrepreneur. Nevertheless, it should be noted that some parts of the law, commonly regarded as obstacles for franchising in Russia, can be overlooked by stating the issues in the franchise agreements. In some parts the law gives an opportunity to agree otherwise by stating "unless provided otherwise in the contract". Furthermore, companies like *Kodak* avoid the law by using an agreement of "quality control services", even though their operation clearly is franchising. Finally, there is no indication that franchisors would have faced problems related to the legislation.

Table 9.6 summarizes the strengths, weaknesses, opportunities and threats (SWOT) for international franchising in Russia. The managerial implications that can be derived from the current analysis include: (1) Use and take advantage of local legal advice, plan your franchise agreements carefully and follow the Russian legislation. (2) Create relationships with the local decision-makers and be present. (3) Make a long-term investment plan and build up necessary infrastructure inside the country. (4) Find the right partner. (5) Adapt your franchise system to local conditions and support the franchisees in their daily business operations. (6) Invest on quality and respect the local culture, language and people. To sum up, one could say that the most important thing one needs to concentrate on is *partner management*. To be able to start a business in Russia and run it successfully depends much on the company's ability to create relationships. To achieve mutual trust one has to be present in the market. It is not enough to know your business partners, but also, you need to build up relationships with various stakeholders, including local and governmental authorities.

Table 9.6: SWOT Analysis for Franchising in Russia

Strengths

1. Franchising represents a less risky entry mode. Sharing the economic risk is essential when entering into an unstable business environment.
2. Franchising enables a faster entry and growth because various resources will be acquired from franchisees.
3. Franchising is regarded as an effective business method because independent entrepreneurs are assumed to be more motivated than salaried employees.
4. International franchising may be better accepted in a host country because most of the revenues will stay in the country. Accordingly, it is possible that local entrepreneurs do not face so much crime and political pressure than international companies do in Russia.

Weaknesses

1. Since franchising is not a well known or common business method in Russia, franchisee recruitment procedures can be rather time- and resource consuming.
2. Training and control of franchisees may acquire more efforts than normally.
3. Franchisee selection criteria may have to be reconsidered in Russia. For instance, it is probable that that many of the potentially successful franchisees only want to be investors who are not willing to participate in daily business operations.
4. Russia's unique culture and language create conditions that require changes in the business concepts and operations. Franchisors need to get familiar with the Russian way of doing business.

Opportunities

1. A large consumer market, an increasing income rate, and a growing middle class with a high purchasing power are all positive factors in the eyes of the foreign investors.

2. The main trends of the Russian economy have been stabilization and growth during the past four years. Economic reforms have been implemented and are expected to continue.
3. Franchising is starting to develop in Russia. Franchising organizations are promoting the growth of franchising.
4. The existence of a growing number of potential franchisees with resources required for buying a franchise. Overall, entrepreneurship is beginning to flourish. The government is starting to support entrepreneurship.
5. A strong need and interest in high quality Western products.
6. The population is rather centralized.
7. The number of educated and skilled labor force is plentiful.

Threats
1. Political instability: Black economy, corruption and crime are too common.
2. Economic instability: Political instability has a negative effect in Russian business life.
3. Legal instability: Russian legislation and taxation are still rather complicated.
4. Infrastructure in the county is highly underdeveloped.
5. Franchising legislation creates business conditions that are clearly unfavorable from the franchisor point of view.
6. Protecting intellectual property can be challenging in Russia. The problem is not so much the legislation itself, but the insecurity concerning the enactment of the court decisions.
7. The availability of financing is rather poor.

The present study contributes to the prior research by summing up previous studies and analyzing the franchising environment in Russia. However, there is still an evident gap of empirical research on franchising in Russia. Thus far all investigations have been cross-sectional. Longitudinal research is needed. Instead of descriptive analysis, a more prescriptive, managerially oriented approach should be applied. Previous studies are rather limited and fragmented. Case studies of both successful and unsuccessful entrants should be conducted and past case studies ought to be updated. Particularly, the normative analysis should focus on the entry phase of the internationalization process, including entry mode choice, franchisee recruitment and franchise system development. Finally, since the Law on Contract of Commercial Concession is regarded as an entry obstacle, the enforcement of the law should be investigated.

NOTES

[1]The results were reported in two separate papers (Welsh and Swerdlow 1991; Swerdlow and Welsh 1992).
[2] In the USA, GDP per capita was 40,047 USD in 2004.
[3] Small business is an enterprise of up to 100 employees and an annual turnover of no more than 470,000 USD.

APPENDIX I

Shortcoming of Franchising Law in Russia

- ❑ Registration of contracts of commercial concession (article 1028) is an absolutely unjustified measure, because it is very hard to imagine any negative impact of unregistered contracts. Agreements usually contain confidential information that might be disclosed to a third person while going through registration bodies. Practice of Russian registration chambers shows that this claim will result in another bothering procedure of "registration for the sake of registration". We can see no reason in registering of agreements for the usage of objects already defended by patent legislation. Once a patent is registered, it's enough, because all franchise contracts include articles on the rights to use a certain brand. (Mailer 2003) Contract registration is in any case a common procedure in Russia and thus franchising makes no difference in relation to other business methods.
- ❑ Remuneration to the franchisor usually has a complex nature, that is why in the article 1030 the conjunction "and" should be used instead of "or". Principally this side of relations between two parties should be regulated by the contract, and not by the Civil Code of Russian Federation. (Mailer 2003) In practice, this does not seem to have an effect, because many franchisors operating in Russia charge several franchise fees.
- ❑ In franchising the quality control over goods and services, produced by franchisee, is the *right* of franchisor, but not his *obligation,* as it's said in the article 1031. This liability of the franchisor is unrealistic, because franchisor is obviously unable to provide such control, if he has substantial number of franchise outlets. (Mailer 2003) However, the article sets the obligation "unless provided otherwise by the contract of commercial concession", which implies that it is possible to agree otherwise.
- ❑ Article 1034 "Right-holder's Responsibility for Claims Filed Against User", stating that the franchisor shall be held subsidiarily liable for claims against the franchisee, contradicts the main principle of the franchise system - the sovereignty of franchisor and franchisee. Subsidiary liability gradually decreases the advantages of franchising in comparison with development by establishing corporate branch enterprises. (Mailer 2003)
- ❑ The statement, that the franchisee "shall have the right on the expiry of the contract term to renew the contract on the same terms" (Article 1035) is not justified, as in 5 - 10 years (usual

term of the contract) conditions could substantially differ. Franchisor shall only "have the right to refuse to renew the contract, provided that within three years after the expiry of the contract term he will not conclude with other". (Mailer 2003) The perpetual right to renewal on the same terms without any permitted leeway to adjust to changing circumstances, business practices and laws makes the education possibilities limited to what one would expect in a managed economy, not in a free one (Mendelsohn 1996). There are a lot of reasons that could emerge in the process of business for the franchisor not to renew the contract with the franchisee. The franchisor should have the right to change his system. Insisting on renewal of the contract "on the same terms" cuffs his hands and legs. (Mailer 2003)

❑ The possibility of termination of the unlimited contract by simply notifying the other party six months in advance, as written in the Article 1037, is highly disputable. Usually both parties make substantial investments into the business. The usual practice is that the franchise contract would be terminated only in case one of the parties violates its obligations. Unmotivated termination of the contract could result in serious financial loses for one of the parties. (Mailer 2003) Anyway, the article can be overlooked by simply stating the contract term in the agreement.

❑ According to the article 1039: "Should the rightholder change his firm name or commercial mark the rights to use of which constitute a complex of exclusive rights, the contract of commercial concession shall remain valid with respect to the rightholders´ new firm name or commercial mark, unless the user demands cancellation of the contract and compensation of losses." The statement is very strange and it is not clear, where such right emerges from, and what "comprehensive reduction" is. (Mailer 2003)

REFERENCES

Alon, I. (2004), "Key Success Factors in the Franchising Sector in the Retailing Sector," *Proceedings of the Southwest Academy of Management*, (45th Annual Meeting) Orlando, Florida (March 3-6).

Alon, I. (2001), Interview: International Franchising in China with Kodak. *Thunderbird International Business Review*, 43(6), 737-754.

Alon, I. and M. Banai (2000), "Executive Insights: Franchising Opportunities and Threats in Russia," *Journal of International Marketing*, 8(1), 104-119.

Alon, I (1999), *The Internationalization of U.S. Franchising Systems (Transnational Business and Corporate Culture Problems and Opportunities)*, New York: Garland Publishing.

Alon, I. and D. McKee (1999), "Towards a Macro Environmental Model of International Franchising," *Multinational Business Review*, 7(1), 76-82.

Alon, I. and M.K. Toncar (1999), "Franchising Opportunities and Impediments in Russia," *Proceedings of the 13th Annual Society of Franchising Conference*. March 6-7, 1999. Miami, FL, USA.

Alon, I., M. Toncar and D. McKee (2000), "Evaluating Foreign-Market Expansion for International Franchising Expansion," *Proceedings of 14th Annual International Society of Franchising Conference*. Feb. 19-20, 2000. San Diego, CA, USA.

BBC (2003), US Shares Russia Poll Concerns. 9.12.2003. Retrieved in 9.12.2003, from http://news.bbc.co.uk/2/hi/europe/3300483.stm

Central Bank of the Russian Federation (The) (2003), Main Macro Economic Indicators in 2003. Retrieved in November 10, 2003, from http://www.cbr.ru/eng/statistics/credit_statistics/print.asp?file=macro_03_e.htm

Christy, R.L. and S.M. Haftel (1992), "Franchising: Entry and Developmental Strategies in the Former Soviet Union," *Proceedings of the 6th Annual Society of Franchising Conference*. Feb. 1-2, 1992. Palm Springs, CA, USA.

Christy, R.L. and S.M. Haftel (1993), "Pizza Hut in Moscow: Post-Coup System Development and Expansion," *Proceedings of the 7th Annual Society of Franchising Conference*. Feb. 7-8, 1993. San Francisco, CA, USA.

Dant, R.P. (1995), "Motivation for Franchising: Rhetoric Versus Reality," *International Small Business Journal*, 14(1), 10-32.

Doherty, Anne Marie and Barry Quinn (1999), "International retail franchising: an agency theory perspective," *International Journal of Retail and Distribution Management*, 27 (6), 224-236.

Economist (The) (2005), Retrieved in June 2, 2005, from http://www.economist.com/countries/Russia/

Ernst andYoung (2003), *Russia Law Brief*. EY LAW February 2003. Registration Procedure for Franchise Agreements. Retrieved in November 11, 2003, from http://www.ey.com/global/download.nsf/Russia_E/Law_Feb_03/$file/EYLaw_02_03 e.pdf

Gorovaia, N. (2003), "Performance of Franchising Networks: Conceptual Framework," *The Proceedings of the First EMNet-Conference on "Economics and Management of Franchising Networks"*. June 26-28, 2003. Vienna, Austria.

Grunhagen, Marko, Robert A. Mittelstaed (2002), "Multi-Unit Franchising: An Opportunity for Franchisees Globally?" in *International Franchising in Industrialized Markets: North America, the Pacific Rim, and Other Countries*, Dianne H.B. Welsh and Ilan Alon, eds., CCH: Chicago, IL.

Kamins, J. (2002), Analysis of Key Franchising Factors Cross-Sectioned by Country of Eurasia, and Region of Russia 2002. BISNIS Franchise Development Matrix 2003.

Retrieved   October   10,   2003,   from
        http://www.bisnis.doc.gov/bisnis/isa/franchise/EurasiaFranchMatrixBISNIS.xls
Kaufmann, P.J. and H. Leibenstein (1988), "International Business Format Franchising and
        Retail Entrepreneurship: A Possible Source of Retail Know-how for Developing
        Countries," *Journal of Development Planning*, 18, 165-179.
Kellman, B. (1989), "Legal Aspects of Forming and Managing an American Franchise or
        Commercial Enterprise in the Soviet Union," *Proceeding of the 3rd Annual Society of
        Franchising Conference*. Jan. 29-31, 1989. Bal Harbor, FL, USA.
Kuzmina, E. (1997), Franchising in Russia. *U.S. and Foreign Commercial Service and U.S.
        Department   of   State*.   Retrieved   in   August   4,   2003,   from
        http://www.bisnis.doc.gov/bisnis/isa/9707fran.htm
Mailer, A. (2003), "Analysis of the Chapter 54 of the Civil Code of Russian Federation
        'Commercial Concession',". In *Franchise Opportunities Guide in Russia*. Moscow,
        Russia: Russian Association for Development of Franchising.
Mendelsohn, M. (1996), "Russia's Franchise-Unfriendly Code," *Franchising World*, 28(5), 44-
        45.
New York Times (2003), Russia's Voting for Parliament Bolsters Putin. 8.12.2003 Retrieved in
        December   9,   2003,   from
        http://query.nytimes.com/gst/abstract.html?res=F10D17F73B590C7B8CDDAB0994
        DB404482
Picot-Coupet, K and G. Cliquet (2003), "Retail Franchising As an Entry Mode in Eastern
        European and Russian Markets in Transition: Literature Review and Research
        Perspective," *Proceedings of the 17th Annual International Society of Franchising
        Conference*. Feb. 14-16, 2003. San Antonio, TX, USA.
Pizanti, Inbar and Miri Lerner (2003), "Examining control and autonomy in the franchisor-
        franchisee relationship," *International Small Business Journal*, 21 (2), 131.
Quinn, Barry and Anne Marie Doherty (2000), "Power and control in international retail
        franchising - Evidence from theory and practice," *International Marketing Review*,
        17 (4/5), 354-372.
Roehl, W., S. Swerdlow and D.H.B. Welsh (1999), "Organizational Commitment, Job
        Satisfaction, Training and Other Important Factors in the Success of Managing a
        Franchise Operation in Russia: A Research Agenda for the Future," *Proceedings of
        the 13th Annual Society of Franchising Conference*. March 6-7, 1999. Miami, FL,
        USA.
Russian Association for Franchise Development (2003), "*Franchise Opportunities Guide in
        Russia*," Moscow, Russia.
Sarkisov, O. (2002), Franchising in Russia. *U.S. and Foreign Commercial Service and U.S.
        Department   of   State*.   Retrieved   in   August   4,   2003,   from
        http://www.bisnis.doc.gov/bisnis/country/020930RusFranchise.htm
Shane, Scott and Chester Spell (1998), "Factors for New Franchise Success," *Sloan
        Management Review*, 39 (3), 43-50.
Swerdlow, S., W. Roehl and D.H.B. Welsh (2001), "Hospitality Franchising in Russia for the
        21st Century: issues, strategies and challenges," In Welsh, D.H.B. and I. Alon, (2001)
        *International Franchising in Emerging Markets: Central and Eastern Europe and
        Latin America*. Chicago, IL, USA: CCH Inc., 149-170.
Swerdlow, S. and D.H.B. Welsh (1992), "The Future of Franchising in the U.S.S.R.: A
        Statistical Analysis of the Opinions of Soviet University Students," *Proceedings of
        the 6th Annual Society of Franchising Conference*. Feb. 1-2, 1992. Palm Springs, CA,
        USA.
Transparency International (2005), Global Corruption Report 2005. Retrieved in June 2, 2005,
        from http://www.globalcorruptionreport.org/
U.S. Department of Commerce (2002), Russia Fact Sheet 2002. BISNIS Resource Center.
        Retrieved   in   October   20,   2003,   from
        http://www.bisnis.doc.gov/bisnis/bisdoc/2002RSFactsheet.htm

Welsh, D.H.B. and I. Alon (2001), "A Look at International Franchising in Emerging Markets," In Welsh, D.H.B. and I. Alon, (2001) *International Franchising in Emerging Markets: Central and Eastern Europe and Latin America.* Chicago, IL, USA: CCH Inc., 33-41.

Welsh, D.H.B. and S. Swerlow (1991), "Opportunities and Challenges for Franchisors in the U.S.S.R.: Preliminary Results of a Survey of Soviet University Students," *Proceedings of the 5th Annual Society of Franchising Conference.* Feb. 9-10, 1991. Miami Beach, FL, USA.

World Bank (2003), World Bank Indicators 2003. Retrieved in November 11, 2003, from http://www.worldbank.org/data/wdi2003/index.htm

World Bank (2005a), World Bank Indicators 2005. Retrieved in June 2, 2005, from http://www.worldbank.org/data/wdi2003/index.htm

World Bank (2005b), Russian Economic Report. Retrieved in June 2, 2005, from http://www.worldbank.org.ru.

World Economic Forum (2004), Global Competitiveness Report. Retrieved in June 2, 2005, from http://www.globalcorruptionreport.org/gcr2005/download/english/corruption_research_%20I.pdf

Zeidman, P.F. (1995), "Franchising in Russia: Sorting It All Out," *Franchising World,* 27(6), 34-35.

Chapter 10
Franchising in the Philippines

Ilan Alon
Crummer Graduate School of Business, Rollins College

J. Mark Munoz
Tabor School of Business, Millikin University

INTRODUCTION

With a population of around 80 million, and proximity to the neighboring Asian markets the Philippines has become an important franchise hub in South East Asia. In a report prepared by the Philippine Franchise Association, it was stated that the Philippine franchise industry grew ten times over the last five years. According to the association, the franchise success rate of 90% was significantly higher than the 25% success rate of traditional retail ventures (Philippine Franchise Association 2003).

Much research has appeared on the subject of international franchising in emerging markets in recent years (e.g., Welsh and Alon 2001; Alon and Welsh 2001). However, previous research on emerging economies has been too general to apply to specific countries because of the great variance in consumer incomes, average education levels, transportation and logistical systems, human resources, and marketing information among countries that are collectively referred to as transitional economies (Batra 1997). Interestingly, the Philippines is in a unique category of its own. Though its economic environment is parallel to those of emerging locations, it has a rich pool of highly skilled professionals that match those in developed countries. Philippine executives are considered to be among the Asia's best.

According to a report provided by the Philippine Franchise Association, the number of franchisors in the country has been steadily increasing. Table 10.1 shows the phenomenal growth of the franchising sector in the Philippines, in addition to the number of foreign franchisors, local franchisors, and the percentage of foreign franchisors. The data points out to the fact that since 1996, the total number of franchisors grew almost six fold, the number of international franchisors operating in the Philippines still exceeds the number of local franchisors, although the proportion of foreign franchisors has declined somewhat.

Table 10.1: Franchise Growth, Foreign vs Local

Year	Foreign Franchisors	Local Franchisors	Total	% of Foreign Franchisors
1995	47	64	111	58%
1996	94	92	186	49%
1997	135	115	250	46%
1998	280	162	442	37%
1999	306	202	508	40%
2000/2001	360	348	708	49%

Source: Data from the Philippine Franchise Association

FRANCHISING ENVIRONMENT IN THE PHILIPPINES

The franchising environment in emerging markets can be judged from political, legal, economic, financial, and social perspectives. These environmental factors have shown to be of high research value to international franchisors in choosing a host country for expansion (Alon and McKee 1999). Table 10.2 summarizes the favorable and unfavorable factors associated with the franchising environment in the Philippines.

Table10. 2: Business Environment in the Philippines

Environment	Description	Favorable/ Unfavorable
Political	-Moderate to high political risk, government instability, emphasis placed on personal relationships, and loyalties	-Unfavorable
Legal	-Recent implementation of the Intellectual Property Code	-Favorable
	-Uncertainty on the evenness or fairness of implementation	-Unfavorable
Economic	-Market potential of about 80 million	-Favorable
	-Large pool of skilled labor and management talent	-Favorable
	-Monetary instability	-Unfavorable
	-Moderately developed infrastructure	-Favorable
	-Spread out population concentrations	-Favorable
	-Moderately mature market with opportunities available in developing geographic locations	-Favorable
	-Competitive climate	-Either

Environment	Description	Favorable/ Unfavorable
Financial	-Large financial sector with extensive resources and infrastructure	-Favorable
	-Currency Devaluation	-Unfavorable
	-Declining bank lending rates	-Favorable
	-Declining inflation rate	-Favorable
	-Fiscal Transparency	-Favorable
Social	-Positive attitude towards US products	-Favorable
	-Cultural affinity	-Favorable
	-Language compatibility	-Favorable
	-Threats to peace and order	-Unfavorable

Political and Legal Environment

The level of political risk in the Philippines may be described as moderate to high. Philippine-style democracy is present at all political levels and is marked by individual loyalties and an interlocking system of personal relationships (US Department of State, 2001). In the 2002 Corruption Perceptions Index conducted by Transparency International, the Philippines ranked 77, and had the same ranking as Pakistan, Romania, and Zambia. With regard to national security, the country continues to face peace and order challenges both from the Muslim separatist movement in the region of Mindanao (Moro Islamic Liberation Front, MILF), and the communist insurgency group (New People's Army, NPA).

Despite pervasive interlocking relationships, corruption, and occasional insurgency of Moslem separatists, the Philippine government has taken proactive measures to create an investment friendly business environment. A report by the US-Asean Business Council pointed out that the Philippine Constitution guarantees the basic rights of all investors and enterprises. The following investor rights are guaranteed:
(1) Freedom from expropriation without just compensation,
(2) Right to remit profits, capital gains, and dividends within the guidelines of the Bangko Sentral ng Pilipinas (BSP), the country's central monetary authority,
(3) Right to remit the proceeds of the liquidation of investments,
(4) Right to obtain foreign exchange to meet principal and interest payments on foreign obligations.

In addition, the country is a member of the Multilateral Investment Guarantee Agency (MIGA). Investments in MIGA member countries are protected against risks associated with host government restrictions on currency conversion and transfers, expropriation, war, revolution or civil disturbance. The agency serves as a guarantor and co-insurer for investment risks associated with contract repudiation by the host government. (U.S.-Asean Business Council, 2003)

With regard to franchising in particular, foreign-based franchisors typically enter the Philippine market by appointing a franchisee. The franchisor is accorded the right to collect a fee for the use of the name or trademark. In addition, royalties on sales may be collected. Philippine retail laws (Retail Trade, Republic Act 1180) prohibit foreign equity positions in franchises. In many cases, American franchisors are franchising in the Philippines through the use of licensing agreements (US Department of State, 2001).

In conjunction with the government's trade liberalization policies, prior laws pertaining to patents, trademarks, and copyrights have been replaced with the Intellectual Property Code of 1998. With the new law under effect, franchisors are not required to register their franchises in the condition that contract agreements do not violate provisions under Section 87, and meet all required provisions under Section 88. As a result of the new law, ceilings on royalties were removed and have paved the way for the introduction of varying master franchise fees ranging from $100,000-$400,000. Table 10.3 outlines the mandatory clauses under Section 88 of the Philippine Intellectual Property Code of 1998. Table 10.4 presents clauses of prohibition under Section 87 of the Philippine Intellectual Property Code of 1998. It is still unclear if in fact the implementation of the Philippine Intellectual Property Code may have been marred by corruption and the extension of privileges to individuals or companies that possess close relationships with government officials.

Table 10.3: Mandatory Clauses - Section 88, Philippine Intellectual Property Code of 1998

1	The laws of the Philippines will govern the interpretation of the same and in the event of litigation, the venue will be the proper court where the licensee has its principal office
2	Continued access to improvement in techniques and processes related to the technology will be made available during the period of the technology transfer arrangement
3	In the event the technology transfer arrangement will provide for arbitration, the Procedure of Arbitration of the Arbitration Law of the Philippines or the Arbitration Rules of the United Nations Commission on International Trade Law (UNCITRAL) or the Rules of Conciliation and Arbitration of the International Chamber of Commerce (ICC) will apply and the venue of the arbitration will be the Philippines or any neutral country
4	The Philippine taxes on all payments relating to the technology transfer arrangement will be borne by the licensor

Source: (U.S. Department of State, 2001)

Table 10.4: Prohibited Clauses - Section 87, Philippine Intellectual Property Code of 1998

1	Those which impose upon the licensee the obligation to acquire from a specific source capital goods, intermediate products, raw materials, and other technologies, or of permanently employing personnel indicated by the licensor
2	Those pursuant to which the licensor reserves the right to fix the sale or resale of the products manufactured on the basis of the license
3	Those that contain restrictions regarding the volume and structure of production
4	Those that prohibit the use of competitive technologies in a nonexclusive technology transfer arrangement
5	Those that establish a full or partial option in favor of the licensor
6	Those that obligate the licensee to transfer for free to the licensor the inventions or improvements that may be obtained through the use of licensed technology
7	Those that require payment of royalties to the owners of patents for patents which are not used
8	Those that prohibit the licensee to export the licensed product unless justified for the protection of the legitimate interest of the licensor such as exports to countries where exclusive licenses to manufacture and/or distribute the licensed product(s) have already been granted
9	Those which restrict the use of the technology supplied after the expiration of the technology transfer arrangement, except in cases of early termination of the technology transfer arrangement, due to reason(s) attributable to the licensee
10	Those which require payments for patents and other industrial property rights after their expiration, termination arrangement
11	Those which require that the technology recipient will not contest the validity of any of the patents of the technology supplier
12	Those which restrict the research and development activities of the licensee designed to absorb and adopt the transferred technology to local conditions or to initiate research and development programs in connection with new products, processes, or equipment
13	Those which prevent the licensee from adapting the imported technology to local conditions, or introducing innovation to it, as long as it does not impair the quality standards prescribed by the licensor
14	Those which exempt the licensor for liability for non-fulfillment of his responsibilities under the technology transfer arrangement and/or liability arising from third party suits brought about by the use of the licensed product or the licensed technology
15	Other clauses with equivalent effects

Source: (U.S. Department of State, 2001)

Economic Environment

The Philippines has an auspicious environment that for franchise growth according to the Philippine Franchise Association (2003). With 7,107 islands and a potential customer base of around 80 million, the country is predisposed to attract international franchisors. Data featured at the CIA World Fact Book indicated that in 2002, the Philippines' estimated GDP was $379.7 billion, and the GDP posted real growth rate of 4.4%, and GDP per capita of about $4,600 (CIA World Fact Book, 2004). The country's infrastructure is good when compared to other emerging markets. Table 10.5 shows some basic statistics on the Philippine infrastructure.

Table 10.5: Selected Information Depicting the Philippine Infrastructure

Electricity	Electricity production is at 45.21 billion kWh
Telephone main lines	6.98 million
Mobile phone users	11.35 million
Telephone system	Good international radiotelephone and submarine cable services; domestic and inter-island service adequate
Television broadcast stations	75
Televisions	3.7 million
Internet users	4.5 million
Highways	Paved – 42,419 km, Unpaved – 159,575 km
Ports and Harbors	15
Airports	257

Source: The CIA World Factbook, 2004

The Asia Pacific Management Forum conducted a recent survey on the best city to do business in Asia. The survey explored locations that may be described as possessing the ability to serve as a central hub or headquarters when doing business in the Asian region. Factors looked at in the survey included : quality and convenience of business facilities (including value for money), business travel factors, business accommodation, business climate, communication facilities including quality of internet connections, functionality of government and financial controls/protection/tariffs/duties, and political risk. One of the major Philippine cities, Manila ranked number 3 in the survey. It posted a ranking higher than popular Asian destinations like Hong Kong, Singapore, Jakarta (Indonesia), Tokyo (Japan), Sydney (Australia), and Shanghai (China), (Asia Pacific Management Forum, 2003).

The country has a labor force of an estimated 33.7 million in 2002, with 45% engaged in agriculture, 15% in industry, and 40% in the service sector. Data from the Economist Intelligence Unit point out to the fact that the labor cost per hour of $0.73 in 2002 has virtually remained unchanged since 1999 (Economist Intelligence Unit, 2004).

Financial Environment

Since 1992, the value of the Philippine peso has declined significantly as measured against the US dollar. The exchange rate in 1992 hovered around P 25.00 to 1 US$, in 2003 the rate was P55.00 to 1 US$ (Banco Central ng Pilipinas, 2004). This significant currency devaluation is partly attributable to the Asian crisis of 1997 and partly to the political instability that continually lingered in the country. This landscape has affected foreign franchisors in the Philippines since the devaluation adversely affected consumer spending, increased the cost of importation, and challenged the revenue streams of the local franchisees. Nevertheless, the landscape also forced the introduction of productivity enhancements and heightened the creativity levels among franchise operators.

Since 2003, there were 18,644 banks and non-banking financial institutions in the Philippines with total resources amounting to 4,542.7 billion pesos (Banko Sentral ng Pilipinas, 2003). This data suggests that there is adequate capital and infrastructure available within the country to adequately support franchise development and expansion.

Additional data provided by the Philippine Central Bank point out to the fact that the Bank Average Lending Rates have declined from 16.2% in 1997 to 9.5% in 2003 while Inflation Rates have also decreased from 5.9% in 1997 to 3.1% in 2003.

Potential Philippine franchisees utilize a wide range of options to acquire business capitalization. Casanova (2003) cites typical financing options to include: business owners or franchisor, friends, family, and relatives, banks and non-traditional sources (ie, loan sharks), and the local community. More recent approaches have taken the form of equity participation through the use of venture capital firms, angel investors, and public listing. Additionally, capital support for franchisees are available through the Small Business Guarantee and Finance Corporation (SBGFC) and a specialized loan program for franchise operations recently implemented by the Development Bank of the Philippines (DBP).

Social Environment

The franchise industry in the Philippines has proven to be resilient and sustainable. Franchising continues to be one of the fastest growing sectors in the economy. The growing demand for new products and services attest that there is plenty of room for new players and many opportunities for U.S. companies (U.S. Department of State, 2001). Philippine consumers hold a favorable disposition towards American brands, resulting to US franchisors' market dominance with over 70% of the entire market. Successful businesspeople typically look at franchising as a viable investment option in expanding their business operations. There are excellent franchising opportunities in food and services-based franchises according to the U.S. State Department (2001).

The Philippine culture has demonstrated familiarity and affinity for the American value system. Philippine consumers have long been exposed to US products, films, music, and various mass media advertising. The United States traditionally has been the Philippines' largest foreign investor, with about $3.3 billion in estimated investment as of end-2002 comprising 22% of the Philippines' foreign direct investment stock (US Department of State 2001). Millions of Filipinos reside in the US and travel back to the Philippines paving the way for widespread cultural convergence. Furthermore, 94% of Filipinos speak English (Philippine Franchise Association, 2003).

The country has been a staunch US supporter in the war against terrorism. Despite this, the locally-based Muslim separatist group (MILF) has been continually linked to the al Queda terrorist network of Osama bin Laden. The group was allegedly responsible for a spate of bombings and kidnap-for-ransom activities in the country. This landscape has bred fear among the local residents as well as potential international investors.

COMPETITIVE LANDSCAPE OF FRANCHISING IN THE PHILIPPINES

Though, evidence of franchising was present in the Philippines as early as 1910 with the entry of the Singer sewing machines, resurrected in the 1960s with A&W Restaurants, it was only in the late 1990s that the growth picked up. Data gathered from the Philippine franchise association point out to the growth of foreign franchisors from only 47 in 1995 to 360 in 2001. Franchising in the Philippines is far from maturity. The growth may be attributed to several factors including population increases, evolving consumer tastes and preferences, creative product introductions, and intensified marketing efforts designed to create a demand.

Despite the recent growth, a researcher for the Center of Food and Agri-Business at the University of Asia Pacific, Ronald Mark Omaga, stated that "Mr. Samie Lim, president of the Philippine Franchise Association believes the market for franchises in the Philippines is still young, unlike markets in the US and Canada." (Omaga, 2004). In addition, not all international franchisors have tapped into all the 21 provinces in the Philippines with a population exceeding 1 million. Domestic franchisors are cognizant of the growing opportunities in untapped and developing locations and will likely be active participants in future franchise expansions.

The local environment may also be described as highly competitive in certain sectors, especially for the food and retail businesses. Largely, the battle grounds for franchises are in large malls and well-developed urban locations. As a result, competitive pressures relating to price, quality, service, productivity, and operational efficiencies exist. This landscape is attractive in a sense that there is evidence that a market exists and forces franchisors to be at their creative best. However, the landscape becomes unattractive when survival tactics lead to price wars and other forms of unhealthy rivalry.

Data featured in a report by the Philippine Franchise Association suggest that while food franchises dominated the Philippine franchising scene in 1995, since 1996 non-food franchises have started to dominate the market. Table 10.6 shows the evolving sector composition of franchisors in the Philippines.

Table 10.6: Ratio of Philippine Franchisors, Food vs. Non-Food

Year	Food Franchisors	Non-Food Franchisors
1995	70%	30%
1996	48%	52%
1997	47%	53%
1998	47%	53%
1999/2000	40%	60%
2001	41%	59%

Source: Philippine Franchise Association, 2004

In 2001, there were 290 food franchises, and 418 non-food franchises. Food franchises typically include bakeshops, bars and cafes, convenience stores, ice cream parlors, pizza parlors, restaurants, and water refilling stations. Non food franchises include beauty parlors, business services, clothing stores, computer training schools, laundry services, video shops, computer training schools and similar ventures.

The dominant presence of US franchises in the Philippines has become evident with the high visibility of food franchises such as McDonald's, Kentucky Fried Chicken, Dunkin Donuts, Greenwich, Domino's, Sbarro, Starbucks, Dairy Queen and many more. US non-food franchises including: Roto Rooter, Computer Assisted Learning, Postnet, Computer Tots, Levi's, Wrangler, Calvin Klein, Revlon, Esprit, Guess, Gap and several more. Omaga (2004) lists selected foreign and local food franchises in the Philippines with data gathered from the Philippine Franchise Association. Table 10.7 and 10.8 show selected franchisors (food and non-food) that chose to operate in the franchising sector in the Philippines.

Table 10.7: Selected Foreign Food Franchises in the Philippines

7-Eleven	Dreyer's	Numero Uno Pizza
Aji-Ichiban	Dunkin Donuts	Orange Julius
A & W Restaurant	El Pollo Loco	Outback Steakhouse
(Friday's) American Bar	Famous Amos	Pizza Hut
Au Bon Pain	Fat Tuesday	Pizza Inn
Auntie Anne's Pretzels	Fiorgelato	Pho Hoa Vietnamese
Baskin & Robbins	Flamers Charbroiled	Noodle House
Beavertails	Foster Freeze	Popperoo
Bee Cheng Hiang	General Nutrition Center	Quickly Health Drinks
Food Stuff Pte. Ltd.	Haagen Daz	Sbarro
Benihana	Hard Rock Café	Seattle's Best
Bennigans	Henry J.Beans Bar & Grill	Shakey's
Blue Bunny Ice Cream	Hotdog on a Stick	Shooters of Bar
Brownies Fried Chicken	Italianni's	Starbucks Café
& Burgers	Kenny Rogers Roasters	St. Cinnamon
Burger King	KFC	Subway Sandwiches
Café Appasionato	Kublai	Sushi Bar
California Pizza Kitchen	La Creperie	T-Salon
Candy Bouquet	Lifestream	Texas Chicken
Carl's Jr.	Little Caesars	TGI Friday's
Charmy Foods	Lord Stow Bakery	Thai BBQ
Cinnabon	McDonald's	The Country's Best Yogurt
Cinnzeo	Meat Shop	Tony Romas
Chili's Grill & Bar Rest.	Mini Stop	UCC Ueshima Coffee Co.
Country Style Donut	Mister Donut	US Health Juice Bar
Country Waffles	Mrs. Fields Cookies	Weigh Eat All
Dairy Queen Ice Cream	Nacho Fast	Wendy's
Delifrance	New Jersey's Chicken	Wimpy Hamburger
Dippin' Dots	New Zealand Natural	Winchell's Donut
Dome Café	Ice Cream	Yogen Fruz
Domino's Pizza	Oliver's Super Sandwich	

Source: Philippine Franchise Association

Table 10.8: Selected Local Food Franchises in the Philippines*

Alex III Restaurant	Giacominos	Nacho King
Almon Marina	Goldilocks	New Kamemeshi House
AM/PM Store	Goto King	Orbitz Pearl Shakes
Ang Tunay na	Granny's Chicken	Padi's Point
Pancit Malabon	Greenwich	Pancake House
Angelino's	Grocerific	Pancit ng Taga Malabon
Barbeque Stik	Henlin	Pancit Malabon Express
Better Than Ice Cream	Herc's Pizza	Potato Corner
Big Mak	Pasta Presto	Potatobilities
Binalot	Ho-Lee Chow	Racks Restaurant
Brothers Burger	Ilonggo Grill	Red Ribbon
Burger Machine	Jack's Pizza	Rice Time
Cabalen Restaurant	Jellagoo	Rolling Pin
Candy Corner	Jollibee	Shago
Candy Mix	Josephine Restaurant	Scoop Shop
Candy World	Jaunchito's Bibingka	Sinangag Express
Casa Ilongga	Julie's Bakeshop	Slim Jims
Chichapops	Korean Palace	Smokey's
Chopstix	Kowloon House	Sugar House
Chowking	Le Coeur De France	Supermelt Ensaymada
Cindy's	Lot's A Pizza	Swift Shop
Coffee California	Majestic Ham	Taco Mio
Coolman Halo-Halo	Max's Restaurant	Tapa King
Dimsum & Dumplings	Merced Bakeshop	Taters
Don Don	Miggy's Super Tacos	Tom Sawyer's
Don Henrico's	Minute Burger	Tropical Hut Hamburger
During's	Monterey Meats	Universe Cybercafe
Europa Delicatessen	Mongolian Barbeque	Zagu Foods
Ferrino's Bibingka	Mongolian Stop	

*excludes water refilling stations
Source: Philippine Franchise Association

An article featured in the website of the Women into the New Network for Entrepreneurial Reinforcement (WINNER) network in the Philippines cites several underlying reasons for the growth in Philippine franchising "One is the expanding local customer base, which represents 14% of the total ASEAN market, and the current 3.6% growth (as of 2000) in personal consumption habits of consumers. Another is the growing preference for convenience shopping, technological breakthroughs improving operations efficiency and facilitating expansion, and the promotion on the growth of small and medium enterprises. Still another is the rising quality of the workforce which multiplies productivity (Winner Network, 2004).

It is a common practice for international franchisors to offer attractive financing options and marketing support to their franchisees in the Philippines in order to facilitate the completion of deal structures. Local franchisees that receive extensive support from their international franchisors are provided a more convenient and expedited route towards business success.

The Philippine Franchise Association is aggressively attempting to position the Philippines to become the franchise hub of Asia. Cited reasons that contribute to the likelihood of the achievement of this goal are as follows:

(1) A large majority of Filipinos speak English,

(2) The country has an inherently huge population that is estimated to reach 100 million by 2014,

(3) Continually growing franchise sector,

(4) Proximity to neighboring Asian markets by airplane Taiwan (1.4 hours), Hong Kong (1.4 hours), Singapore (3 hours), Thailand (3 hours), China (3.25 hours), Malaysia (3.3 hours) South Korea (3.5 hours) , Japan (4 hours), and

(5) Large pool of skilled labor and managers in diverse fields. In addition, the Philippines offers relatively low labor cost that makes it ideal as a test market or jump off point for the rest of Southeast Asia.

The infrastructure in major metropolitan cities like Manila, Cebu and Davao is comparable to that of developed locations in Asia. Entering the Philippine market to establish a regional headquarter for Asia may soon become an appealing option to international franchisors.

Domestic franchisors in the Philippines have also started to explore international markets. Dominant food franchisors in the Philippines include Jollibee, Goldilocks, Chowking, and Max's. Non-food franchisors include Penshoppe, Kamiseta, Crystal Clear, and Bench.

A popular local food franchisor, Jollibee has started to successfully penetrate foreign markets as a result of their ability to build on a niche market of overseas Filipinos who have retained a strong preference for Filipino cuisine (Winner Network, 2004). Jollibee has over 400 outlets in the Philippines alone, and has enjoyed sustained success in the local market. The Inquirer News Network (2004) mentioned the company's recent acquisition of an 85% stake in Belmont Enterprises Ventures Ltd, the group that owns and operates the 77-store Yonghe King Restaurant chain in China. The acquisition increased the Jollibee store network to 1,065 worldwide from the current 988 and has turned the company into a major force in the Asian restaurant business. Jollibee's international presence includes US, Hong Kong, Brunei, Indonesia.

An article at International Franchise Association website (2003) stated that Chairman of the Philippine Franchise Association, Samie Lim is confident that franchising is on its way to become one of the top 5 industries in the Philippines in the next 10 years. The article quoted Samie Lim as saying that "The Philippines is likely to become a mature market with a total of 1,500 franchises in the next eight years...this is still an infant industry which we can export to China."

The Department of Trade and Industry in the Philippines has lent support to the franchising industry by embarking on a program called "Order Negosyo." Negosyo is a Philippine term for business. The objective of the government program is to invite interested individuals, especially overseas Filipinos, to explore business opportunities related to franchising. Included in the list of local franchisees are : Bench (clothing), Business Box (business services), Goto King (food), and Mr. Quickie (repair service). Franchise fees range from P 200,000 – P 4,000,000 (approximately $3636 to $72,727), (Department of Trade and Industry, 2004).

A Philippine Franchise Association Report cited a USAID-funded study that identified the growth areas for Philippine franchising to be: Business Services, Security Services, Printing and Publishing, Food and Beverage, Car Service and Accessories, Health Services, Cosmetics and Toiletries, Maintenance and Cleaning, Laundry Services, Hotels and Motels, and Retail.

De la Cruz (2003) quoted the president of the Association of Filipino Franchisers, Inc. (AFFI) Pacita Juan as saying, "You do not franchise a fad because this does not last very long. You should be franchising a trend. The trend now is coffee shops, laundromats, and home delivery." The Philippine Franchise Association's vision for the Philippine market in the next five years is anchored on a three-pronged approach. Table 10.9 presents an overview of the planned expansion strategy.

Table 10.9:Philippine Franchise Association Strategic Vision and Expansion

Scale	Strategy
Large	International expansion – through the use of territorial master franchise for Asia-Pacific, assisting in the exportation of top Philippine franchisors, attracting international franchisors to use the country as a regional hub for Asia-Pacific
Medium	National Expansion – expand existing franchises into the provincial areas and broaden networks to operate over 100 units
Small	Develop Small and Medium Enterprises (SME's) – by bringing successful provincial franchise concepts into metropolitan locations, and by making franchise more affordable (under $20,000)

Source : Philippine Franchise Association, 2004

STRATEGIC CONTROL MEASURES

International franchising into fast-growing and emerging locations may lead to notable opportunities and threats. Contractual safeguards and the early anticipation of potential challenges heighten the likelihood of success. There is a need for the establishment of an efficient contractual relation between a franchisor and a franchisee in a manner that best utilizes the franchisor's system know-how and the franchisee's local market knowledge (Caves, Murphy 1976). The approach is beneficial in the context of optimizing revenue streams over the long-term.

The institutional arrangement of franchising is deeply anchored on initial fees and royalty rates (Dnes 1996; Lyons 1997). Dnes (1992) elaborated on the screening theory suggesting fixed fees and related investments eventually attract highly entrepreneurial franchisees. Klein (1980) and Williamson (1985) identified the transaction cost model and pointed out that upfront fees binds the franchisee and prevents the possibility of opportunism.

With regard to the selection of franchisees in the Philippines, however, international franchisors need to find the intricate balance between the availability of capital and talent. There are a multitude of honest, well-trained, entrepreneurial managers capable of devoting time and energy in operating franchises but are constrained by capital. Additionally, lower-cost local franchises are widely available. The utilization of the screening theory and the transaction cost model have to be applied within an appropriate context and perspective.

Caves and Murphy (1976) point out to the challenge of franchisor investment returns when there exist a dependence on the franchisee's inherent capabilities to nurture and deliver core management functions such as marketing and human resources development. In the case of the Philippines, international franchisors are served well by integrating a long-term and growth-oriented viewpoint in franchisee selection and strategy formulation.

A variety of strategies have been utilized in recent years to better define the relationship between a franchisor and a franchisee. In a research report by Windsperger (2001) selected contractual measures were enumerated : Exclusivity Clauses to protect the franchisors brand name (Marvel 1982), Tying Clauses to ensure standards and quality procedures are strictly followed (Meese,1996), and Resale Price Agreements to reduce the risk of brand riding (Mathewson, Winter 1986).

When franchising in a market like the Philippines, understanding and implementing an optimal mix of contractual arrangements may prove to be beneficial.

MARKETING FRAMEWORK FOR INTERNATIONAL FRANCHISING ENTRY

The normative framework of market entry into the Philippines has five components: (1) price, (2) promotion, (3) place, (4) product, and (5) mode of entry. In Table 10.10, the authors summarize the international normative model of entry in to the Philippines.

Table 10.10: Normative Framework of Market Entry in the Philippines

Price of final products	-Charge lower prices than the US markets ; US products and services often can command higher prices than comparable Philippine goods -Use limited assortment and local input to achieve low prices
Franchises	-Use low franchise fee in relation to royalties to achieve quick economies of scale -Use high franchise fee in relation to royalties to hedge against risk and bond the franchisee to the contract
Promotion	-Use U.S.-style promotion, including direct and indirect marketing methods -Use more informative and less comparative advertising
Place	-Enter through the major cities in the National Capital Region like Quezon City or Manila, because these cities have the best distribution networks, infrastructure, and consumer demand -Use several distribution networks according to geographic specialization -Build firm-specific distribution systems where none exist
Product	-Limit product selection -Provide consistent service at affordable prices -Use local production to remain competitive
Mode of Entry	-Find a suitable partner -Use the National Capital Region as entry point -Set up mall stores -Expand selectively to provincial areas

Price

A critical consideration in international franchising is sensitivity to prices in the context of franchise fees and final price of the product. Batra (1997) notes that Western brands are generally higher-priced than domestic brands in transitional economies. In the Philippines, a wide selection of competing products and alternative purchase options are available to consumers, practicality in pricing is therefore a suitable adaptation to the business environment.

As a result of the substantial depreciation of the Philippine peso in recent years, the purchasing power of consumers has weakened and the financial health of prospective franchisors may have likely declined. Sensitivity to price issues would lead to a franchisor's stronger and more sustainable relationship with franchisees and would be a positive contributor to the franchise's success.

Omaga (2004) stated that there has been a notable movement in Philippine franchising from the more expensive food franchise operations like McDonald's or Jollibee that run into millions of pesos to cheaper franchise alternatives like small stall franchises namely Zagu, Orbitz Pearl Shakes, Nacho King, and Potato Corner carts.

The agency theory suggest that a price structure that has a high initial fee relative to royalties bonds the franchisee to the franchise agreement and reduces the need for monitoring the franchisee across borders, which increases the likelihood of internationalization (Alon 1999b). While charging high initial fees relative to royalties may limit the level of risk for international franchisors, this marketing strategy may make the franchise less marketable in the foreign location. It is notable that foreign-based franchisors in the Philippines utilize rates and fees that are beyond the reach of the average Filipino executive or businessman. Additionally, it is possible that the restrictive fees would only attract already wealthy individuals who are engaged in several business ventures and who would not be inclined to take on a hands-on approach in the franchise operation. High fees may also limit the participation of skilled and competent Filipino executives who have the talent and the desire to manage the franchise but lack adequate capital to pay for the franchise fee. Based on the research of Omaga, here we present a selected list of popular food franchises in the Philippines, a brief description, and the franchise fees in Table 10.11.

Table 10.11: Selected Popular Philippine Franchise with Estimated Fees*

Franchise	Description	Peso Fees	In US $
Jollibee	Country's largest fastfood chain ; varying capitalization	P17-25 million	$309K-$454K
Max's Restaurant	Specializes in fired chicken, started franchising in 1998	P10-20 million	$181K-$363K
Zagu Foods	Popularized the pearl-tea or pearl shake in the country	P240,000-P532,000	$4.3K-$9.6K
Red Ribbon	One of the most successful bakeshops in the country	P8-10 million	$145K-$181K
Shakeys	One of the biggest pizza parlor in the country	P6-8 million	$109K-$145K
Mister Donut	One of the leading donut shops	Dine-in (P500,000 – P1 million Take-out (P300,000-P400,000)	Dine-in ($9K-18K) Take-out ($5K-$7K)

Note: The computed fees were based on the exchange rate US$1 = P55.

Omaga's research also point to a growing franchising trend involving smaller-scale food business like fruit juices, natural fruits, halo-halo, processed dried fruits, fruit jams, quick shrimp meals, fish rolls and sandwiches, squid balls, ground "brewed" coffee, soluble "instant" coffee, and cyber-bar coffee-tainment. These operations are offered in non-traditional formats such as kiosks, carts, and trailers which lead to lower rental and operational costs. Furthermore, franchise fees range only from P50,000-P100,000 ($909-$1818).

The Department of Trade and Industry in the Philippines (2004) indicated that the franchisee investment range of $3636 to $72,727 by local franchisors (under the Order Negosyo Program) typically includes : Franchise fee, Marketing study, Store design, Layout assistance, Training programs, Leasehold improvements (outlet construction), Equipment, Signage, and Pre-opening marketing expense and pre-opening supplies.

Promotion

Advertising is a central component in product or service promotion in the Philippines. There are over a hundred advertising agencies in the Philippines, several of them utilize the structure and systems of their US counterparts. Advertising expenditures in 1999 was in excess of $ 800 million with television taking 63%, print 19%, and radio 17% (U.S. Department of State, 2001). With a wide selection of television and radio stations, newspapers, and consumer magazines to choose from franchisors have a ready access to the market segment that they wish to capture.

A number of US firms have used the direct-marketing or multi-level marketing with success in the Philippines. Companies like Tupperware, Avon, and Sara Lee have gained significant in-roads in the market. This also speaks to the fact that brand perception an important factor to consider when promoting a product in the country.

A successful local franchisor in the Philippines, FH/Folded and Hung, pursued an aggressive branding strategy. Vanzi (2003) noted that the company continually provides assistance to franchisees through site selection, store design and layout, intensive hands-on training, marketing and promotional support, and through the integration of a well-planned operating system geared towards maximizing profitability.

Batra (1997) recommends the downplaying of the foreign origin of the products in transition countries due to a consumer's national pride or a "buy local" mentality. While this strategy may work in other transition economies, the quality perception of Western brands would likely work to advantage of the international franchisor in the Philippines.

Place

U.S.-based franchises such as McDonalds, Kentucky Fried Chicken, Levi's, and Wrangler are highly visible in major cities in the Philippines. Many of these franchises are located in major shopping malls in the National

Capital Region (NCR), as well as other key cities in the Visayas and Mindanao regions. The Winner Network (2004) alluded to the fact that colorful frontages and logo designs in the malls have resulted to the mall franchises becoming landmarks and meeting points. The mall outlets offer accessibility, affordability, and convenience that have converged social classes.

As a result of business and consumer congestion in the major cities, the prices of rental properties can be prohibitive and finding a large unused space can be challenge. Occasionally, there are rental spaces that become available in malls due to lease expirations or bankruptcy. These locations are ideal for a franchise start-up due to high foot traffic that exists almost every day of the week. The Department of Trade and Industry (2004) suggest that when located in a mall, the preferred locations are near cinemas, near food courts, near main entrances, or near entrances of main parking lots. The high visibility gained from a mall location, coupled with ease of integration with national advertising and promotions, can contribute to a franchise success.

When locating outside a mall preferred locations include those that are near : churches, public markets, schools, municipal halls, loading and unloading transportation points, and populated residential areas. Alternately, good locations should be within commercial areas and locations with heavy pedestrian traffic (Department of Trade and Industry, 2004).

With regard to distribution, a disparity clearly exists between urbanized and rural locations. While systems in major cities are thorough and efficient, those in rural locations can bog down and result in delays. According to the U.S. Department of State (2001), approximately 85% of the Philippine foreign trade pass through the Port of Manila and 90% of imported products are subsequently distributed to other key cities with the use of trucks and inter-island vessels. Therefore, establishing a franchise initially in the National Capital Region allows a franchisor to tap into a relatively efficient distribution system. Batra (1997) recommends that multinational enterprises in transition economies invest in cost-effective distribution systems to reduce unit prices, develop relationships with select dealers, provide credit and inventory financing to members of distribution channels, and design ways to collect better and more timely market information. While this approach may not be critical in the urbanized cities in the Philippines, it would be appropriate when franchisors start to expand to rural locations in the country.

The Philippine 2002 report by the Census of Population and Housing pointed out that from 1995-2000 the annual population growth rate in the Philippines averaged 2.36%. The report stated that more than half of the 76.5 million population in the 2000 census were located in the Luzon region (55.97%), followed by Mindanao (23.70%), and the Visayas (20.30%). Twenty one (21) provinces in the country had a population of over 1 million. The provinces of Pangasinan, Cebu, Bulacan, Negros Occidental, and Cavite had populations in excess of 2 million. With regard to urban cities, three cities in the Capital

Region and one city in Mindanao had a population of over 1 million. The most populated cities are Quezon City (2.17 million), Manila (1.58 million), Caloocan City (1.18 million), and Davao City (1.15 million), (Philippine National Statistics Office, 2002).

The data suggests that population concentrations are spread out across the country, paving the way for several opportunities for franchise expansions in various locations. Furthermore, population data suggest that the country has an inherently young population with 64% of the population classified in the 0-29 age group.

Product

The consumer expectation in urbanized and metropolitan Philippine cities is comparable to that of major cities around the world. It is therefore a sound strategy for franchisors to be adequately prepared to consistently deliver top-rate quality products and service.

The success of FH/Folded and Hung in the Philippines is attributable to the branding strategy employed by a local managing company, Adenip, Inc. The company has positioned itself as a leading retailer of top quality affordable clothing for men and women. Strategies leading to the company's product success are : strong consumer recognition and loyalty, product excellence, and the introduction of constant innovation that is attuned to the evolving consumer tastes and preferences (Vanzi 2003).

Moreover, the often creative and innovative nature of competing Philippine entrepreneurs could exert a significant pressure on new foreign entrants. International franchisors need to be prepared modify their product or readjust their planned strategy to respond to a competitive and evolving business landscape. Vanzi (2003) notes that comprehensive franchise support packages and innovative business models are offered by franchise operators such as Gourmet's Xpresso Coffee Bar (coffee outlet), Great Image (photo and digital imagery), CIE School System (education), Memory Magic (photo finishing), and Saigon Best (Vietnamese cuisine).

Filipino entrepreneurs are quick to pick-up on American franchising and marketing approaches and use them on local products. Hookway (2004) narrates the case of Ariel Manalac, a seller of duck embryos (*balut*) that are known to be a Filipino specialty and local aphrodisiac. In essence, Manalac implemented five strategic approaches to sell more of the duck embryos:

(1) Product innovation – rather than just offering the traditional product, he introduced special sauces curry or chili to make the taste appealing to a wider market. Additionally, research and development for tempura and tortilla versions of the balut are under way,

(2) Quality control – a chef has been hired to ensure consistent and high quality standards

(3) Location – traditionally the product is sold on the streets by roving vendors shouting "baluuut!", he located his outlets in upscale residential communities that are accessible to a large number of moneyed residents,

(4) Marketing – he conducts market research, designed a logo and patented it, and secured a nutritional content endorsement from the Philippine government,

(5) Franchise – he already has a well developed franchising plan and enlisted the support of a franchising consultant. Plans are underway to expand the franchise to international locations with a large number of Filipino residents.

The Philippine market may be described as price sensitive. Upward price adjustments that may seem minor in the eyes of a Westerner may have a direct and lasting adverse effect to product sales. It is not unusual to see retailers in Philippine malls aggressively offering 50-70% discounts on selected product lines.

Modes of Entry

The four fundamental ways foreign franchisors chose to enter the Philippine market are listed in order of decreasing level of internalization: (1) sole ventures, (2) joint ventures, (3) direct international franchising, and (4) master franchising (Alon 1999a). With respect to the environmental factors that affect franchising modes of entry, a number of factors are proposed. In sum, countries that offer a high levels of economic market potential, a low levels of political instability and risk, a legal environment that protects intellectual property, an efficient court system, and a social environment that is auspicious to franchising are more like to attract franchising investment.

Sole ventures are often pilot operations that are designed to promote franchisors' trademarks aggressively, conduct market research, and modify products and services to cater to local needs. Though, used in the Philippines this is not a predominant entry mode. Joint ventures are implemented by establishing a partnership agreement with a local partner. Direct franchising is also used in the Philippines, particularly through a wholly owned venture, a joint venture, or a home-based franchising system. The Australian Trade Commission (2004) suggest that the most viable franchising entry modes in the Philippine market is through the use of: (1) joint venture with a local firm, or (2) appoint a local company to act as a master franchisee and lead the network expansion in the country.

Master international franchising refers to the contractual agreement between the franchisor and an independently owned sub-franchisor to develop a specified number of franchises in a given area in exchange for the exclusive right to use the business format for a specific period (for a review of master franchising agreements, see Justis and Judd 1986). Alon (2000) proposed that master international franchising is growing mode of entry into emerging markets and developed a model that explains the use of master international franchising by examining the organizational factors of franchising companies. Since, master franchising contracts may take up to 10-20 years, the franchisor is exposed to problems associated with selecting the wrong master operator, quality issues, legal disagreements. In the case of a dispute between the franchisor and the master operator, the master operator may retain the franchisees because they are used to working with the master operator and are reluctant to deal with the franchisor (Burton and Cross 1995). This is essentially the reason why some franchisors decide to test an international market by initially operating company owned outlets.

Hayes (2004) discussed one of the notable master franchise success of the Philippine entrepreneur, Reynaldo Concepcion. Conception owns eight American master franchises namely Days Inn, Century 21, Pizza Inn, The Medicine Shoppe, Century Business Services, Hertz, Blockbuster, and Tutor Time. Many of these ventures continued to be successful despite the economic downturn and political challenges that plagued the Philippines in recent years.

Entering the Philippine market requires careful planning and preparation. We propose five (5) approaches deemed critical to establishing a successful international franchise operation in the Philippines. The recommended steps are as follows:

(1) Find a suitable partner. There are several instances worldwide where international franchising operations were marred by an error in partner selection. The Australian Trade Commission (2004) suggest that regardless of whether an international franchisor decides to enter the Philippine market via a joint venture or a local master franchisee, selection of a partner should be done judiciously as it makes a large impact on the success of a foreign franchise. Potential franchisees may be found during franchise exhibitions in Manila or the other major cities. The American Chamber of Commerce, Philippine Chamber of Commerce, US Embassy, and the Philippine Franchise Association are ideal starting points to meet and gain information on potential franchisees.

(2) Identify and Utilize Strategic Control Measures. Establishing ventures in foreign locations often necessitate some form of adaptation and adjustment. The fact that the culture, market and business conditions, socio-political landscape, and infrastructure could be different from home markets thorough contractual safeguards have to be in place. Sensitivity to existing disparities have to be factored into the company's strategic planning.

(3) Use the National Capital Region as entry point. The supporting infrastructure and distribution systems in the Philippines are well

developed in urban locations, such as the National Capital Region. The cities of Manila, Quezon City and Caloocan are in the National Capital Region and have a population of over 1 million. These locations also have a wide presence of world-class advertising and marketing support facilities. It makes strategic sense to establish the initial franchise in these locations while further gaining an understanding of the business dynamics of the country.

(4) Set-up Mall Stores. A number of Western franchises have experienced success as a result of their presence in major malls. Benefits associated with a mall presence include : high visibility, large foot traffic, convenient consumer access, image building, and easy to complement with national advertising campaigns. Though, space availability and lease rates may be issues to consider, select opportunities do exist and can prove beneficial.

(5) Expand selectively to provincial areas. The Philippine population is spread out across different provinces. Several provinces have a population of over 1 million. There are issues to consider with regard to infrastructure development, peace and order, and ease of product distribution in certain provinces. Nevertheless, a well-thought out expansion strategy allows an international franchisor to tap into unique market opportunities that may exist in these developing locations.

CONCLUSION

The Philippine market offers an innately large consumer base that is attractive for franchise operators. Its strategic location makes the country an appealing option as a franchise hub to launch a future Asia-Pacific expansion. Additional favorable factors include: Wide use of the English language, Cultural affinity with American values, low labor cost, large pool of skilled labor and management talent, and moderately well-placed infrastructure. The competitive climate that exist in the more urbanized locations in the country forces new entrants to creatively innovate and adapt quickly to the environment in order to succeed.

Challenges associated with the lingering political instability, weak currency, corruption, and peace-and-order problems in the Philippines are serious issues international franchisors need to face head on. There is no clear indication as to when these challenges will be mended. However, for the more valiant and aggressive franchisors willing to face the current risks in hope of long-term gains, and who are prepared to introduce flexible contractual arrangements, the Philippine market appears to be a unique investment haven.

REFERENCES

Alon, Ilan (2000), "The Organizational Determinants of Master International Franchising," *Journal of Business & Entrepreneurship*, 12 (2), 1-18. (Lead Article)

Alon, Ilan and Dianne Welsh, eds. (2001), *International Franchising in Emerging Markets: China, India and Other Asian Countries*, Chicago IL: CCH Inc. Publishing.

Alon, Ilan (1999a), " International Franchising Modes of Entry," in *Franchising Beyond the Millenium : Learning from the Past*, John Stanworth, David Purdy, and Cheryl R. Babcock, eds. Miami : Society of Franchising.

Alon, Ilan (1999b), *The Internationalization of U.S. Franchising Systems*. New York : Garland Publishing.

Alon, Ilan and David L. McKee (1999), "Towards a Macro Environmental Model of International Franchising," *Multinational Business Review*, 7 (1), 76-82

Asia Pacific Management Forum (2004), Best City in Asia for Living, [available at http://www.apmforum.com/travel/asia-city-business.htm?action=results&poll_ident=19]

Australian Trade Commission (2004), Franchising to the Philippines, (accessed March 2004), [available at http://www.austrade.gov.au/australia/layout/0,,0_S2-1_CLNTXID0019-2_2-3_PWB1962660-4_-5_-6_-7_,00.html]

Banco Central ng Pilipinas (2004), Philippine Exchange Rates, [available at http://www.bsp.gov.ph/Statistics/spei/tab12.htm]

Batra, Rajeev (1997), "Executive Insights : Marketing Issues and Challenges in Transitional Economies," *Journal of International Marketing*, 5 (4), 95-114.

Burton, F.N. and A.R. Cross (1995), "Franchising and Foreign Market Entry," in *International Marketing Reader*, S.J. Paliwoda and J.K. Ryans, eds. London: Routledge, 35-48

Casanova, Christine (2003), Franchise Financing : The Filipino Way (accessed March 2004), [available at http://www.tsinoy.com/bizguanxi/BizMatters.cfm?ID=641]

Caves, R.E., F. Murphy (1976), Franchising : Firms, Markets, and Intangible Assets, Southern Economic Journal, 42, 572-586

CIA – The World Fact Book (2004), The Philippines, [available at http://www.cia.gov/cia/publications/factbook./print/rp.html]

De la Cruz, Anne R (2002). "Short Cuts : Franchisees begin with established business procedures to succeed." Philippine Business Magazine : Volume 9, No. 4 (accessed March 2004), [available at http://www.philippinebusiness.com.ph/archives/magazine/vol9-2002/9-4/cover_p3.htm]

Dnes, A.W. (1992), Unfair Contractual Practices and Hostages in Franchise Contracts, Journal of Institutional and Theoretical Economics, 148, 484-504

Dnes, A.W. (1996), The Economic Analysis of Franchise Contracts, Journal of Institutional and Theoretical Economics, 152, 297-324

Department of Trade and Industry (2004), Franchising (Order Negosyo), (accessed March 2004), [available at http://www.dti.gov.ph/contentment/9/17/107/272.jsp]

Economist Intelligence Unit (2004), Country Data – Philippines [available at http://www.economist.com/countries/Philippines/profile.cfm?folder=Profile%2DEconomic%20Data]

Hayes, John P. (2004) "Master Franchisees Take Franchising Around the World" Franchise Handbook.com, (accessed March 2004) [available at http://www.franchise1.com/articles/article.asp?articleid=54]

Hookway, James (2004) "Filipino Hopes to Hatch a Duck-Embryo Empire" *Wall Street Journal Online* (accessed March 2004), [available at http://www.startupjournal.com/ideas/retailing/20020607-hookway.html]

International Franchise Association (2003), Franchising Sector to Become Philippine's Top Export, (accessed March 2004), [available at http://www.franchise.org/news/newsbriefs/story8]

Inquirer News Network (2004) " Initial Payment : Jollibee pays $11.5M for China-based fastfood chain (accessed March 2004), [available at http://money.inq7.net/topstories/view_topstories.php?yyyy=2004&mon=03&dd=27&file=5]

Justis R. and R. Judd (1986), "Master Franchising : A New Look," Journal of Small Business Management, 24 (3), 16-21.

Klein, B. (1980), Transaction Cost Determinants of Unfair Contractual Arrangements, American Economic Review, 70, 356-362.

Lyons, B.R. (1996), Empirical Relevance of Efficient Contract Theory : Inter-Firm Contracts, Oxford Review of Economic Policy, 12, 27-52

Marvel, H. P. (1982), Exclusive Dealing, Journal of Law and Economics, 25, 1-25

Matthewson, F. R. Winter (1985), The Economics of Franchise Contracts, Journal of Law and Economics, 28, 503-526

Meese, A.J. (1996), Antitrust Balancing in a Near Coasean World : The Case of Franchise Tying Contracts, Michigan Law Review, 95, 111-165

Omaga, Ronald Mark G (2004). *Traversing the Way of Franchising*. An article featured at the Canadian Agri-Food Trade Service, (accessed March 2004), [available at http://atn-riae.agr.ca/asean/e3227.htm]

Philippine Franchise Association (2004), *Franchising : Duplicating the Success of your Business* [A report submitted to the authors in MS Powerpoint format on March 2004]

Philippine National Statistics Office (2002), *Results from the 2000 Census of Population and Housing* [available at http://www.census.gov.ph/data/pressrelease/2002/pr02178tx.html]

Transparency International (2002) Corruption Perceptions Index FY 2002, [available at http://www.transparency.org/cpi/2002/cpi2002.en.html]

U.S. Asean Business Council (2003), *Doing Business in the Philippines*, [available at http://www.us-asean.org/Philippines/business_guide/]

US Department of State (2001), *Philippine Country Commercial Guide FY 2001*, [available at http://www.state.gov/www/about_state/business/com_guides/2001/eap/philippines_ccg2001.pdf]

Vanzi, Sol J. (2003), "Franchise Business Yielding Success Stories in RP", *Philippine Headline News Online*, (accessed March 2004), [available at http://www.newsflash.org/2003/05/be/be002575.htm]

Welsh, Dianne and Ilan Alon, eds. (2001), *International Franchising in Emerging Markets: Central and Eastern Europe and Latin America*, Chicago IL: CCH Inc. Publishing.

Williamson, O.E. (1985), The Economic Institutions of Capitalism, Free Press, New York.

Windsperger, Josef (2001), Complementarities in Franchising Networks : A Property Rights Approach, (accessed May 2004), [available at http://www.isnie.org/ISNIE01/Papers01/windsperger.pdf]

Winner Network (2004), *Franchising : A fine way of doing business* (accessed March 2004), [available at http://www1.winner-tips.org/article/articleview/150/1/17/]

Chapter 11
Conversion Franchising in Slovenia

Igor Pavlin
International Center for Promotion of Enterprises (ICPE)

Ilan Alon
Crummer Graduate School of Business, Rollins College

INTRODUCTION

Definitional issues relating to franchising are important as far as emerging markets are concerned since these countries are in the process of legitimizing the sector. The legitimization of the sector is vital for its establishment, growth and long-term viability. This was also the case in the 1960s in the United States, when there was a need to differentiate between real "franchise systems" and those that market themselves under the franchising umbrella but in actuality are "pyramid sales organizations" or plain distributorships. Franchising regulations, court decisions, and industry associations have helped legitimize the franchising sector.

In Slovenia, there are two reasons to reflect upon the definition of franchising. The first one is heuristic, demanding validity of classifying our case as a prospective franchise system. The second one relates to the "would-be franchise system" as a potential member of the national franchise association. When will a given operation fulfil the requirements implied in the definition of franchising?

Stanworth and Hoy (2003) have adapted a widely accepted definition of franchising containing most of the recognisable, relevant elements apparent in many self-defined franchise systems in the EU.

"Franchising is a business form essentially consisting of an organisation (the franchisor) with a market-tested business package centred on a product or service, entering into a continuing contractual relationship with franchisees, typically self-financed and independently owner-managed small firms, operating under the franchisor's trade name to produce and / or market goods or services according to a format specified by the franchisor." (Curran and Stanworth, 1983)

The definition is suitable to Slovenia as a member state of the EU. It implies, but does not specify, the contents of the contractual relationship in terms of "know-how" – its transfer from the franchisor to franchisee, as well as the amount of continuous services extended from franchisor to franchisee that have become the most critical subject of the commercial relationship between the franchisor and franchisee of a business- format franchise system.

The definition of franchising in the European Code of Ethics for Franchising contains more detail (EFF, 2003):

> "Franchising is a system of marketing goods and/or services and/or technology, which is based upon a close and ongoing collaboration between legally and financially separate and independent undertakings, the Franchisor and its individual Franchisees, whereby the Franchisor grants its individual Franchisee the right, and imposes the obligation, to conduct a business in accordance with the Franchisor's concept.
>
> The right entitles and compels the individual Franchisee, in exchange for a direct or indirect financial consideration, to use the Franchisor's trade name, and / or trademark and /or service mark, know-how[1], business and technical methods, procedural system, and other industrial and /or intellectual property rights, supported by continuing provision of commercial and technical assistance, within the framework and for the term of a written franchise agreement, concluded between parties for this purpose."[2]

The above definition in the Code as a self-regulatory act of the European franchise industry contains some additional provisions regarding the marketing background of franchising, intellectual property rights, definition of know-how and continuing provision of commercial and technical assistance, which cannot be established without a careful consideration of the franchise agreement of a system.

On the basis of the additional details contained in the definition, a franchise system may or may not be accessed into the regular membership of a national franchise association in the 17 European countries where such associations exist, depending on meeting criteria such as

- The established legal separation of the two firms (franchisor and franchisee);
- The quality of business packages (membership is not possible if operational manuals do not exist);
- The minimum number of units that have been functioning for a defined period. (This requirement recognizes both the time needed for a network

to become viable as well as proof of its viability through a number of the existing franchise units on top of pilot units and the piloting period.)

From a research perspective, the validity of the empirical research is strongly conditioned with the ability of researchers to establish correspondence between a pre-defined phenomenon of franchising and the selection of networks that can meet the minimum standards of this definition. Validity can be confirmed by checking franchise agreements and establishing their match with a definition—which in most cases is not a very easy job, given the confidential nature of franchise contracts. Simple checks of the agreements and operational manuals constitute just one step of their verification; it would be more difficult to establish the matching of an agreement with its practical implementation.

In the absence of such possibilities, researchers could qualify a network as a franchise system on the basis of the following criteria:
- A network defines or calls itself a "franchise network";
- There is a legal verification of each contract at the court or by another national authority (mostly in cases of specific franchise legislation);
- The system is a member of the national franchise association. This is especially important in Europe.

In our case study, the difference between the requirements of the definition and the existing structural and functional set up of a "would-be" franchise system has heuristic implications.

The conditions for franchising in Europe may differ especially from the US (Bezemer, 2001), due to the smaller size of markets served as well as to a multitude of cultural and legal differences. The nature of "partnership" or "networking" may even disqualify such systems from being recognized as franchise systems. By just assuming the existence of a proper franchise system (e.g. on the basis of the EFF definition of a franchise system), one may fail to realize the following situations:
- There is no clear legal / factual separation of the two sides in a "franchise relationship". There is no factual sell-purchase of goods between franchisor and franchisee that is provided by the franchisor or his suppliers. Franchisee sells goods on the account of franchisor, although the franchisee may have an independent legal identity otherwise, or transfers revenues, keeping "provision" or "commission" for his services. The nature of this relationship resembles agency.
- There is little or practically no know-how that franchisors would transfer to franchisee, although there is a clear separation in terms of the wholesaling-retailing role in addition to sell-purchase contracts. In such cases there would not exist even a systematic operational manual, but rather ad hoc directions by the franchisor. The nature of the relationship would resemble a simple distribution system.
- One of the traders forms a voluntary chain to benefit from the economies of scale in purchasing and selling goods. The chain will evolve into a

"cooperative franchise system", which could gradually be transformed into a real franchise system. Although users may define the system as a franchise system, there is a way to go before it is, in fact, a "franchise system."

In EU countries in general—and in smaller, transitional economies of the contemporary EU in particular—examples can be found of all three of the above-stated situations. In Slovenia, the transitional conditions—such as lack of business experience of the existing and would-be franchisees, lack of capital with franchisees and lack of favourable financing schemes for franchising, unsettled prices of real estate, shortcomings related to the enforcement of law, and others transitional elements—have contributed to the development of quasi-franchise systems (Pavlin, 2001). It is our contention that for a developing country, standards for the establishment of a "franchise" need to accepted and enforced for the purpose of collecting data, monitoring the sector, and ensuring its development. Nevertheless, contingencies may need to be developed to accommodate the needs of transitioning countries that may not follow the model of developed markets in the establishment of a franchise system. The case of BHS discussed later in the chapter is an example of such development.

HOW INDEPENDENT IS THE FRANCHISEE?

There is also an interesting phenomenon, documented by Kaufman and Stanworth (1995) for the USA and UK, that up to one-half of franchisees have had previous self-employment business experience. In Slovenia, franchisors value previous business experience by franchisees (Pavlin, 1998). The company that has limited its recruitment of franchisees to the gradual conversion of current workshops into franchise units has demonstrated the drive towards understanding a franchise system as a network of units with a better bargaining position and better chances for survival. To take advantage of scale, standardization, and brand recognition, many stand alone entrepreneurs consider franchising as an option.

The independence of a franchisee is a complex phenomenon that cannot simply be reduced to a general stereotype "quasi-entrepreneur," closer to the status of an employee than to the status of an entrepreneurial capitalist. On the other side, firms in various forms of networks -cooperatives, clusters, as well as firms subordinated to large companies - may all have their existence provided only as parts of chains, either in vertical or horizontal.

Different layers of government, financial institutions and larger firms all determine / reduce the level of autonomy of nominally independent entrepreneurs. An "independent venture" is subject to various national and local government permits re location, standards of services, accounting standards, and government regulations concerning safety, hygiene, the wellbeing of employees and protection of the environment. An entrepreneur's independence is curtailed by the strict criteria of provision of venture capital / bank loans, available SME support systems, various grants, tax relief, etc. Additionally, in the transitional environment the disorder in payments within buyer-supplier networks can marginalize or ruin small firms, especially those in capital-intensive businesses.

Considering the above-mentioned limitations of independent entrepreneurs, the reduced negotiating position of atomised small firms can mean a comparative advantage for franchised units. As Stanworth and Curran put it (2003, p. 37), the franchisor shields franchised units from external pressures, which may result in substantial franchisee autonomy. Again, the drawbacks of transitional conditions may worsen the assumed advantages of an "incubation" of franchisees.

By focusing on economies of scale, one can find a growing number of companies that are becoming parts of one or more chains, deliberately or unwillingly (Bezemer, 2001). An independent venture within a changing market condition can either continue to strive in market conditions of increased competition or that venture has to become a unit of a voluntary chain / franchise network.[3] A voluntary chain / franchise system can provide

- Purchasing economies of scale for input components of their final products and services;
- Negotiating position with large suppliers of goods and services;
- Targeted responses to consumer demands in terms of price and quality, within the given distribution structure of goods and services;
- Reformulation of the simple act of selling production-driven products or services by providing long-term service of standard quality to the consumer (lines of credit, leasing, servicing, guarantees, combined services etc.);
- Responses to the changing habits and changing needs of their consumers (employed women, at-home elderly, pre-school children, etc.) in terms of time, place and manner of delivery.

The process of joining a voluntary chain (to be later converted into a franchise system) represents modernisation in terms of adjustments to the handling of orders, keeping and shortening of delivery times, and fulfilling the expectations of customers.[4]

CONVERTING VOLUNTARY CHAINS INTO FRANCHISES

In general, franchise systems tend to evolve in the following ways (Mendelsohn, 1992, World Intellectual Property Organisation, 1994, Forward and Fullop, 1995):

- Establishing a franchise network by replicating a successful business concept with typical start-up pilot operation – following a textbook approach to franchise development;
- Conversion of company-owned stores into franchises;
- Conversion of existing, independent businesses into franchise units either via voluntary chain, interim stage or directly;
- Starting franchising as a spin-off operation of the main business;
- Beginning franchising via master franchise by importing a foreign concept;
- Establishing franchising with a subsidiary of a foreign chain;
- Starting franchising as a joint-venture operation of the "principal" with a foreign company;
- Arrival of a foreign concept through a direct franchise arrangement;
- Purchasing a foreign direct franchise for its replication within its own distribution network as a mode of diversification of the main business (as a company owned chain managed by the company-hired managers).

Classical approaches to franchise-system development normally begin with testing and replication of successful business concepts. At the outset, such systems develop and implement a franchise package including operational manuals and a franchise support system, develop a franchise agreement, and develop recruitment and selection tools for prospective franchisees. Simultaneously, the pilot operation(s) serve(s) this development process. The actual testing stage continues with the recruitment and launching into business of the first franchisees. This can be the period of greatest (concept) vulnerability.

Studying franchising as an instrument of SME development and growth conversion of voluntary chains into a franchise network—as well as an improvement of a cooperative franchise system—may deserve special attention. A proper choice of a well-phased strategy and well-conceived approach with tailor-made advisory and franchisor development support systems on a national level may enhance the process and make it less erratic. Conversion of company-owned shops into franchises of a large wholesale-retail system seems to be rather easy, after a proper distribution pattern has been strategically designed. This also implies the formatting of franchise units within a differentiated system of company-owned and franchise operations. The important elements in the development of the franchise format are the expected entry profile of a franchise—including leadership, managerial and technical experience—(franchisee) financial potential as well as the overall viability of such a franchise format.

Studies in the development and conversion of voluntary chains and cooperative forms[5] of business into franchise units, including the acquisition of smaller franchise chains by larger ones, could be most interesting for transitional economies and may help the elaboration of viable national economic development strategies.

One of the questions in a recent e-mail survey of the European Foundation for Management Development (EFMD, 2003) was whether franchising could be considered as an alternative to classical start up. Several authors have touched upon this topic in discussing the possibility of using franchising as a tool for SME development (Pavlin, 1996A, 1996B and 2001; Shangavi and Pavlin, 1991; Shangavi, 1991; Jeanmart, 2000; Chong, 1994). Using the respective cases of policies and actions in some Asian countries (Singapore, Malaysia, Philippines, and others), one has to anticipate both the shortcomings of transitional economic environment as well as the proper action of the SME support services for franchising. One may agree that proofs of deliberate use of the franchise approach for SME development or even studies that would propose fast growing SMEs that use franchising as a growth strategy have not been well documented (Kirby and Watson, 1999).

As far as Central Europe is concerned, another question may arise: Is there potential for building indigenous franchise systems that may first thrive in local environments and eventually cross borders within the rest of the EU? Entrepreneurship in these countries, according to the Global Entrepreneurship Monitor (Rebernik, et al, 2003), confronts specific barriers. Slovenia is positioned quite low in terms of new entrepreneurial activities. From our database, we may conclude that fast-growing small firms have not often used franchising as a growth strategy.

In what follows, I will present the case of BHS in Slovenia, a typical case of a "bottom-up" approach[6] to franchising that converted a voluntary chain of automotive repair services and shops into a franchise system.

THE TRANSFORMATION OF AUTO REPAIR WORKSHOPS INTO VERTICALLY-INTEGRATED FRANCHISED RETAIL OUTLETS

Service workshops run by mechanical craftsmen served local customers who had limited choices due to the geographical dispersion of alternative services. Specific and non-standard needs of customers, trading favours (exchange of services, products and favours) and individualized services—depending on the skills of the individual service workshop—were positive consequences of this type of supply. Improvements in road and highway connections have increased alternative possibilities, brought closer modern shopping centres and alternative and specialized services, e.g. tire specialists, brake specialists, car-body specialists, quick services related to regular motor servicing and others. In addition, binding customers of new vehicles only to authorized service units in the guarantee period has changed the supply as well as demand side in this sector.

The increase in the use of private cars in Slovenia in the last ten years has been the highest in comparison to other countries in Central Europe or even in countries of the EU. However, in the last few years the market of used cars has also increased, especially after the joining of Slovenia to the EU. This represents an opportunity for fast car-servicing in the post-guarantee period.

Automotive and tire repair services in Slovenia remained dispersed all over this relatively sparsely inhabited country. There are dozens of larger importers and wholesalers of spare parts and tyres and hundreds of independent repair workshops, tyre repair services and automotive shops. There is also a fierce competition in the Slovenian car and car-repair market, yet there is no system of prices of services and spare parts. The borders between wholesale and retail trade do not exist anymore (Marinsek, 2002). One of the main reasons for presenting this case is their beginning, typical for franchise systems in other parts of Europe (e.g. Bezemer, 2001).

At the same time other changes have contributed to the appearance of an ever-growing market niche such as

- Change in the value systems of the buyers of cars – buying older cars (a shift in mentality – valuing real estate or growing investment opportunities;
- Change in transport habits resulting in the shift from the use of public transport to private car transport;
- The availability of cheap and durable second-hand cars with guarantees by seller makes it possible for less affluent consumers (18+ school generation, unskilled workers, older less well-to-do population) to acquire a car;
- Possession of more than one car within a family;
- Strict enforcement of regulations concerning winter equipment (winter tires, chains, etc.) provides new market niches in retailing of spare parts as well as in servicing.

International competitors in the quick-service automotive market have not yet crossed the Slovenian borders. When such international players do enter the Slovenian market, the role of exclusive importers / wholesalers will also change. BHS voluntary franchise system emerged from these conditions.

The modern franchise supply model would provide the consumer with a choice of different worldwide used and recognised products and services – e.g. spare parts, tyres, car-care products on the side of distribution and standardised but limited "fast service" intervention with formalised guarantees for services and products, possible delayed payments and credit arrangements for expensive purchases.

The question about the consumer benefits within such a system has been asked by different researchers (see, e.g., Freyburger and Cutter, 2000). Is it a "consumer choice" issue in terms of the variety of products and services offered or is it a "consumer satisfaction" issue in terms of tailor-made responses to a wide spectrum of less demanding needs in terms of short time of delivery, convenience, standard reliability of products and services, value for money, etc. (see, e.g., Curran and Stanworth, 1983; Rubin, 2003).

BHS (Bartog Hitri Servis – Bartog Fast Service): THE CASE OF AN AUTOMOTIVE REPAIR SERVICE CHAIN

BHS started a "voluntary chain" by inviting would-be associates to a meeting—these were automotive repair service owners who were pre-disposed to the idea of joining. Earlier, they had learnt about the functioning of similar chains of services at home and abroad. The idea of the chain-of-service workshops came when BHS (at that time an independent service workshop) management did a "benchmarking" study of distribution and franchise chains in international firms such as ATU, Speedy, Midas, Vergolst, S point, etc. They realized they could not simply copy foreign models that were primarily related to large urban centres; Slovenia does not have such centres. Therefore, they tried to make use of the potential of the existing workshops and protect them against an impending recession. Currently, there are 47 associated car-repair workshops in the chain, all of whom had been independent services in Slovenia.

BHS improved the functional features of their business including the level of cleanliness, orderliness, customer relation behaviour and common identity features. BHS is thus serving a market niche characterised by both low cost as well as by differentiated products and services. In terms of Porter (1985), the parameter of their market niche "the segment of the products / services" is limited to simple and periodic vehicle maintenance and repairs. The geographical spread has not changed while the franchisor has been progressively converting the "voluntary chain" into a franchise network. BHS is able to service vehicles that are not tied into specific producer-dictated terms and conditions for after-sale warrantees, which may require servicing within a manufacturer-mandated chain of subcontracted workshops.

Their repertoire of products and services has thus changed – it has become standardised within the purview of their product line, quickly adapting to customer concerns. Quick service has become part of their reputation. Attentiveness to customers' concerns in a friendly manner, even while applying a standardised set of procedures in defining problems / needs, has strengthened their competitive advantage. This combination of customer care and standardised systems resembles the description of mobile franchise systems by Preble and Hoffman (1998). Of course, the standardization of BHS services does not mean uniformity of high-quality services only for the sake of economy of scale, but also for the sake of shortening the waiting periods of customers on one side—providing services at expected technical standards of quality leads to increased customer satisfaction. Similarly, as in the case of "hamburgerology" (Boas and Chain, 1976), speed in the service part of the business is one of the main constituting elements behind standardisation and economies of scale.

Franchising for BHS will thus be a form that enables adjustments to the changed distribution of automotive spare parts and car care products, which allows the company to benefit from economies of scale in purchasing. This benefit continues in that it allows economies of scale in retailing by contractors, and at the same time increasing standards of service-quality, shorter delivery times, and a greater ability to cope with changes in technical requirements as a result of improved vehicle technology.

Currently, the principal—Bartog—has two company-owned units where they test their supply, organization and standards. They also financially help their partner workshops to get suitable bank loans on the basis of their warranties.

The benefits for joining the BHS chain of shops and services, looked at from the perspective of an individual entrepreneur, follow:

- Purchasing of goods under better conditions. (The BHS principal has a well-established track record of purchasing spare parts, car-care products and tyres, from reputed producers.);
- Building a visible customer-friendly chain of services, starting from the reception desk to placing the order, delivery of and guarantees for services;
- Using the increasingly well-known trade name and logo of BHS in addition to the already well-known name of the company in the local environment;
- Standardised system of inspection of engines, replacement of parts that require replacement with parts that are at the quality level of the original parts (though branded parts may be several times more expensive (Marinsek, 2002);
- Continuous benchmarking of critical parameters within the system;
- Continuous market analysis of competing companies;
- Problem solving related to functioning in the local environment.

One of the most important aspects of the development of their franchise system has been gradualism in building up individual instruments that will ensure internal coherence of the system, understanding of the strength of their service, including the shop with spare parts on one side and efficient service on the other. Individual units originally led by entrepreneurs have traded part of their earlier autonomy for their increased survival potential within the system with different types of autonomy as already discussed. The strategic alliance aspect meant gaining from the synergy of the "umbrella service centre" (Bezemer, 2002). The current role of the "integrator – franchisor" does not seem disputable. On the brink of the possible arrival of international franchise chains in this field, "old-fashioned craftsmanship" could become obsolete and hardly competitive.

The franchisor's development potential has become convincing for those who were invited to join and who agreed and eventually passed the test of "recruitment." The recruitment differed from a typical recruitment of franchisees where the franchisor would focus on the following basic elements:

- Business experience of the candidate;
- His/her leadership and management potential;
- Capital available to the would-be franchisee;
- Attitude that would enable his/her functioning within the system;
- His/her age and health characteristics.

In addition to these criteria, BHS's recruitment included a detailed diagnosis of the existing company, a feasibility study and its convergence within the system that focused upon

- The local market potential of individual would-be franchisees;
- The prospects of converting the workshop into a unit of the chain which would broadly satisfy the minimum requirements of a future franchisor;
- Already acquired goodwill within the local environment;
- The current and prospective financial performance;
- The need for additional training in technical and managerial aspects of functioning within the BHS system.

If eligibility was established, development of the conversion plan proceeded, and the business would be slated to begin business plan specific to unit performance.

The technical skills required within the automobile service were taken for granted and were not made an asset of the system, which would charge franchisees for their transfer through training. One may observe an evolution similar to that observable within standard bottom-up approaches, especially for smaller systems, where know-how was assumed to include the technical skills of would-be franchisees (Pavlin, 1996). Pavlin's research results in 2001 confirmed this finding. Nevertheless, management service fees are assessed for common marketing and the building of special signs with the chain logo, flags and other image-related items.

In the contract, the business partner[7] agrees to use special forms and procedures in dealing with customers, to use only the homologated spare parts, and to follow the guidelines regarding customer-friendly posting of prices. At this time, the lead partner still does not collect initial fees from joining entrepreneurs, covering costs through the sales of spare parts to partners.

Each entrepreneur joining the system has been allowed to continue offering customary services to his old customers. There was an emphasis on customer relations, new elements of receiving orders, and handling customer requests. They became the major element that the voluntary chain has brought into the functioning of their new partners. The importance of this component has been researched and demonstrated as important in the research of the automotive repair businesses in France by Freyburger and Cutter (2000).

The chain deliberately did not require the partner's premises to be decorated with "marble and gold," although they required a decent, clean, well-equipped setup that would offer quality of services. An overly decorous environment might suggest (to customers) that the price being paid for services was related to this surface issue, rather than to the goods and services themselves.

The chain has adjusted to the geography of dispersed and more-or-less urbanized settlements in Slovenia. Gradual adaptation of common features such as use of logo on company premises, marked vehicles, letterheads and uniforms, customer-servicing procedures is in progress. There is a strong emphasis on creating commitment and a feeling of belonging to a common network as a parallel to creating a converging company culture, yet each partner is allowed to present himself as a distinct entrepreneur. The debate on the dependence versus independence of individual entrepreneurs in this case is subordinated to the urge for survival of earlier independent businesses. The strength of each unit seems to be reinforced by belonging to the system, yet the level of independence / contracted dependence relies on the quality of participative leadership through the strings of the evolving franchise system.

The level of integration of the entire system within unique standards of performance, product/service mix, their quality and rules of handling orders and delivery seems to be proportionate to the intensity of abolishing/diminishing signs of economic independence that can be described as:

- A strong connection between the trade name of the firm / entrepreneur and its reputation;
- The unique features and individual reputation of specific services and favours;
- Idiosyncrasies pertaining to each business as a "family business,"e.g., dependence on the specificity of available human resources in terms of Williamson (1985);
- Informal rules and specific features of the informal economy;

All of which result in strong borders among the firms within the network.

INTERNATIONALIZATION OF SLOVIAN FRANCHISING: THE CASE OF BHS

Several Slovenian companies have established or will establish international franchise chains in ex-Yugoslav regions. Some other companies follow a similar route: e.g., Merkur (home accessories, construction material); Mercator (a food-store chain); jewellers (Goldsmith Celje); and others. One may assume that franchising for some of these companies may not represent a pro-active strategy as it does for BHS, but may be a response to a limited success within the international environment, especially within demanding EU markets.

Some of these retailers may not have a globally relevant product to internationalize. Their organisational structure may also not support operational development through methods such as organic growth. They may apply franchise approaches that are relatively unfamiliar to them. Even nationally, within Slovenia, franchising has often been used by companies for reasons of easier access to the capital without rigorous screening of candidates in periods of fierce international competition (Pavlin, 1998). In addition they may perceive expansion to these (regional) markets as a rather limited operation, as they are culturally or psychologically still quite distant (or risky) for the retailer, or too small to justify additional international operations within the corporate expansion (see also Quinn and Alexander, 2002: 272; Forward and Fulop, 1996).

BHS had decided to grow internationally even before the intention to finalize the process of evolution into a franchise system that would comply with the European definition of franchising[8], especially in terms of

- A well refined / tested franchise operational manual;
- A standard format for each franchise in terms of size, technology, definition of services, service attitude and behaviour;
- A balanced franchise agreement with essential elements defined in the Code of ethics;
- Protected know-how provided by franchisor.

Among the reasons for internationalization followed by the company one can agree that BHS followed basically the strategy of responding to international opportunities rather than expanding abroad in order to compensate for the threatening lack of domestic opportunities in terms of Williams (1992). This statement has to be confined to the current size of the system, encompassing 45 units; in other words, it may be approaching saturation within the rather small Slovenian market where all major automobile brands are selling and servicing cars through licensed chains at rather high standards.

Another important fact is that markets in the former states of Yugoslavia are still attuned to Slovenian brands and products. This fact makes BHS a qualified competitor in the region, able to use its ties to the Slovenian business community, knowing the cultural, economic and geographical characteristics as a cause for internationalization. Further, BHS has been proactive, acting early to capitalize on markets that have emerged after the recent war in this region.[9]

At the same time, this region is associated with substantial risks for business format franchising. Infringement in the use of trade names, including violations of industrial and intellectual property rights, may not be prosecuted at the same level or rigour as in the EU. The risk does not stem necessarily from the non-existence of regulations protecting such rights but from problems related to enforcement (Zeidman, 1994). There may even be problems related to unresolved ownership rights over real estate.

CONCLUSION

One of the most important transformations within the chain evolving as it evolves into a franchise network requires not only technological but also administrative innovations. The transition from craft-related, individualized provision of services to an industrial type of provision of services requires, at the same time

- The introduction of recruitment techniques, diagnosing the subcontractors' companies to become contracting partners in the process of gradual evolving into franchisees;
- The management of new members, as franchisees become sui generis management;
- Changed – friendly, but standardised customer service procedures;
- A strong reliance on modern ITC technology in handling orders /delivery as well in the repair process;
- The marketing of "package services";
- Using marketing as a tool for informing customers of new types of supply and service, thus creating standardised demand in terms of expectations of the kind, type and quality of services at any service unit, an independent franchise, within the network;
- Standard list re supply of products, with a defined share of sales (e.g. 20%), a defined choice of goods that could be purchased from a non-defined supplier or franchisor.

A gradual enhancement of the institutional structure—i.e., the business format of units, a softening of the borders between firms—will have to occur. However, this transformation will not bring entrepreneurs close to employee status in spite of increased quality-oversight in terms of the theory of the firm (Rubin, 1978: 50-55). This expectation is based on the existence of strict operational manuals and various forms and subjects of training, along with the concurrent development of franchise support services, which would—in concert with performance-monitoring mechanisms— lead to the strengthening and homogenisation of standards of services throughout the system.

In the conversion process one may well realise that each individual entrepreneur will have to be brought to similar operating efficiencies, adopt a renewed life-cycle stage, as well as improve the fit between his and other units as well as harmonising its future transformation with the strategic guidelines of the lead partner in the chain–evolving franchisor. This unique development strategy implies also a streamlining of the innovation process within the network. Benefiting from joint development and marketing synergies was one of the key reasons for those that have decided to join the chain within the increasingly competitive market. Innovations expected by franchisees can be well built into the common technical base of services.

Centralized commanding that could be opposed by a segment of franchisees may jeopardise the existence of the entire transitional system. Participative style in strategic decision-making seems to be of great importance. The increased use modern ICT technology together with acquiring fast feedback mechanisms can serve in further enhancing of the system. Allowing different fields and levels of individualisation at this stage will gradually lead to more and more standardised supply of goods and services. The administrative innovation of the system means creating a unique structure for the franchisor / franchisee relationship.

In the case of BHS, one can expect that the extent of tying individual units into a unique network with a common identity under the same trade name will be a progressive but all-encompassing process. The name of the process that we can witness in this case is reducing the levels of complexity to more manageable proportions.[10] We are speaking about simplification of different arrangements with different suppliers or subcontractors at higher prices and longer times of delivery, time-consuming re-negotiation of short-term trading agreements, etc. These simplifications result in higher standards of quality, as well as shorter delivery times at lower prices.

A necessary step will be conversion based upon a proper franchise agreement. Changes that will be unavoidable in this process in relation to franchisees, especially those that will require abolishing specific aspects of the present autonomy of member entrepreneurs, may be painful but essential. The case of Coca-cola re-engineering as shown by Felstead can inspire the agents of change in the BHS chain, although there are only indirect similarities (Felstead, 1993 A and B).

NOTES

[1]"Know-how" means a body of non-patented practical information, resulting from experience and testing by the Franchisor, which is secret, substantial and identified;
"Secret" means that the know-how, as a body or in the precise configuration and assembly of its components, is not generally known or easily accessible; it is not limited in the narrow sense that each individual component of the know-how should be totally unknown or unobtainable outside the Franchisor's business;

"Substantial" means that the know-how includes information which is of importance for the sale of goods or the provision of services to end users, and in particular for the presentation of goods for sale, the processing of goods in connection with the provision of services, methods of dealing with customers, and administration and financial management; the know-how must be useful for the Franchisee by being capable, at the date of conclusion of the agreement, of improving the competitive position of the franchisee, in particular by improving the franchisee's performance or helping it to enter a new market.

"Identified" means that the know-how must be described in a sufficiently comprehensive manner so as to make it possible to verify that it fulfils the criteria of secrecy and substantiality; the description of the know-how can be set out in the franchise agreement, in a separate document, or recorded in any other appreciable from.

[2] The purpose of the European Code of Ethics has been to uphold a self-regulatory approach to good and fair business practice in franchising in Europe. The founding members of the European Franchise Federation drew up the European Code of Ethics in 1972. This initiative was followed, appreciated and commended by the European Commission. Since then it has evolved and has been amended to fit the changes and evolution of franchising in Europe. It was last amended in September 1989. The European Code of Ethics for Franchising applies to the relations between franchisor and franchisee, Master franchisee and franchisee, but not to franchisor and Master franchisee – according to article 6 of the Code (EFF, 2003)

[3] International chains of Belgian origin are progressively rounding up their system of hypermarkets, supermarkets, and various forms of smaller units - convenience stores. There would hardly be any place for supplies to independent shops that would not fit into the concept of their system that includes company-owned units, as well as franchised stores (Pavlin, 2001B). Similar is the case of another system in different market conditions. The chain Mercator (in 2002, 1,5 billion € turnover), competing with Interspar, Tus, Leclerc and some others, finds itself in a similar situation. Bezemer (2001) reports that in 1999 in the Dutch retailing industry 85% of stores were either company owned by a large corporation or belonged to a voluntary chain or franchise. Approximately half of them were company owned. Independent shopkeepers owned only 15% of units. The share of independent shopkeepers continues to decrease. Units included into the voluntary chains, which would cooperate simply for the reason of purchasing goods under better conditions, are gradually being replaced by franchising as a more defined business format that fosters cooperation under a common identity with the remaining company-owned and managed units. This same process can be seen in Slovenia.

[4] Especially in the retail industry, the introduction of voluntary chains and cooperatives has played a very important role. Well-documented cases include that of Econ-Minimart, a voluntary self-help scheme and NTUC Fairprice franchise (Chong, Li-Choy, 1994).

[5] In 1995 Chong Li Choy, presented the case of the Singaporean Minimart...........

[6] Among classifications of different origins of franchise systems, one can observe starting franchise networks from the bottom up and / or, from the top down (Stanworth, Curran). BHS may be a case of the former.

[7] Partner in this text does not mean a partner in terms of the definition of partner in the Model declaration on the information relating to the qualification of enterprise as an SME by the Commission (2003), but simply a cooperating, autonomous enterprise.

[8] The EU definition of franchising has been discussed earlier

[9] For reasons of internationalisation of franchise systems see Quinn and Alexander (2002). In their terms the BHS concept would fall within Path 1 of international franchising. It concerns operations that have experience of franchising in the domestic market where internationalisation through a franchise entry method is the logical development.

[10] Stanworth (1996) refers to the complexity that can be seen as a catalyst for innovations designed to reduce levels to more manageable proportions.

REFERENCES

Bezemer J. Notes of the presentation of Jan Bezemer on the financing of franchise networks. ICPE Conference; April, 2003; Ljubljana, Slovenia.

Bezemer J. Developments in franchising present new challenges. Paper presented at the 15th Annual Conference of International Society of Franchising; 2001; Las Vegas.

Boas M., Chain S. (1976). *Big Mac: The Unauthorised Story of McDonald's*. New York: Meator, 1976.

Chong L.C. (1994). Franchising as an instrument for business Transformation: The Singaporean experience. *Public Enterprises* 1994; 14 (1-2): 115-119.

Commission of the EU. Commission communication. Model declaration on the information relating to the qualification of an enterprise as an SME; May 20, 2003; Brussels.

Curran J., Stanworth J. (1983). Franchising in the modern economy / towards a theoretical understanding. *International Small Business Journal* 1983; 2 (1): 8-26.

EFF. (2003). European Franchise Federation: The European Code of Ethics for Franchising. Retrieved May 5, 2003 from: http://www.eff-franchise.com

EFMD. (April, 2003). European Foundation for Management Development. Survey on EISB – Entrepreneurship, Innovation and Small Business.

Felstead A. *The Corporate Paradox: Power and Control in the Business Franchise*. London & New York: Routledge, 1993.

Felstead A. Beyond the boundary: exercising control without ownership - the case of Coca-Cola in Germany. Paper presented to the Department of Business Studies, University of Edinburgh; March, 1993.

Forward J., Fulop C. Large established firms' entry into franchising: an exploratory investigation of strategic and operational issues. The International Review of Retail, Distribution and Consumer Research 1996; 6 (1): 34-52.

Forward J., Fulop C. (1992). Large firms and franchising. The NatWest Centre for Franchising Research 1992; City University Business School, London.

Frauenhuber W. (1993). Franchising in Europe: Situation and strategies. Public Enterprise 1993, 13 (1-2); ICPE series: Franchising in Asia and Europe.

Freyburger R., Cutter, P. (2000). Is the know-how transmission from franchisor real and assessable? An empirical survey in the French car maintenance sector. Paper presented at the 14th Annual International Society of Franchising Conference; 2000; San Diego, California.

Hoffman R. J, Preble J. F. (1991). Franchising: Selecting a strategy for rapid growth. Long Range Planning 1991; 24 (4): 74-85.

Jeanmart P. (2000). Development of SMEs and franchising in accessing countries to EU. Report of the President of the EFF; in Fransizing 2000; 2; newsletter of the Slovenian Franchise Association.

Hoy F., Stanworth J. (2003). Franchising: a conceptual overview. In *Franchising: An International Perspective*, F. Hoy & J. Stanworth, eds.London: Routledge.

Kirby D., Watson A. (1999). Franchising as a small business development strategy: A qualitative study of operational and "failed" franchisors in the UK. Journal of Small Business and Enterprise Development 1999; 6 (4): 341 -349.

Kaufman P., Stanworth J. (1995). The decision to purchase a franchise: A study of prospective franchisees in the U.A. and the U.K. *Journal of Small Business Management* 1995; 33 (4): 22-33.

Quinn B., Alexander N. (2002). International retail franchising: A conceptual framework. *International Journal of Retail and Distribution Management* 2002; 30 (5): 264-276.

Manrinsek I. BHS Slovenian car repair chain. Presentation at the Annual Conference on Franchising at the Slovenian Chamber of Commerce and Industry; May, 2002; Ljubljana, Slovenia.

Mendelsohn M. *The Guide to Franchising (5th edition)*. London: Cassel, 1994.

Pavlin I. Franchising in Central Europe: Case of Slovenia. In *Franchising in Emerging Countries*. Dianne Welsh & Ilan Alon, eds. Chicago: CCH Press, 2001a.

Pavlin I. Notes on the field visit to Carefour and Delhaize 2001b; Brussels. Belgium.

Pavlin I. Franchising development in Central European countries. Editorial Introduction, Franchising Research: An International Journal 1996b; 1(1): 33-40.

Pavlin I. Franchising, a fast-track induction into entrepreneurial survival and growth in transitional economies, 1996. EFMD European Small Business Seminar: Developing Core Competencies in Small Business for the 21st Century; September, 1996b; Vaasa, Finland.

Preble F. J., Hoffman R. C. (1998). Competitive advantage through specialty franchising. *Journal of Consumer Marketing* 1998; 15 (1): 64-77.

Porter M. *Competitive Advantage*. New York: Free Press, 1985.

Rebernik M., Tominc P., Glas M., Psenicny, V. Kako podjetna je Slovenija? (How entrepreneurial is Slovenia?). Global Entrepreneurship Monitor, Slovenia 2002. Faculty of Business Economics; 2003; Maribor.

Rubin P. (1978). The theory of the firm and the structure of the franchise contract. In *Franchising: An International Perspective*, F. Hoy & J. Stanworth, J.. eds. London & New York: Routledge.

Sanghavi N. Retail franchising as a growth strategy for the 1990s. *International Journal of Retail and Distribution Management* 1991; 19 (2): 4-9.

Sanghavi N., Pavlin I. (1996). Franchising and small business development: The case of transitional economies. ICSB 41st World Conference proceedings, Volume 3, pp. 85-99; 1996; Sweden.

Stanworth J., Price S., Purdy D., Zafiris N., Gandolfo A. Business format franchising: innovation and creativity or replication and conformity? Franchising Research: An International Journal 1996; 1 (2): 29-39.

Stanworth J., Curran, J. Colas, burgers, shakes and shirkers: Towards a sociological model of franchising in the market economy. In *Franchising: An International Perspective*, F. Hoy & J. Stanworth, eds. London & New York: Routledge, 2003.

Williamson O. E. *The Economic Institutions of Capitalism*. New York: Free Press, 1985.

Williams D. Motives for retailer internationalisation: Their impact, structure, and implications. Journal of Marketing Management 1992; 8: 269-285.

Zeidman P. F. (1994). International franchising: the Central and Eastern European experience. Public Enterprise 1994; 14 (1-2): 104-114; ICPE, Ljubljana, Slovenia.

IV. Cases in International Franchising

Chapter 12
Franchising with Kodak in China

Ilan Alon
Crummer Graduate School of Business, Rollins College

INTRODUCTION

"To be the leader in the world, you have to be the leader in China"
George Fisher, Eastman Kodak's Chairman

Kodak, a Fortune 500 company, headquartered in Rochester, New York, has sought opportunities to both develop and market photographic and imaging products and services in China. China is not only a tremendous source for "cheap labor" and resources that attracts foreign direct investment, but also an emerging economy with the largest consumer market in the world.

Kodak's products include films, photographic papers and plates, cameras, projectors, chemicals, processing equipment, audiovisual equipment, copiers, microfilm products, applications software, printers, and other imaging products and services. The company's sales and profits are divided as follows:

- Consumer imaging accounted for 53% of 1999 sales and 56% of profits;
- Professional imaging 13% and 16%;
- Health imaging 15% and 20%; and
- Other imaging 19% and 8% (E-trade, 2000).

The company's other imaging segment consists of professional motion imaging, document imaging, and digital & applied imaging.

Consumer Imaging

Consumer imaging is the largest segment of Kodak's business both in term of sales and in terms of profits. This business segment also contains Kodak's franchising operations abroad.

For 1999, the consumer-imaging segment had registered $7.4 billion in sales (SEC, 2000). The consumer imaging business manufactures and markets both traditional and digital products. Films, photographic papers, processing services, photo-finishing equipment, photographic chemicals, cameras and projectors are part of the product portfolio of the traditional products. Digital storing media, software, other digitization options, and online services make up the new-age products and services.

Kodak has found innovative ways to bridge the traditional film and digital technologies in an effort to stimulate demand for all its products. For example, the Kodak Picture Maker, which can produce photo enlargements from prints, complement the traditional services using high-technology imaging processors (Kodak, 2000a).

THE POTENTIAL FOR KODAK'S PRODUCTS IN CHINA

China is unarguably one of Kodak's most promising emerging markets. "If just one half of China's population used but one 36-exposure roll per year - three pictures a month - that would add 500 more pictures taken per second. That is the equivalent of adding another U.S. or Japan to the world photographic market" (Swift, 1999: 2).

The size of the population, however, is not the only driver of economic growth for Kodak's products in China. Economic and technological improvements, trade liberalization and demand for film products is likely to stimulate Kodak's business potential in this emerging market.

Economic and Technological Improvements

Chinese standards of living and disposable income are growing, and minority segments in the population are becoming increasingly affluent. From 1980 to 1997 the country's economy has exhibited double-digit growth rates, making it the seventh largest economy in the world (World Development Report, 1999). The company estimates that demand for photographic products and services grows at twice the rate of GDP growth (Swift, 1999).

If the demand for film in China mirrors other emerging markets, the company expects the per capita film consumption to increase from less than half a roll a year to about three once income reaches about $10,000 (Swift, 1999). China's per capita GNP adjusted to purchasing power is currently about $3,570 (World Development Report, 1999).

China is making enormous strides in all areas of technology, the economy and society, catching up rapidly with the west. For example, the number of Internet users has been doubling every six months and is expected to exceed 100 million in the next four years. Technological dualism is persistent as traditional and modern elements are juxtaposed. While 90% of the population own televisions, only 30% have running toilets (Rand, 2000).

Trade Liberalization

China is expected to join the World Trade Organization (WTO) shortly. China's entry into the WTO will result in lower tariffs and trade restrictions that will allow Kodak to become more competitive in the Chinese market. For example, the basic 35-millimeter, $15 "point and shoot" camera manufactured in China is the best selling camera in India. Because of government regulation, the company cannot sell the camera in China (Rand, 2000). Such problems will be rectified once China enters the WTO.

Demand for Film Products

Several socioeconomic factors are likely to increase the demand for film products in China during the coming decade. Strong family tradition coupled with massive migration to the cities is likely to accelerate the demand for pictures to bridge the physical distance created by the new economic landscape. The one child policy advocated for years by the government has led to lavish attention showered on youngsters in the form of toys and travel, which leads to many "Kodak moments". Finally, pictures are used as a method of educating children about moral issues, respect to tradition, authority and the elderly (Swift, 2000).

Only 15% of China's households presently own a camera, up from 11% in 1996 (Rand, 2000). Despite the low penetration of cameras in the market, the Chinese photo market is large and profitable. As the penetration of cameras will increase, so will the demand for photographic products and services.

KODAK'S INVOLVEMENT IN CHINA

Kodak is a world leader in imaging with operations that span over 150 countries and employ about 80,000 employees worldwide (Kodak, 2000a). Emerging markets are key to Kodak's future growth and competitive advantage. According to David Swift (1999), Chairman and President of Greater China Area, emerging markets are expected to grow from $2.2 billion in revenues in 1998 to as much as $4.0 billion by 2004. Given China's enormous population and cultural affinity for taking pictures, the country provides a cornerstone for Kodak's emerging market strategy.

Today, Kodak is heavily involved in the Chinese market and sees it as a major growth market for the future. The company's total investment in China - over $1.2 billion - rivals that of General Motors, Ford and General Electric and includes, in addition to the consumer imaging business, an investment in all of Kodak's business segments.

Building Markets in China

Until 1993, Kodak's involvement in China had been rather modest. The company had 30 employees operating in only three cities (Shanghai, Beijing and Guangzhou) and its market share was dead last. The situation has changed for the better after the 1993 appointment of a new chairman of Kodak, George Fisher, who previously led Motorola into China and recognized the opportunities there. Under his leadership, Kodak has:

- Created a Greater China Region division
- Moved Senior Executives and highly competent Chinese-speaking marketing professionals into the region
- Opened 11 representative offices
- Developed relationships with distributors, wholesalers, and government agencies
- Expanded retail presence for Kodak's products

In addition, to position itself as a leader in the imaging sector and to fend off competition, Kodak made a significant investment (about $1.2 billion), consolidating and modernizing the entire Chinese photographic industry and manufacturing facilities of the government. The decision to invest was primarily based on four operating principles:

- Make products where you sell them
- Make world class products using world class technology
- Get costs into local currency to hedge against fluctuations and devaluations
- Accept short-term risk and volatility for long-term growth (Swift, 1999).

Kodak's Achievements in China

The Chinese market has rewarded Kodak for its well-constructed strategies:

- In 1999, sales of Kodak films in China exceeded sales in Germany (formerly Kodak's largest foreign market for photographic products). Kodak's Chinese revenues are currently more than $300 million.
- Revenues of China's operation in 1999 grew 36% while profits mushroomed 58%, which compares favorably with Kodak's global growth of 5% and 13%, respectively.
- China is Kodak's 10th largest export market.
- Kodak is the best selling film in China, with a 40% market share.
- Kodak Express with 5,500 outlets in 500 cities is the largest retail chain in China.

KODAK EXPRESS OUTLET

In the international environment, the definition of franchising is not clear because in many markets, particularly emerging ones, franchising along with its legal framework have not evolved to the level of the United States. Kodak uses the term "Quality Monitoring Network" for its franchising system in order to avoid falling under the Chinese franchising regulations.

Kodak's Express outlets are managed as franchises in that (1) they utilize independently owned outlets, (2) which are obligated under contract (3) to buy and display 100% Kodak products and services, and (4) utilize Kodak's store specifications including display of the Kodak brand, logo, and signage. The entrepreneur has to front the startup operational costs and bear the risk of failure.

The Kodak Express chain is, therefore, a network of Chinese owned and operated stores that are identified with Kodak's global brand name, closely resembling what is considered to be a franchise relationship in the company's home market.

The stores provide for Kodak:

- A front-line retailing presence
- A wide distribution of Kodak products/services and brand name
- A strategic asset for Kodak in China for market development (Swift, 1999).

Kodak Express outlets have experienced rapid growth since 1993. There are currently about 5,500 independent Kodak outlets in more than 500 cities (Rand, 2000; Swift, 1999). These outlets are located in major cities particularly on the east coast. Since 71% of China's population (about 900 million) lives in rural dwellings, potential exists for network expansion in the peripheral regions and in the western regions of the country (Rand, 2000). Kodak signs up entrepreneurs at the rate of three per day and is planning to grow its franchising system to 8,000 outlets by 2001 (Swift, 1999).

To achieve this lofty goal the company is prepared to re-design its merchandising every two years, introduce new products and services through aggressive marketing efforts (including both push and pull elements), and design 12 prototype "imaging centers" utilizing digital photographic technology (Rand, 2000).

The company is pursuing a more intensive and extensive distribution of its Kodak Express outlets. The company, through the Kodak Express outlets, plans to launch grass-root marketing development programs that will rent cameras, educate consumers on the value, fun and simplicity of photography, and encourage more photo taking and sharing. The company will use stores on wheels to extend to smaller cities (Swift, 1999). It will also open outlets in Chinese post offices, in retailing areas, and in larger stores of multinational companies such as WalMart.

The company will also sell master (multi-unit) franchises. In January 2000, the company signed an agreement with Multi-Asia to open 20 film-processing and digital-imaging service stores under the name of Kodak Express. Each store will require sales area from 45 to 130 square meters, an estimated investment of RMB 500,000 to RMB 1 million and with a payback period of 18-24 months (Kodak, 2000b).

In order to help spur the demand for and success of its independently owned franchised Kodak outlets, the company has lowered the costs of ownership, provided extensive training and marketing support, and offered prospective store owners a mortgage secured by Kodak's photo-finishing equipment from the International Commercial Bank of China. The financial support and market-based loans to would-be small business owners is unusual in China's cash driven society (Rand, 2000).

METHODS

An in-depth interview questionnaire, developed by Dahlstrom and Nygaard (1999), was used for our interview. The research instrument was developed for the purpose of understanding ownership decisions in U.S.-based franchising networks. The questionnaire was slightly modified and shortened to fit the Chinese context.

We used double translation to ensure that the meanings of questions were not lost. The English version was translated to Chinese and then back into English twice by two university-trained bilingual translators in Shanghai, China on June 2000. Both translations were then evaluated to see if they converge and if they reflect the original intention of the interview questions. The interview took place in July 2000 in Shanghai, China.

The process of doing research in China is different from the process followed in the West, and reveals some of the intricacies of doing business there. Neither the interviewee nor the interviewers wanted to be identified by name. The interviewers, which were previously government employees, as well as the facilitators, preferred to remain anonymous despite the tremendous contributions they have made. Furthermore, Guanxi - a link of people who developed a mutual relationship - was used to secure the interview, locate an appropriate interviewer, contact potential interviewees, translate the questionnaire and the answers, and allow for the smooth exchange of information. The total amount of money required to conduct this research was significantly reduced due to personal connections.

THE INTERVIEW

We interviewed one of the managers in charge of developing the Shanghai franchising system of Kodak's express stores. Shanghai is the biggest consumer market in China with about 16 million people. The city already buys more Kodak films than Hong Kong and is now rivaling New York City in consumption, providing a lucrative market for many entrepreneurs (Rand, 2000).

1. What are the main products of your chain stores?
We are mainly in the business of developing films, and retailing printing paper, cameras and related equipment. The developing service in traditional chains accounts for more than 90% of the whole business. However, in half of the newly developed stores the developing service only accounts for 60-70%. The retailing business as a whole is on the increase.

2. How many chains stores are running under the name of "Kodak"?
There are almost 200 stores running in Shanghai and this year the number will increase dramatically.

3. How many stores are owned by "Kodak" Company?
Nearly 20%.

4. Who owns the real estate property of these stores?
The franchisee, that is, the investor.

5. Why do you want to run the two different kinds of stores?
Because we want to let the brand name of Kodak extend to every corner of people's lives and everybody could feel the service of Kodak.

6. What are the problems you will face first when you choose a store location?
The major problem we consider is whether the location we choose has the potential market (power) of sales and a large traffic of people. We think a

place that is suitable to open a store is in business areas, scenic spots (tourist destination), living residence, schools, concentration place of corporations & organizations, and concentration place of traffic (such as the exit of subway).

7. After you find a location, will you decide to set up your own store or run the franchisee store?

It depends. If the place is very attractive and there are no Kodak stores in its neighborhood, we will set up our own store. Otherwise, we will wait for investors or those franchising investors.

8. For a franchisee store, what is the capital requirement?

The new store owner needs to invest in the equipment that can develop and enlarge color films, rent, decoration, furniture and floating (active) capitals. The equipment (machine) mentioned above are 2 kinds: one is domestically produced and the other is imported from other countries. Accordingly, the price is:

Soweni 955E, RMB 107,500;

Ruorishi QSS2600, RMB 234,000;

Ruorishi QSS2611, RMB 630,000

Ruorishi QSS2301, RMB 840,000.

Each franchisee can equip himself/herself according to his/her own needs and conditions. What's more, the new store's acreage should be more than 20 square meters. Thus, the decoration cost is around RMB 20, 000. The furniture for business use needs RMB10,000 and the floating capital needed is around RMB 20,000.

9. Is there any big difference in operation cost between the franchisee store and stores owned by company itself?

There is not a lot of difference and actually they are quite similar. But still there is some difference, which is unavoidable.

10. If the store doesn't run well, how much will be lost in the initial investment?

It is very difficult to say. The loss is about 30% of the initial investment, but still it depends on your following work, whether you change your business scope or continue to run the developing store. In the latter part, the equipment can be reused and thus some loss can be offset.

11. If a store went into bankruptcy, how do you calculate the salvaged value?

It depends on the special circumstance. If we calculate in 5 years, then every year the depreciation will be around 20%.

12. How much is the management training cost? How many parts does it include?

It is divided into two parts: the training at the early stage and at the later stage. The former includes skill training after buying the equipment and it is free. The latter includes training meetings 3-4 times per year, such as the training of staff and superintendents in stores and how to manage the engine room (the room that has the developing equipment). This part of the cost is very small.

13. Are there any other operational costs?
Expenses at the earlier stage, such as recruiting personnel and applying for licenses should be counted in. There is no subsequent (following) cost.

14. How many parts does the franchisee fee contain? What does each cost?
No franchisee fee (in 3 years). Later there will be extra and special items. But the franchisee store should promise the following things:
1) 100% to use Kodak films and liquid medicine, and the stock must be purchased from the assigned supplier.
2) 100% to make sure that it displays Kodak films and products.
3) 100% to put Kodak ads and puff. If it is an open-up store, it must accept the operation idea of our company and the regulations in the storefront design as well. It must use 100% of the loyal films.

15. What are the royalties charged from the franchisee?
There is no need for the franchisee to turn in any profit, but the franchisee must display 100% of Kodak's products and buy its equipment from Kodak.

16. Will you have other investments in the franchisees?
Yes. Every year there are 3-4 training meetings and the sales rep will go to each store regularly to instruct the franchisee how to run the store and manage it.

17. Do you get the information on sales continuously from your franchisee stores?
Normally, we need to get the business operation information of those stores. Besides asking directly, we can get the purchasing information from suppliers and thus we come to some conclusions. But there are many proprietors that make falsifications in the report, which increases the difficulty of getting reliable information.

18. Is this information gained through the computer?
Not at this moment, but all the computers in Kodak stores will be in the network in the future.

19. Is the investment in computer included in the franchisee fee?
No, this should be calculated in addition. But there is a trend in the future to include it in the franchisee fee.

20. How often do you communicate with your franchisees?
Once or twice every month, the sales rep would visit and supervise franchisee stores periodically. At the same time, the training meeting (3-4 times every year) serves as a good channel for communication.

21. How do you assess the product quality and service quality of the franchisee stores?

Regional representatives will assess the product and service quality in each store on their tours of inspection. At the same time we could assess it from feedback of customers[1].

22. Considering the price, new product, store location, store front, working time and running the store, how much decision power belongs to the franchisee?

The decision power lies with the franchisee, but Kodak provides a suggested retail price. The franchisee can adjust the price accordingly. Once the new product comes out, Kodak Company will advertise and promote a lot to assist the marketing of new products. As to renting the storefront, it is decided by the franchisee. With regard to choosing a location, it should follow the basic requirement of Kodak Company, otherwise, Kodak Company will involve itself in it and the assessment won't be passed.

23. Do you have a general plan for the number of the franchisee stores and stores owned by company? Why?

No. Since the current film-developing market is not saturated and there is a huge potential in increase, the number of franchising stores is not controlled.

24. Do you plan to expand the scale of franchisee stores?

It depends on the needs of customers and the market.

CONCLUSION

Kodak's consumer imaging division accounts for the majority of sales and profits, and China constitutes one of the fastest-growing consumer markets for photographic products and services in Kodak's global portfolio. Despite its immense population of over 1.2 billion people, China is a difficult market to penetrate. The cultural, economic and political systems in China are markedly distinct and require flexible and innovative approaches.

What lessons can one draw from Kodak's experience in China? Kodak success in China has been based on three major strategies:

- Franchise for rapid distribution
- Invest in business infrastructure with a long-term planning horizon
- Tie close relationships with multiple levels of government

Franchise for Rapid Distribution

Kodak's Express outlets have been increasingly used as a method of distribution to China's vast consumer market and will likely continue to play a major role in Kodak's future penetration of the market. Kodak franchises its stores to achieve rapid distribution of its products and services, to build brand-name equity, and to penetrate remote, and often less desirable, regions.

There are a number of similarities between the structure of Kodak's franchising system in China and developed franchising systems in the U.S.

(1) The proportion of franchised outlets in Kodak's system (80%) in China is similar to the resulting proportions of franchised outlets observed in developed franchising systems in the U.S., which range from 70 to 90 percent depending on the industry.

(2) Similar to U.S.-based franchisors, Kodak prefers to own the most profitable locations and franchise those locations that are more remote from critical population centers and high traffic and tourist areas. The company does not seem to target a particular ratio of franchisee owned outlets, but is likely to favor franchising in remote and less desirable locations.

(3) The initial investment by the franchisee can cost as much as RMB 890,000 (about $ 107, 488), not including rent. This amount is comparable to an investment in a U.S.-based franchising unit. However, considering that the average GNP per capita in the United States is 33 times higher than that of China, the capital requirements are high when viewed in terms of local purchasing power.

(4) The operations of the franchise-store and parent-store are very similar in terms of cost and management. Training is provided to employees in the use of the equipment and the management of the store.

Unlike most business-format franchisors in the U.S., royalties or advertising fees are not imposed on would-be entrepreneurs probably because monitoring is difficult and because quick expansion is desirable. Since monitoring and enforcement of company policies at the franchisee level is difficult in China, the company depends on selling the input materials to the franchisee, including ones relating to film processing, store layout, and final products/services sold. The company, therefore, does not depend on royalties, but rather on purchases of input products, similar to some product-name franchises in the U.S.

Invest with a Long-Term Planning Horizon

Consistent with practices of major multinational corporations in developing countries (Alon and Banai, 2000), Kodak has made a significant investment in infrastructure development. The strategic decision to invest over $1.2 billion in the Chinese market was based on Kodak's perception that China is one of the most important consumer markets in the world. This is exemplified in the opening quote by Kodak's Chairman, George Fisher: *"To be the leader in the world, you have to be the leader in China."*

The investment is also consistent with the previously discussed Kodak's operating philosophy of making products where you sell them, getting costs into local currency, and accepting short-term risk for long term growth. George Fisher claimed that success in China hinges on Kodak's ability to further China's interests in addition to its own and, therefore, Kodak should pursue *long-term mutual benefit* (Swift, 1999). Appendix 1 discusses the impact of this investment on China.

Tie Close Relationships with Multiple Levels of Government

Because in China many of the key resources are controlled by government, negotiations with the government were a non-trivial task, especially in light of the burdensome bureaucratic and multi-level structure of the Chinese political arena. Kodak's negotiations included four provincial governments, three city governments, a number of tax authorities and multiple government ministries as well as seven companies and several banks and trust companies (embodying varying levels of government control). To coordinate the negotiations among the various stakeholders, a central coordinating committee consisting of senior officials was formed (Swift, 1999).

The deal that emerged from the negotiations was beneficial to both Kodak and the People Republic of China. Kodak received:
- A business with acceptable projected income and rates of return
- A temporary monopoly to work with Chinese sensitizing factories
- An effective control of legal entities that direct operations
- A royalty compensation for use of proprietary imaging technology
- A relief from liability of non-productive assets and previous debt

On the other hand, the Chinese have:
- Rationalized and improved their imaging industry
- Substituted some products previously imported and created a potential for exporting
- Generated tax revenues rather than a drain on government resources
- Reduced industry debt to equity ratio
- Obtained leading imaging technology
- Increased the quality and quantity of long-term employment (For more detail see appendix 1).

Kodak has followed a multifaceted strategy of building a brand name and retailing presence via Kodak Express, setting up manufacturing sites using western technologies and innovative management, developing governmental relationships, and recently establishing alliances with state-of-the-art domestic firms, such as Sina.com and Etang.com. Kodak was able to leverage the resources, both physical and human, to position itself competitively worldwide.

Large companies with plans that span over the long-term horizon need to consider China a priority in their overseas expansion to obtain a first-movers advantage over their competitors. Kodak's expansion into China has proved to be profitable and with much future potential. By developing unique relationships with suppliers, wholesalers, distributors, entrepreneurs, and government officials, Kodak has erected barriers to market entry that will be difficult for competition to surmount.

APPENDIX 1

THE IMPACT OF KODAK ON THE BUSINESS ENVIRONMENT

This section was included as an appendix to the chapter for two reasons. First, there is a debate in the literature of globalization, in general, and international franchising, in specific, on whether internationalization has a positive or negative impact on the host country. Second, a lot of controversy surrounds the question of whether China should join the WTO. Particularly, its proposed entry into the WTO has worried union leaders and activists of human rights, workers' rights, and the environment. This appendix was constructed to review the impact that Kodak had on the business environment in China.

Much of the information in this section is borrowed from the presentation of David Swift (1999) and the special issue about China written by Rand (2000) and published by the Democrat and Chronicle, a newspaper based in Rochester, the city in which Kodak is headquartered.

In the case of Kodak in China, Kodak has stimulated the small business sector, created jobs, increased the economic efficiency and global competitiveness of China's imaging sector, enhanced the standard of living and working conditions of labor, improved ecological conditions, and increased the tax base of the industry.

Spurring Development of Small Businesses and Entrepreneurship

The company supports budding entrepreneurs through extensive distribution, brand name advertising, and relationships with the governmental agencies. The loans to prospective independent Kodak Express owners, the manufacturing and distribution infrastructure, and the marketing support of a multinational company form the basis for the development of small entrepreneurial businesses in China. Kodak provides company-based marketing program, which includes extensive distribution of Kodak outlets and signage and monumental billboards in key tourist areas, such as the "Bund" in Shanghai, leading to a highly recognized brand name.

The benefits to potential buyers of Kodak's franchises are similar to the ones experienced in the West: being in business for yourself, but not by yourself. Entrepreneurial freedom to adjust prices and to choose locations is granted to franchisees along with guidelines from the company

Creating and Destroying Jobs

The unemployment problem in China - 15 million in cities and 130 million in rural areas - has prompted the Chinese government to favor companies that can deliver jobs. The net impact of Kodak's on job creation in China is positive. Since 1995, the Chinese workforce has expanded from 316 to 5,556, a 1,658% increase. On the other hand, the consolidation of the government's six state-owned factories into three when Kodak became involved cost about 4,000 people their jobs. The remaining jobs created are more competitive by global standards, however.

In addition, Kodak's franchise chain in China spans around 5,000 outlets. If each outlet employs 3-5 full-time employees, another 20,000 jobs on average are created.

At the same time that Kodak was expanding jobs in China, many jobs were cut in Kodak's domestic market. While the company denies causation, the evidence is compelling. Kodak's U.S. workforce has decreased its domestic workforce by 20% since 1995 to 43,000. Sixty five percent or 28,000 of these jobs were cut in its home city, Rochester, New York. Nonetheless, much of the Kodak film sold in China is manufactured in Rochester and packaged in China. And given that China is Kodak's 10th largest export market, one can argue that China has helped maintain jobs at home. The net impact on jobs at the home is not clear.

Increasing Economic Efficiencies and Global Competitiveness

Kodak has restructured and modernized China's entire imaging sector, by consolidating factories, opening new state-of-the-art manufacturing facilities, and positioning the industry for supplying domestic and even international demand for imaging-related products and services.

The consolidation of the government's six state-owned factories, while cutting jobs, has rendered these factories competitive by world standards, able to operate efficiently and export effectively to neighboring markets. As mentioned before, the new industrial development can withstand international competition and exert its power abroad as well.

Introducing Western Work Standards and Improving Standards of Livings and Working Conditions

With the Western work standards also come the harsh realities of the market economy. Kodak is not a parental, nurturing company offering life-long employment. The threat of a layoff is always lurking. Jobs are not guaranteed. 450 jobs in Wuxi were eliminated when a photochemical plant was closed. Workers work hard to meet individual and group performance to keep their jobs. Kodak, however, guarantees pay for work, and provides steady income to many.

Workers report that the working environment is energizing and empowering, providing incentives for self improvement and rewarding hard work and cooperation. In the Xiamen factory that employs 1,200 people, for example, 10% of workers' salary depends on meeting tough environmental and performance goals.

In the Xiamen factory for $100 a month workers are willing to work hard and diligently. While by American standards, this salary seems miniscule, it is a respectable wage in China that can buy one a living. On average, workers' salaries in factories Kodak purchased went up 30%, but the workload doubled. Some employees' salaries tripled and a few became millionaires. Mr. Yu, for example, who is the sole distributor of film and other products to more than 400 outlets is also an owner of 10 express stores. He makes about RMB 10 million - about $1.2 million - a year.

The rise in the standard of living has allowed the affected employees to buy homes, furniture, consumer goods, durables, and education for their children. Kodak has also improved the working conditions of many of its employees by providing social amenities and Western-style working conditions. For example, Kodak has provided bus service from downtown Xiamen, onsite cafeterias, 40 hour work week, 40 hours of training per year, and brighter job prospects for its employees. It also cut down carrying loads from over 30 lbs to less than 10 lbs, reducing the number of injuries.

Improving Ecological Standards

Kodak employs western pollution and environmental standard in its operations in China. It installed oil-fired boilers, for example, in its new film-making plant in Xiamen last year, despite the permission to use cheaper coal-burning fuel, which causes air pollution.

Increasing the Tax Base

The creation of new businesses as well as profit generating potential of the factories greatly increased the tax base of the industry. For example, Kodak has paid more taxes in the first 6 months of operations than Fuda Co., one of the purchased factories, had in 14 years. It is Xiamen's largest taxpayer.

Summary

China, as a whole, also benefited from Kodak's operations. Aside from the tangible rewards of jobs and tax revenues, Kodak has helped China streamline its market into the global economy by encouraging entrepreneurship and introducing Western-style work processes, procedures and conditions. The company has also participated in the "creative destruction" of the economy, which increases the efficiency and productivity of its resources. The mutual interdependence of Kodak and China is likely to foster a deeper and closer relationship between the two entities for years to come[2].

NOTES

[1] Aside from the difficulties of monitoring sales, checking on product quality is highly elusive. While regional representatives are supposed to assess the product and service at the franchisee level, we found some quality problems both of product and service at one particular store in Shanghai. For example, the pictures we developed were developed backwards (evident by the lettering on the back of the developed film). When we tried to take advantage of a promotion to laminate one picture out of each roll, we found that an employee had grouped all of our rolls into one envelope, making it very difficult and time-consuming to find the appropriate negative. Overall, however, we felt that the service was courteous, quick, of acceptable quality, and affordable (about $2 per roll).

[2] At the macro-environmental level, it is unclear how U.S. foreign policy, particularly with regard to the insistence on the independence of Taiwan and the enforcement of human, workers' and environmental policies, will impact future relationships between the People Republic of China and U.S.-based companies. Foreigners' occupation of China during WWII, the U.S.-led (accidental) bombing of the Chinese embassy in Belgrade, Yugoslavia during the conflict in Kosovo, and the U.S. desire to build a missile defense system at home, have made China suspicious of Westerner's actions. Bilateral tensions can increase the political and country risks of U.S.-based multinational companies, icons of western economic imperialism. However, companies that contribute to the Chinese economy, such as Kodak, are less susceptible to negative governmental intervention.

REFERENCES

Alon, Ilan, and Moshe Banai, "Franchising Opportunities and Threats in Russia," *Journal of International Marketing*, 8 (3), 104-119.

Dahlstrom, Robert, and Arne Nygaard (1999), "Ownership Decisions in Plural Contractual Systems: Twelve Networks from the Quick Service Restaurant Industry," *European Journal of Marketing*, 33 (1/2) 59-87.

E-trade (2000), Company Research, Eastman Kodak (EK) member's only reports (retrieved Oct. 9, 2000; www.etrade.com).

Kodak (2000a), Kodak Business Overview, (retrieved October 19, 2000) www.kodak.com.cn/CN/en/nav/aboutKodak/overview.shtml.

Kodak (2000b), "Multi-Asia Partners with Kodak to Venture into Photographic Business in China," (retrieved October 19, 2000), www.kodak.com.cn/CN/en/corp/pressCenter/pr20000124.shtml.

Rand, Ben, "The New China: Rochester's New Frontier," *Democrat and Chronicle: A Special Report*, (June 25), 1-8.

Security Exchange Commission (retrieved September 2000), www.sec.gov/archives/edgar/data/31235/0000031235-00-000004.txt

Swift, David (1999), "Remarks of David Swift Chairman & President, Greater China Region Eastman Kodak Company," in Goldman Sachs 21st Century China Conference, (September 26-28), 1-8.

World Development Report (1999), *Knowledge for Development*, Washington DC: World Bank.

Chapter 13
The Internationalization of Marks & Spencer

Ilan Alon
Crummer Graduate School of Business, Rollins College

INTRODUCTION

This case study describes the internationalization of Marks & Spencer (M&S), a giant British retailer. In the late 1990s, the company suffered a series of misfortunes, both at home (Britain) and abroad: company sales have dropped, stock prices and market capitalization were substantially reduced, and overseas profits have declined. In January 1999, following a terrible earning announcement, the company announced that it had formed a marketing department, forcing the company to become more proactive and market driven. To head the department, M&S promoted James Benfield, a 17-year veteran of the retailing giant who worked as a former head of menswear, home furnishings, and direct mail.

For years, M&S' marketing philosophy was simple: produce high quality products under a recognized brand name at affordable (but not cheap) prices, and advertise through word-of-mouth. However, in recent years, this marketing philosophy has come under attack as the company started loosing its competitive stance. The move to develop a marketing department was a departure from a long tradition of production/manufacturing emphasis. The problem facing James Benfield: how can M&S emerge from the slump and reposition itself as a fierce global competitor in the international marketplace?

BRIEF BACKGROUND

Marks and Spencer of Britain (often referred to as Marks & Sparks by locals) is a general retailer that sells clothes, gifts, home furnishings, and foods under the St. Michael trademark in the UK, Europe, the Americas and Far East. The company also operates financial services segment, which accounted for about 3% of the company's 1998 profits (Dow Jones Industrial 1999).

Marks & Spencer (M&S) started as a stall in 1884 by Michael Marks in the Leads market using a L5 loan from a wholesaler. The company stressed value and low prices as a hallmark for development. By 1901, the company acquired 35 outlets as well as a new partner, Tom Spencer. By 1949 all the company's stores carried mostly private label (St. Michael) products produced by British suppliers (De Nardi-Cole 1998).

For many years the company's mission has been to offer consumers quality, value, and service. The company relied on five operating principles to achieve its mission:
(1) Developing long-term relationships with suppliers,
(2) Providing value through a narrow merchandise selection at affordable prices,
(3) Supporting local (British) industry (De Nardi-Cole 1998),
(4) Promoting from within (The Economist 1998), and
(5) Using a single brand name St. Michael for most of its products (Financial Times 1999).

These operating tenets have gained M&S the support of British producers, consumers, and workers. The sixth largest employer in British manufacturing, the textile industry, with over 354,000 workers, owes a large part of its existence to M&S (The Economist 1999c). M&S has encouraged British textile manufacturers to keep factories at home, which led to a better check on quality and more flexibility in manufacturing and distribution (The Economist 1999c). The British have responded with affection. A British writer described M&S as "quintessential British institution, woven into the fabric of our national life, as firmly lodged in our psyches as furniture in the front room" (Financial Times 1999, p. 10).

CURRENT BUSINESS SITUATION

Using the business model described above, M&S had achieved impressive growth rates and market shares in many of its business segments. By 1994, the firm had 18% of the UK retail market, 33% of women's undergarment market, and 20% of men's suit market (De Nardi-Cole 1998). The company has 40% of the nation's underwear market and 14% of the clothing market - only retailer in Europe to have double-digit market share (Financial Times 1999). M&S food market share has been around 4.3% (M&S Press Releases 1999). The impressive market shares have gained M&S the reputation of a leading retailer in the United Kingdom.

The euphoria, however, did not last as M&S caught investors and business spectators off guard. In 1998, the company's stock fell 34%

(Business Week 1998). Pretax profits fell by as much as 41% (to $1.09 billion) and market share declined, for the first time in years, by almost 1% (The Economist 1999a). In May 1999, the company reported full year profits of L630 million, a 50% fall from 1997-1998 (Financial Times 1999). Warburg Dillon Read, an investment bank, reduced its profit expectations for M&S by 10% for 1999-2000 (Dow Jones Industrial 1999).

Overseas profits have declined from their 1996-1997 high of L100 million (Financial Times 1999) to a loss of L15 million, before exceptional items, for fiscal year 1998. Sales measured in local currencies were down by 3% (M&S Press Releases 1999).

Table 13.1 shows the financial snapshot of the company. It also compares key financial measures of M&S (Britain's leading retailer) with those of Wal-Mart (US leading retailer).

Table 13.1: Snapshot of Marks & Spencer Compared To Wal-Mart

	Marks & Spencer	**Wal-Mart**
Market Capitalization	$18 billion	$204 billion
Sales	$13.3 billion	$150.7 billion
% of Sales Overseas	16%	17%
No. of Countries	34	10
Revenue	$14 billion	$144 billion
Return on Assets	13%	10%
Return on Equity	18%	23%
Current Ratio	0.98	1.30
Price-Earning Ratio	31	44
52 Week Price Trend	-31%	63%

* Compiled by the author from Dow Jones Industrial (1999), Market Guide (1999), Economist (1999d). Retrieved June 1999.

The company blamed consumer confidence and a strong pound for the decline in sales and company's value. M&S Press Release (1999) stated that the deterioration in 1998-1999 profits has been the result of (1) a shortfall in expected sales, (2) a slowdown in overseas markets, and (3) the purchase of Littlewoods stores for L90 million. Recessionary business environment in Europe and the Asian crisis have put a great strain on global profitability. At the same time, domestic and international competition has intensified both from specialty retailers and mega merchandisers, such as Wal-Mart.

Stockholders and business analysts were not convinced that the company's problems were merely external. M&S stock has underperformed other British retailers by more than 25%. They blamed M&S management for dull merchandising, poor inventory control, and lagged response time to competitive environmental conditions (Business Week 1998. Industry commentators have criticized the color, size and shape of their clothes, the lousy retailing climate, the unglamorous stores, the overpriced products, and the personal service (Financial Times 1999).

COMPETITION

The core values of M&S: quality, affordability and service came under the greatest attack, not from critics, but from competitors. Retailers such as Top Shop, Kookai, Miss Selfridge, Jigsaw, Oasis, Warehouse and the Gap offer more fashionable designs and trendier labels. Other retailers, such as Next, Debenhams and BhS, offer better values. Food chains, such as Tesco, Waitrose, and Sainsbury's have moved into prepared foods (Financial Times 1999). M&S is being challenged in every single business segment it competes. By its own admission, M&S has not changed quickly enough to react to accelerating competition, which resulted in unacceptable fall in profitability and market share (M&S Press Releases 1999).

MARKETING AT MARKS & SPENCER

Product

M&S products can be divided into three lines of business: (1) general merchandise, (2) foods, and (3) financial services. General merchandise include clothing, undergarments, handbags, footwear, goods for the home, children toys, books and cosmetics.

The food business carries a wide range of prepared foods, perishables, ethnic foods, meats, alcoholic and nonalcoholic beverages. Among the eclectic selection of foods are chocolate-covered ginger biscuits, salmon *en croute*, chicken tikka sandwiches, and mushroom risotto (Financial Times 1999). The company is currently changing its food offerings with new bistro style meals and introducing juice and coffee bars in some stores (Marketing 1999).

Finally, the company also sells financial services including a store credit card, personal loans, personal equity plans, unit trusts, and life insurance. M&S credit cards are the only ones accepted by the company in its British stores, where M&S does not accept major credit cards such as Mastercard, Visa, Discover or American Express. Customers deposit money into their M&S credit cards and can get up to 20 times the purchasing power. For example, with a deposit of $100, the customer gets a line of credit of $2000 (De Nardi-Cole 1998). The company has also diversified into life assurances and group pension contracts (M&S Press Releases 1999). While the financial segment is relatively small (about 3% of profits), it is the fastest growing segment of M&S operations. Profits over 1998 increased by 24% to L111 million, while the number of card accounts increased to 5.2 million (M&S Press Release 1999).

The St. Michael brand name has been used on most of the products sold through M&S. The brand, therefore, is used on a wide range of products targeting everyone from middle aged patrons to kids. M&S expertise has been delivering consistently high quality products under the St. Michael brand name. A commentator in Financial Times (1999), however, suggested that the company follow the example of Debenhams (a competing retailer) and use sub-brands to target specific segments of its market.

Price

Marks and Spencer followed a value price strategy from its inception, starting with Michael Marks who put all his products for a penny in one side of the store with a sign saying "Don't ask the price, it's a penny." Since M&S has concentrated on middle class customers, it has continued value pricing strategy. Although most of its suppliers have been from Britain, which has higher textile manufacturing costs than some developing nations, M&S was able to maintain its value by developing strong economic bonds with suppliers. Through its economies of scale in buying, M&S has been able to require manufacturers to adhere to strict quality standards and to bargain lower prices for its customers (De Nardi-Cole 1998).

Due to the recent strength of the sterling and the large British manufactured content in the stores, profit margins has substantially declined in recent years. Yet, M&S has managed to remain moderately priced. For example, a pair of casual pants in one major European city cost about $50.

In anticipation for the Euro conversion, the company features prices both in local currency and Euros in its European stores. It also has limited conversion tables by the cashiers.

Place

M&S stores come in two basic formats. The first format is a general merchandise store, with its basement dedicated to foods, while the second offers foods only. The average size of the store ranges from 35,000 to 40,000 square feet (3,252 to 3,716 square meters), with a minimum of 100,000 square feet (9,290 square meters) for remote locations. In recent years the firm has been aggressively increasing square-footage of their stores (M&S Annual Report 1998).

M&S tries to locate its stores on the Main streets of major cities, claiming that it seeks "to build critical mass around capital cities or across important conurbation, such as the Rhine-Ruhr area in Germany" (M&S Annual Report 1998, p. 1). Paris, the most significant market in Europe, for example, hosts 20% of the country's population and 10 out of the 20 M&S stores in the country (M&S Annual Report 1998). The company owns a very valuable global portfolio of property, with footholds in prime cities and districts across the world (Financial Times 1999). Competition for prime space, however, has made it necessary to locate in more remote locations.

In 1994, M&S started to aggressively focus on building distribution networks to supply its growing global operations (De Nardi-Cole 1998). The focal point of this network, however, has remained in the United Kingdom.

Promotion

M&S has mostly tried to avoid advertising and has relied on word-of-mouth. Word of mouth advertising was very powerful, not to mention cost-effective. The trade name of St. Michael has become synonymous with quality in a broad segment of products. While the St. Michael brand has been very successful over the years, by focusing on St. Michael products, the company does not get the marketing backing of popular brand names.

In the past the company used advertising only in rare cases, such as when M&S was introducing a new product or retail format or when brand name recognition was low, as in the case of its store introduction in Paris (De Nardi-Cole 1998). M&S' media spending was about L4.7 million, compared to L18.8 million of 10 other leading retailers (Jardin 1999b). After recent years of bad financial statements, the company has significantly increased the advertising budget to about L20 million (Jardin 1999a). The company has already invited advertising agencies to pitch and is planning its second-ever television campaign focusing on M&S products (Marketing 1999).

INTERNATIONALIZATION OF MARKS & SPENCER

M&S experimental involvement with internationalization began in the 1940s. Unlike most service firms, however, the company began exporting its St. Michael brands overseas as a way to test the waters (recall that the company did not own manufacturers, merely branded their merchandise using the St. Michael private label). Briggs (1992) estimated that in 1955 the company was exporting about $1,146,000 worth of merchandise.

Early internationalization of the company was mostly due to domestic factors. Internally, the company started to feel that it has saturated to domestic market and that expansion will have to come from overseas. Externally, some Labor Party members were suggesting nationalizing the leading domestic retailers (De Nardi-Cole 1998). Internationalization was, therefore, seen as a tool of diversification.

Out of the export business, some international franchising relationships were formed. Importers of the St. Michael brand, who were familiar with the success of the brand in their countries, also bought the business format (including store layout and operating style) from M&S. By the early 1990s, St. Michael franchises were operating in 14 economies including some emerging countries such as Gibraltar, Bermuda, Israel and Philippines (Whitehead 1991). Franchising allowed the company to achieve global presence with minimal economic and political risks. As M&S' familiarity with internationalization grew, more direct modes of entry, such as acquisitions and joint ventures, were being used. By 1996, the company had 645 outlets worldwide, most of which (58%) were in the UK, Europe and Canada (De Nardi-Cole 1998).

Modes of Entry

The internationalization of M&S resembles the theoretical explanations of service firm internationalization (Alon 1999; McIntyre and Huszagh 1995). These theories suggest that service firm become increasingly international as they gain experience, willing to commit more company resource and take additional risks. Retailers will use relatively less risky modes of entry, such as exporting and franchising, in markets where market and political risk are high. Retailers will share ownership where sole ownership is prohibited or restricted. In markets, such as the US and the EU, with significant purchasing power, large population and developed infrastructure, retailers enter through high-control high-risk modes of entry, such as sole-ownership and acquisition.

M&S utilizes various types of modes of entry around the world. The company believes in opening its own stores and expanding through acquisitions in major economies. On the other hand, M&S expands through franchise agreements into countries where a partner's local expertise is viewed as beneficial (M&S Annual Report 1998). The company owns stores in Belgium, Canada, France, Germany, Hong-Kong, Ireland, Spain and Netherlands; and franchises in the rest of the countries including The

Bahamas, Bermuda, Çanary Islands, Cyprus, The Czech Republic, Gibraltar, and Israel (De Nardi-Cole 1998). Whitehead (1991) proposed that the company used franchising in countries that have relatively small population size or low per capita incomes, but sufficiently large to support a small number of stores.

When forming international alliances, M&S often preferred an experienced retailer with significant market share. In 1990, M&S went into its first joint venture with Cortefiel, one of Spain's leading retailers. A joint venture was initially used in Spain because it was felt that the market knowledge and power of an existing retailer will help mitigate the cultural distance, and the sometimes adverse political climate(De Nardi-Cole 1998). In Australia, M&S chose a partner who is an experienced local clothing retailer. In China, the company is looking for a likely candidate as the industrial structure of the economy develops (M&S Annual Report 1998).

Maureen Whitehead (1991) was one of the first researchers which examined international franchising at M&S. Whitehead research revealed that M&S used a franchise format that was a hybrid between first trademark franchising and business-format franchising. Trade-name franchising is based on supply of merchandise and trade marks, such as gas service stations and automobile dealerships, while business format franchising relies on a transfer of formalized operating style. M&S' franchisees need to show short and medium horizon business plans and demonstrate minimum level of turnover. The franchisee pays through merchandise purchases and a percentage of inventory turnover. Franchisees can selectively pick only part of the merchandise, instead of full range of products available through the British owned stores.

Regional Analysis of M&S Internationalization

A truly global firm should have operations in all three regional economic blocks. Since 1975, M&S has increasingly become a global retailer, with presence in each of the major trading block: (1) the Americas, (2) Europe, and (3) Far East. Table 13.2 shows current operating results and comparisons of the three regions.

Table 13.2: Operating Results and Regional Comparisons

	The Americas	Europe*	Far East
Turnover	606	538	128
Operating Profits	17	33	18
Number of Stores (Franchised)	43 (5)**	53 (15)	10 (33)

Source: M&S Annual Report 1998,
* includes some Middle-Eastern states
** not including Brooks Brothers 119, and Kings Supermarkets 22.

The Americas

The first major round of acquisitions M&S made was in 1973 of Canadian People's Department Stores (budget retailer), DiAllaird's (older women's store), and Walker's store (modeled after British M&S format). The executives in M&S saw Canada as a good country to invest in because of its high incomes, solid infrastructure, large middle class, low political risk, and use of English language. Since they perceived little cultural distance, they transferred their business formula almost unchanged from the United Kingdom to Canada. They quickly found that even Canada requires some modifications.

The Canadian stores required customization to local needs including the use of Canadian merchandise, enlargement of food departments, restructuring of inner city store, and opening of suburban stores, much of which the company had little experience with. The changes were made to slow and, by 1988, the stores lost about $7 million. Thereafter, the D'Allaird's stores were closed to cut costs and concentrate efforts on more profitable operations (De Nardi-Cole 1998). In May 1999, M&S announced that it will be closing all 38 M&S stores in Canada by September 1999 (Dow Jones Industrial 1999). The company has decided that Canada no longer fits the strategic future, after several attempts to return it to profit have failed. The cost of withdrawal is estimated around L25 million (M&S Press Releases 1999).

M&S entered the US in 1988 using a similar strategy it used in Canada, trough acquisitions. It bought Brooks Brothers (department store, also nicknamed Brooks Bros) to market its clothes and Kings Supermarket to sell its food line. Unlike M&S, which bought its supplies, these companies owned manufacturing facilities. Brooks Brothers and Kings Supermarkets are similar in format to M&S two store formats.

After the acquisition, Brooks Brothers (M&S largest operation in The Americas) expanded its sports selection, widened its product base, and enlarged its customer base. It opened a few locations in malls targeting a younger market. The company used some products from Brooks Brothers clothing line to sell in the UK and European stores. M&S did not change the names of the US chains, probably because of their loyal customer base, nor did it significantly change the product offerings.

The purchase of Brooks Brothers contributed to continuing innovation in the merchandise mix, offered M&S an opportunity to compete in the largest economy in the world, and gave M&S a foothold in the Far East. While some believed that the purchase of Brooks Brothers was overpriced (30 times 1987 profits), it provided M&S with 21 joint venture stores with Daido Worsted Mills in Japan, three US based factories, a charge card business, and a direct marketing operation (De Nardi-Cole 1998).

For year ending 1998, Brooks Brothers increased its number of stores by 7 (to 119), increased market share of US men's clothing market, improved direct marketing, and invested in a new warehouse management system to increase service efficiency. The chain expects to become more contemporary, broaden its market appeal (particularly to working women), and modernize its brand image (M&S Annual Report 1998).

Kings Supermarkets have also shown satisfactory results, two new stores were added in New Jersey, and new stores are being pioneered in Florham Park. Five new Kings Super Markets are expected to open in 1999(M&S Annual Report 1998).

Europe

M&S entered the European market in 1975. This was two years after the less than successful Canadian acquisition. France was chosen as the gateway country, and Paris the gateway city, to the rest of Europe (M&S Annual Report 1998). After much market research, the company decided to adapt the store to French life styles. The French stores offered snugger fit clothing, a wide selection of French wines, and less British imports. Due to a lack of brand name recognition, the company also relied on advertising to spark interest in the stores (De Nardi Cole 1998). From there, M&S expanded to Belgium (1975), Spain (1990), Germany (1996), and recently to smaller economies, such as Greece, Hungary, Portugal, and the Czech Republic.

The Europe report of M&S includes Eastern and Western Europe including some states in the Middle-East. In Europe the company owns 37 stores (in France, Belgium, Holland, Spain, Germany and Ireland) and franchises 53 stores across the rest of Europe and the Middle-East. M&S plans to open new stores in Spain, Belgium, Holland and Ireland, develop new franchises in Turkey, Dubai and Poland, and increase square footage in Czech Republic, Greece and Cyprus. The company hopes to have 60 stores in Continental Europe by year 2000 (Business Week 1998). It is seeking to increase customization to local national tastes by establishing additional brand names to the already successful St. Michael brand (M&S Annual Report 1998). Still, about 80% of the stock sold in continental Europe is the same as the UK home market, while the other 20% reflects differences in culture, size, climate and local preferences (Glew 1994).

In Europe sales from core stores and recently expanded stores were below expectations for 1998-1999, particularly in the major economies of France, Germany and Spain. Profit margins have deteriorated as the company attempted to maintain good value (M&S Press Releases 1999). Sales in the Middle-East, on the other hand, were particularly strong, including the new operation in Kuwait (M&S Press Releases 1999). To increase profitability of European operations, the company (1) closed unprofitable stores (in Zaragosa and Parinor), (2) acquired full control of the Spanish business, (3) gave more control to local managers, and (4) developed a European buying department to meet local demand (M&S Press Releases 1999).

Far East

The entry into the Far East was twofold. M&S first exposure to business in the Far East occurred indirectly through the purchase of Brooks Brothers (1988), which co-owned affiliates in Japan. Brooks Brothers has 19 years of brand exposure trading experience with Japan. Two Brooks Brothers franchises started in Hong-Kong over 1998. M&S believes that Asia will be a major market for Brooks Brothers because of the region's receptiveness to US culture and brand's aspirational values (M&S Annual Report 1998). In recent years, Brooks Brothers Japan was adversely affected by recessionary conditions in the economy (M&S Press Releases 1999).

The second penetration to the Far East was through the brand name of M&S. M&S clothes are marketed as high quality western style items. M&S opened stores in Hong-Kong, which were supplied through the British home base. All of the wholly owned stores in the Far East are in Hong-Kong, the 33 other outlets are franchised across six other nations in the region. In recent years, the company has expanded to suburban areas of Hong-Kong, a move it believes will help it penetrate the Chinese market (M&S Annual Report 1998). The company already has a resident office in Shanghai with a purpose to evaluate the market and to spark interest in a joint venture there (De Nardi-Cole 1998). During the last couple of years, the company expanded its presence in Thailand, Philippines, Indonesia, Korea and Australia. (M&S Annual Report 1998).

The 1997 Asian crisis has seriously stalled retail sales in the region, and M&S stores were not an exception. Both franchised and non-franchised outlets have been adversely affected by the crisis. Despite the slowdown, the company was able to increase the number of owned and franchised stores by 9 to 43. The company's expansion coupled with the adverse conditions created by the Asian crisis have hampered sales and profitability in Asia (M&S Annual Report 1998). Therefore, no new development is planned in the near future (M&S Press Releases 1999). The company plans to source locally and buy temporarily depressed properties. Hong-Kong will remain a strategic base, despite sales being L20 million below expectations for 1998-1999 (M&S Press Releases 1999).

JOURNALISTIC IMPRESSIONS OF THE COMPANY

Based on the popular business magazine, M&S' international marketing challenges fall into three broad categories: (1) over-reliance on British market, (2) top management's internal orientation, and (3) corporate culture.

Over-Reliance on British Market

M&S relied too much on the British market both for its customers and its suppliers. This over-reliance on the domestic market exposed the company to unsystematic risk. The British market constitutes 85% of sales and 94% of profits. The reduction in profits of 23% in 289 stores in Britain is largely what led to the depressed stock prices (Business Week 1998).

M&S for years has insisted on buying its clothes from domestic manufacturers, a policy that gained it support from its citizenry, but not necessarily its customers. Around 65% of all products sold in M&S stores were manufactured in the UK (M&S Press Releases 1999). The dependence on British suppliers has limited the scope of M&S product offering and innovation, deteriorated its competitive position vis-à-vis retailers which import cheaper garment from abroad, and made its exports products expensive in relation to world markets (The Economist 1998).

The insistence on buying British produced goods has also been unhealthy to M&S suppliers. In response to the M&S' slowdown, suppliers had to cut almost 2,300 jobs. The company broke tradition and has started to encourage suppliers to manufacture overseas (The Economist 1999c). How to lower global production and distribution costs is a key problem the company needs to deal with.

M&S needs to internationalize to further diversify the risk of a downturn in any one economy. Business Week (1998) recently suggested that M&S reduce its dependence on local British market and maintaining international expansion.

Additional international expansion require a great resource commitment, a difficult task during hard economic times. Furthermore, as developed countries become saturated and highly competitive, retailers need to expand to emerging countries, where cultural, economic and political differences exist. Two key problems in seeking international expansion are (1) how to choose a host country, and (2) what should be the mode of entry.

Top Management's Internal Orientation

The top management and board of governors has been inward looking for too long (The Economist 1998). The board is made up of no less than 16 executives, most of whom have spent most of their careers at M&S, and 6 non-executives, one of which is from the co-founding families. A recent article in the *Economist* (1998, p. 68) argued "With M&S now selling financial services and going overseas, the narrowness of experience of M&S' senior managers and board directors is a weakness."

The narrowness of top management is also reflected by the choice between recent bid for the chief executive job to replace Richard Greenbury. Keith Oates, who joined M&S in 1984 as finance director, having built a career with blue-chip companies, has lost the top job to Salsbury, who joined the company in 1970 fresh out of London School of Economics (Gwyther 1999).

The new marketing director, James Benfield, 28 year M&S veteran, has joined M&S as a graduate trainee (Jardin 1999a). Despite his stated desire for new marketing input, his four newly appointed managers for each store type are also M&S employees (Buxton 1999). M&S resembles Sears in that it has been inward looking for too long. Both companies have suffered series of deteriorations to their stock prices (Pitcher 1999).

Top management's international orientation, which is a function of cultural distance, level of education, proficiency in foreign languages, and international experiences, was shown to be an important internal factor of internationalization (Eroglu 1992). M&S top management personnel and board of directors are mostly British born, British educated, male, and have spent most of their careers there.

Corporate Culture

M&S corporate culture has been one of top-down. Decision making was centralized and the company ruled from the top through command and control. Prices, products, colors, and even designs, had to be approved at the top. "Those who were close to the customer weren't listened to or encouraged to be bold and take risks" (Financial Times 1999, p. 8). While the company used famous designers, such as Paul Smith, Betty Jackson and Ghost, it never used their names in promoting the stores nor did it give them much latitude in designing new fashions (Financial Times 1999).

Perhaps the biggest pitfall of M&S has been its attitude "we know best" (Financial Times 1999). This attitude has prevailed in many of its business practices. For example, the company has accepted only M&S credit cards in its British stores, used very limited advertising, and insisted on buying British textiles. M&S' old business model does not fit the new world realities. Competitors struggle for market share by offering increasingly better quality, nicer service, lower prices, and more pleasant shopping experiences. The result is increasing customer expectations that are more difficult to satisfy. Companies that cannot keep up with the pace of change will eventually perish. M&S famous quality and service have not kept pace with modern notions of these terms (Financial Times 1999).

AN EPILOGUE: COMPANY'S RESPONSE TO SLOWDOWN

The company's response to the slowdown and the depressed stock prices has been to reduce number of workers, decrease prices, and rethink the organization of the firm.

Job Cuts

To offset the loss in profitability the company announced cutting 15% of its 1,900 managers in hopes of saving $16.2 million (The Economist 1999b). The company plans to cut additional 350-400 head office jobs and 290 store management positions. Senior management numbers were cut by 25% (M&S Press Releases 1999). The board has been reduced from 22 to 7 (Financial Times 1999). In addition, the company announced that it canceled its 1999 graduate trainee program, which hired about 250 graduate trainees per year, and withdrew offers made recently (Dow Jones Industrial 1999).

Price Cuts

In an effort to become more competitive and trim down excess inventory, M&S cut prices across the board. Many clothing items, including a third of children wear, have been discounted by as much as 15%. The prices of a third of all merchandise has been cut by 2%-3% (Financial Times 1999).

Reorganization

M&S was reorganized into three profit centers: (1) UK retailing, (2) overseas retailing, and (3) financial services. Stores were reclassified from geographic division to four store types: (1) department stores, (2) regional centers, (3) high (main) street, and (4) small stores. This the firm hopes will help it (1) develop specific management skill associated with different store types, (2) tailor merchandise more accurately, (3) reduce administration, and (4) improve staffing and training. The total cost of restructuring is estimated at about L40 million, leading to a L40 million cost savings associated with redundancies starting fiscal year 2000-2001 (M&S Press Releases 1999).

A new marketing department was set up to help create improved (1) competitive analysis, (2) information gathering, (3) proactive communication, (4) advertising clarity, and (4) customer targeting (M&S Press Releases 1999). The department will increase marketing research, develop a coherent brand strategy, and increase the level of advertising. Its marketing thrust will be to cut prices, put more staff on the shop floor and improve visual merchandising (Jardin 1999a). The company will attempt to develop a more balanced sourcing policy to its domestic and international outlets and will review global logistics to streamline distribution and lower costs (M&S Press Releases 1999).

The company will continue to develop their e-commerce web site. A property division has been set up to assess use of real estate. Market cost of assets will be charged to individual stores to better assess performance. Accountability has increased as each profit center is judged individually against its cost of capital, and resources will be allocated to increase shareholders equity value (M&S Press Releases 1999).

REFERENCES

Alon, Ilan (1999), "International Franchising Modes of Entry," in *Franchising Beyond the Millennium: Learning Lessons From the Past*, John Stanworth and David Purdy, eds., Society of Franchising 13th Annual Conference.

Briggs, A. (1992), "St. Michael Marks and Spencer PLC." in *International Directory of Company Histories*, A. Hast, eds., St. James press, 124-126.

Business Week (1998), "Marks & Sparks Isn't Throwing Off Any," (November 16), 64.

Buxton, Philip (1999), "M&S Chief Rejigs Retail Operation," *Marketing Week*, 22 (12), 6.

De Nardi-Cole, Sarah Marie (1998), "Marks and Spencer," in *International Retailing*, Brenda Sternquist, eds., New York: Fairchild Publications, 159-166.

Dow Jones Industrial, "Executive Report Marks & Spencer PLC," http:mrstg1s.djnr.com/cgi-bin/DJIntera..._binding=&get_name=null&searchText=U.MAR, (Retrieved May 26, 1999).

Economist, The (1999a), "Dress Sense," (May 22), 7.

Economist, The (1999b), "Taking Over," (May 15), 5.

Economist, The (1999c), "Business: Unraveling," (January 2), 57-58.

Economist, The (1999d), "Shopping All Over the World," (June 19), 59-61.

Economist, The (1998), "Poor Marks," (November 21), 68.

Eroglu, S. (1992), "The Internationalization Process of Franchise Systems: A Conceptual Model," *International Marketing Review*, 9 (5), 19-30.

Financial Times (1999), "Angst in Their Pants," Weekend FT, June (37), 7-10.

Glew J. (1994), "Meeting the European Challenge (Marks & Spencer)," *European Superstore Decisions*, (Spring) 46-49.

Gwyther, Matthew (1999), "King Richard: A Tragedy in Three Acts," *Management Today*, (April), 78-85.

Heller, Robert (1999), "No Excuse for Room at the Top," *Management Today*, (February), 23.

Jardin, Alexandra (1999a), "St. Michael's Evangelist," *Marketing*, (April 22), 25-28.

Jardin, Alexandra (1999b), "Time for M&S to Follow Tesco," *Marketing*, (January 28), 17-21.

Market Guide (1999), "Wal-Mart Stores, Inc.," (June 5), 1-15.

Marketing (1999), "M&S Doubles Ad Budget in L20m Branding Review," (March 25), 9.

M&S (Marks & Spencer) Press Releases (1999): www.marks-and-spencer.co.uk/corporate/press-releases/19990518.002.html (retrieved 5/27/99).

M&S Annual Report (1998): www.marks-and-spencer.co.uk...ate/annual-report/Europe(Far-East or America)/main.html (retrieved 10/9/98).

McIntyre, Faye S. and Sandra M. Huszagh (1995), "Internationalization of Franchising Systems," *Journal of International Marketing*, 3 (4), 39-56.

Pitcher, George (1999), "Reality Forces UK Retail Giants To Check Out Their Strategic Options," *Marketing Week*, (January 21), 21-24.

Whitehead, Maureen (1991), "International Franchising - Marks & Spencer: A Case Study," *International Journal of Retail & Distribution Management*, 19 (2), 10-12.

Chapter 14
Concluding Remarks

Ilan Alon
Crummer Graduate School of Business, Rollins College

This book brings together contemporary research on service franchising from an international perspective. Herein, I would like to focus more closely on international franchising research and suggest future research directions that might be fruitful.

The conceptualization of international franchising can be seen in figure 14.1. This figure summarizes much of the research that was done on franchising globally. At the core of these conceptualizations are two theoretical frameworks, resource-based and agency theories, which helped researchers explain both why firms use franchising (chapter 2), and why franchisors internationalize (e.g., Alon, 1999). Franchisors internationalize for internal reasons (as shown in figure 14.1) and for competitive and external reasons, such as a solicitation from abroad and market saturation.

Often time, when internationalization is induced from outside influences, the franchisor may not be ready to internationalize and will need to regroup and develop the appropriate dynamic capabilities that will enhance its global competitiveness. Such capabilities may include distance management, international contract enforcement, cultural adaptability, risk management, and partnership management skills (Choo, 2003), not to mention additional human and financial capital and an organizational framework that supports global expansion. Since franchising cuts across multiple industries, the need and development of these capabilities vary significantly. Alon (1999) showed that the internationalization of franchising systems in the hotel, business service and retail industries changed with respect to the organizational antecedents displayed in figure 14.1.

Relationship management is also complicated by the internationalization of the system. In addition to managing relations with store managers, franchisees, and area sub-franchisees of all kind, the international franchisor also needs to manage government relations, multiple regulatory requirements, international economic issues, large and powerful area and

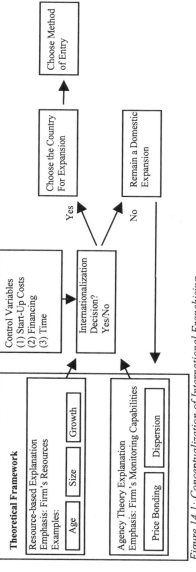

Figure 14.1: Conceptualization of International Franchising

master franchisees, and franchisees which often don't have direct reporting relationship to the franchisor.

For franchisors the decision to internationalize is inflective, altering the competitive and strategic direction of the firm. At the same time that franchisors are considering globalization, they must also give consideration to the appropriate market for their products and to the mode of entry they will initially employ. For US franchisors, the first country of involvement are often English speaking, making the transition easier due to cultural and psychic similarities. As discussed in Chapter 11, Slovenian franchisors may choose ex-Yugoslav countries due to the positive country-of-origin image Slovenian firms have there and a history of economic cooperation.

Chapter 6 discusses a framework for analyzing the environments of franchising for foreign expansion from a US perspective. Economic, demographic, distance and political factors are explored (see figure 14.2). More research can be done on each of the dimensions explored to develop better predictive and prescriptive models that will help franchisors better understand their environments. For example, looking at the economic dimension, it is possible to examine a greater breadth of variables and to analyze them in a way that will allow more accurate estimations of market potential (e.g., Currie and Alon, 2005).

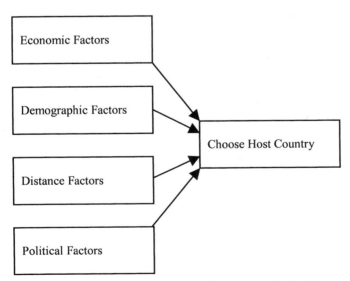

Figure 14.2: Dimensions of International Franchising Market Selection

Simultaneous with the decision to go abroad and the international market selection should be the selection of the mode of entry. Master international franchising has become a popular mode of entry among international franchisors because of its minimal investment commitment and the potential for fast expansion (Chapter 7). This mode of entry, however, has the disadvantage of embodying a low level of control over the brand and operations of the franchisors' agents. Rather than following master franchising as a mode of international market expansion blindly, franchisors are advised to evaluate their environments, industry dynamics, and company's characteristics. Chapters 8 evaluates the company's characteristics, groups them into theoretically-relevant clusters, and explains when master franchising is more prevalent. More research is needed on international franchising modes of entry using data collected for this purpose. Cross-country analysis can explain relevant environmental variables and cross-company evaluations can help in identifying the appropriate organizational mix for different models of expansion. The book offers a number of overlapping country (Russia, Philippines, Slovenia, China, and UK) and company (BHS, Kodak, Marks & Spencer) cases focusing on franchising (Chapters 9-13). More case studies are needed to expand the knowledge base of franchising globally and to provide a database for future research.

Franchisors are advised to also pay attention to the consequences of their entry into the market from the standpoint of their success and from the standpoint of social responsibility. In global markets, the effects of foreign franchisors may sometimes be undesirable and include cultural alienation, conflict and displacement of local businesses (Chapter 3). This is not to say that the net impact is negative. In fact, the evidence shows that there are significant positive economic externalities associated with the introduction of franchising in emerging markets, including economic and entrepreneurship development and consumer surplus benefits, such as price stability and enhanced service delivery experience (Chapter 3). The economic benefits to the locality in terms of employment, output, and economic development are also relevant to developed markets (Chapter 4).

Whether franchising is a superior model of business is still an unresolved question. Chapter 5 shows no significant differences in the ROEs of franchising and non-franchising firms of public firms in a single industry. Clearly, however, more research is needed in this area. Does the relationship between franchising and financial performance hold over time? Is the impact of franchising on financial performance different across industry? Do public firms financial results applicable to non-public firms to which most franchisors belong? Will other measures of performance react the same way to the manipulation of the franchising variable? Does context matter? Is the impact of franchising on financial performance country dependent?

We hope that this book is one in many future books that will stimulate debates about franchising, encourage others to continue to research the topic, and help franchisors wishing to improve their system.

REFERENCES

Alon, Ilan (1999), *The Internationalization of U.S. Franchising Systems* (Transnational Business and Corporate Culture Problems and Opportunities), New York: Garland Publishing.

Choo, Stephen (2003), "Valuable Lessons for International Franchisors When Expanding into East Asia," in *International Franchising in Industrialized Markets: North America, Pacific Rim, and Other Countries*, Dianne Welsh and Ilan Alon, eds., 249-268..

Currie, David M. and Ilan Alon (2005), "Estimating Demand for Kodak Film (with a Teaching Note)," *Ivey Publishing House* (9B04D015, TN 8B04D15).

About the Contributors

Ilan Alon is Associate Professor of International Business and Director of Global Practica at the *Forbes*-ranked AACSB-accredited Crummer Graduate School of Business, Rollins College. Alon's writings have been published in peer-reviewed journals in Europe, Asia, and the Americas, and include the following books on franchising:
- *International Franchising in Industrialized Markets: Western and Northern Europe* (CCH Inc., 2003)
- *International Franchising in Industrialized Markets: North America, Pacific Rim and Other Developed Countries* (CCH Inc., 2002)
- *International Franchising in Emerging Markets: China, India, and Other Asian Countries* (CCH Inc., 2001)
- *International Franchising in Emerging Markets: Central and Eastern Europe and Latin America* (CCH Inc., 2001)
- *The Internationalization of US Franchising Systems* (Garland Publishing, 1999)

Dr. Alon has taught courses on "global franchising" in the China Europe International Business School and Fudan University in China and in MIB School of Management in Trieste, Italy. As a consultant, Alon's experience is extensive and includes the Business Process Outsource industry, Financial industry, Recreational Vehicles industry, Garment industry, Packaging industry, Electronics industry, Real Estate industry, Restaurant industry, Furniture industry, and Education industry.

Noora Anttonen is a Ph.D. candidate at the School of Business & Economics at the University of Jyväskylä, Finland. She earned her M.Sc. (Economics and Business Administration, majoring in Marketing) at the University of Jyväskylä in 2004. Her interest in international franchising began as she was writing her master's thesis focusing on Franchising in Russia – The Challenges of Entry. Noora's publications include conference papers and academic articles on franchising. Besides her academic studies, she is working as a Franchising Development Manager for a Finnish franchisor.

Ralph Drtina, Ph.D., CPA, is a Professor of Accounting and Management at the Crummer Graduate School of Business, Rollins College. His research interests address the use of decision models to achieve organizational objectives. He has published in widely diverse journals, such as the *California Management Review, Accounting Review,* and *Public Productivity Review.* Professor Drtina has held several visiting professorships abroad, including appointments with the Madrid Business School, the Australian

National University, and the University of the Virgin Islands. He was a visiting Fulbright Scholar at the Institute of Education in the island-nation of Mauritius. Professor Drtina's consulting activities focus on the application of models for decision support and performance evaluation.

James Gilbert, Ph.D. is Professor of Quantitative Analysis and Operations Management at the Crummer Graduate School of Rollins College. Jim was Director of Inventory Planning at the DeVilbiss Corporation in Toledo, Ohio. He joined the Crummer School having taught at the University of Georgia, Western Illinois University, and the University of Nebraska-Lincoln. Along with his colleague Richard J. Schonberger, he developed the area of Just-in-Time Purchasing from work originating at the Toyota Manufacturing Company of Japan. These purchasing practices are now used worldwide. His teaching, research, and consulting expertise include just-in-time systems, quality management practices, and quantitative decision support for efficient business systems. Professor Gilbert has received numerous teaching awards from his students, faculty colleagues, universities, and associations. He is a Lilly Teaching Fellow, a Richard B. Russell Teaching Award recipient, a past MBA Teacher of the Year, and several times the Department of Management Teacher of the year. Dr. Gilbert has taught outside of the U.S., teaching Contemporary Quality Management at the Institute d'Administration des Enterprises, Universite' Jean Moulin, Lyon, France. He is past Division Chair of the Operations Management Division of the Academy of Management. Jim served the Production and Operations Management Society (POMS) from 2002–2005 as vice-president for meetings and continues to serve as co-general chair for the 2005 operations management conference in Shanghai, China. Dr. Gilbert has lead consulting projects at Cirent Semiconductors (now Agere Systems), Scholastic Books Fairs, Johnson & Johnson, Scholastic, Inc., Asia Bovea Brown (ABB), HTE, Inc. among others.

Peter Holt has been active in the international franchise community helping companies manage franchise systems in both domestic and overseas markets for nearly 20 years. Mr. Holt has written and lectured extensively on the subject of franchising. He serves as Chairman on the International Affairs Network (IAN) of the IFA. He also serves as Chairman of the Global Marketing Group (GLOMAK), which advises IFA on all its international franchise activities, and is president of P.D. Holt International LLC, a San Diego based consulting firm dedicated to assisting franchisors in all aspects of franchise development. Most recently he was the Chief Operating Officer of 24seven Vending (US) Inc., a New Zealand based, publicly traded company starting a franchise system in the United States. Prior to that, Mr. Holt worked as Executive Vice President for Mail Boxes Etc., the world's largest franchisor of retail centers specializing in shipping, business and communications services. Mr. Holt began his career in franchising at the

International Franchise Association, the oldest and largest trade association in the world serving the interests of businesses that franchise.

Frank Hoy is Director of the Centers for Entrepreneurial Development, Advancement, Research and Support (CEDARS) at the University of Texas at El Paso (UTEP). He is a professor of management and entrepreneurship and holds the endowed Chair for the Study of Trade in the Americas. From 1991 to 2001, Dr. Hoy served as dean of the College of Business Administration at UTEP. Dr. Hoy earned his Ph.D. at Texas A&M University where he developed a small business outreach program for the Texas Agricultural Extension Service. Subsequently, he became director of the Small Business Development Center for the State of Georgia. He moved from the University of Georgia to Georgia State University in 1988 as the Carl R. Zwerner Professor of Family-Owned Businesses. Dr. Hoy's research concentrations are entrepreneurship and economic development, franchising, family business, strategic alliances, and social entrepreneurship. He is a past editor of Entrepreneurship Theory and Practice and is currently the editor for Latin America for the Journal of World Business. His most recent book is *Franchising: An International Perspective*, co-edited by John Stanworth of the University of Westminster.

James Johnson, a native of London, England, is Associate Professor of International Business and Director of the Global Practica program at the Crummer Graduate School of Business, Rollins College, Florida. Prior to relocating to the USA in 1987, he lived and worked in the U.K., Spain, Finland, Yugoslavia, and Mexico. He received his Ph.D. in International Business from the University of South Carolina and previously taught at Old Dominion University in Norfolk, VA, where he conducted regular cross-cultural negotiation training for managers from Deutsche Telekom, Germany. Dr. Johnson's research interests focus on international market analysis, cross-cultural management and cultural training. His research has been presented at major international conferences and has been published in top journals in international business. He is a member of the Academy of Management and the Academy of International Business.

David McKee is Professor of Economics in the Graduate School of Management at Kent State University where he specializes in development economics and economic change. His most recent books, co-authored with Yosra A. McKee and Don E. Garner include *Crisis, Recovery, and the Role of Accounting Firms in the Pacific Basin* (2002), *Offshore Financial Centers, Accounting Services and the Global Economy* (2000), and *Accounting Services, the Islamic Middle East and the Global Economy* (1999). He is the immediate past president of the International Academy of Business Disciplines.

J. Mark Munoz is a Assistant Professor of International Business at the Millikin University in Illinois. He was born in the Philippines, where he also acquired his PhD in Business Management at the University of San Jose. Dr. Munoz is the author of a Philippine book entitled *Land of My Birth*. His 35-country research on globalization and its impact on business led to Best Research Paper Awards in international business conferences, as well as several publications in management journals and commercial business magazines. Dr. Munoz sits as a Board of Director for two Philippine companies, and is listed in the 22nd edition of Who's Who in the World.

Igor Pavlin, Slovenian citizen is head of management and entrepreneurship development at the International Center for Promotion of Enterprises. Mr. Pavlin has designed and implemented over thirty customised international development programmes for policy makers, managers, entrepreneurs, government officials and experts from countries with transitional economies in Europe and in developing world for/in co-operation with UNIDO, ILO, World Bank, and various national institutions. They took place in Europe, South and South East Asia, Africa and in the Caribbean. Mr. Pavlin research focuses on franchising leading to many publications and recognitions by academic and government associations.

Mika Tuunanen is a Senior Research Fellow at the School of Business & Economics at the University of Jyväskylä in Finland. Subsequent of completion of two-year marketing degree from the Kuopio Business College he received B.Sc. (Soc.) from the University of Kuopio, majoring Entrepreneurship and Management. Mika earned his M.Sc. and Ph.D. (Economics & Business Administration; majoring Entrepreneurship) at the University of Jyväskylä. As part of his doctoral studies he served as a visiting researcher at the University of Texas at El Paso. In addition to franchising his research interests include CRM, Marketing research, Entrepreneurial behavior and Quantitative research methods. Mika lectures on franchising and entrepreneurship in several academic and polytechnic institutions. He has been an active member of International Society of Franchising since 1997 and attended several conventions of the International Franchise Association. Mika collaborates closely with the Finnish Franchising Association and contributes to their research, publications and educational sessions. Mika received the association's highest recognition, golden medal for his long lasting support and contribution to franchising community. Mika's publications cover some four dozens of academic articles and conference papers and three textbooks. In 2004, he was one of the four editors of Economics and Management of Franchising Networks published by Physica-Verlag, world's largest academic publisher. In 2005, his Ph.D. dissertation Essays on Franchising in Finland: Empirical Findings on Franchisors and Franchisees, and Their Relationships was the first ever-published doctoral thesis on franchising in Finland. Mika has served McDonald's Finland as a Research Manager. He has also consulted listed companies and he serves as a Chairman of the Board in three companies. Mika is a founder and CEO of Upshots ltd., a company specialized in marketing research and franchise consulting.

Index

Adaptation, 115
Adhocracy configurations, 124
AFFI. *See* Association of Filipino Publishers
Age, 21
   master franchising and, 109–110
Agency costs, 108
Agency problems, 125–126
Agency theory, 11, 21, 81
   critique of, 17–18
   empirical support for, 17
   hypotheses, variables, and measurements
     of, 13t
   in internationalization, 123
   in master international franchising, 108
   overview of, 16–17
   reconciling, 18
   theoretical antecedents of, 13
Aggregate income, 65
al Qaeda, 172
Allied Domecq, 111, 113
Americanization, 39, 40–41
   international franchising and, 45–48
AOL Time Warner, 46
Area development, 105, 125
Arizona State University, 63
Asia, 28, 176
   Marks and Spencer in, 237–238
Asia Pacific Management Forum, 170
Assets
   brand name specificity, 110–111
   sales and, 89
Assets/Stockholders' Equity model, 88, 89
Association of Filipino Publishers (AFFI),
   177
Asterix, 47
ATU, 197
Australian Trade Commission, 184
Auto-repair workshops, 197–200
   conversion of, 195–197

Balance of Payments (BOP)
   international franchising and, 34–35
Bank Average Lending Rates, 171
Bankruptcy, 216
Bartog Hitri Service (BHS), 197–200, 203

internationalization of, 200–202
Baskin Robins, 111, 113, 143
BEA. *See* Bureau of Economic Analysis
Belgium
   international chains from, 204n3
Belmond Enterprises Ventures Ltd., 176
Benetton, 40
Benfield, James, 227, 239
BHS. *See* Bartog Hitri Service
bin Laden, Osama, 172
Blockbuster, 185
BLS. *See* Bureau of Labor Statistics
BOP. *See* Balance of Payments
Brand name asset specificity
   in master franchising, 110–111
Brazil, 38, 111
British Franchise Association, 81
Brooks Brothers, 236, 237
Bureau of Economic Analysis (BEA), 66
Bureau of Labor Statistics (BLS), 66
Bureau of Land Management, 64
Bureaucratization, 42
Burger King, 43–44, 142
Business building
   in retail sector, xv
Business format franchise systems, xv–xvi
   model development in, 94–95
Business-format franchising
   definition of, 12–13

Canada, 135
Capabilities, 38–39
Capital markets, 16
Capital requirements
   of Kodak in China, 216
Carbon-copy configurations, 124
   hypotheses behind, 126
   results of cluster analysis on, 130–131
Center for Franchise in Small Business, 150
Central Europe, 28
Century 21, 185
Century Business Services, 185
CES. *See* Consumer Expenditure Survey
China, 40
   achievements of Kodak in, 213